director multimedia studio

AUTHORIZED

MACROMEDIA PRESS

Director Multimedia Studio Authorized
Macromedia, Inc.

Published by Macromedia Press, in association with Peachpit Press, a division of Addison Wesley Longman.

Macromedia Press
2414 Sixth Street
Berkeley, CA 94710
510/548-4393
510/548-5991 (fax)
Find us on the World Wide Web at:
http://www.peachpit.com
http://www.macromedia.com

Copyright © 1997 by Macromedia, Inc.

All rights reserved. No part of this book may be reproduced or transmitted in any form or by any means, electronic, mechanical, photocopying, recording, or otherwise, without the prior written permission of Macromedia, Inc.

ISBN 0-201-68829-8

Notice of Liability

The information in this book and on the CD-ROM is distributed on an "as is" basis, without warranty. While every precaution has been taken in the preparation of the book and the CD-ROM, neither Macromedia, Inc., its licensors, nor Macromedia Press shall have any liability to any person or entity with respect to liability, loss, or damage caused or alleged to be caused directly or indirectly by the instructions contained in this book or by the computer software and hardware products described herein.

Trademarks

Macromedia and Director are registered trademarks, Director Multimedia Studio, Extreme 3D, Lingo, Macromedia Studios, Shockwave, SoundEdit 16, xRes, Xtras, and the Made With Macromedia logo are trademarks of Macromedia, Inc.
Apple, QuickTime, and Macintosh are registered trademarks of Apple Computer, Inc. Sound Forge is a trademark of Sonic Foundry, Inc. Other product names mentioned within this publication may be trademarks or registered trademarks of other companies.

Printed and bound in the United States of America

9 8 7 6 5 4 3 2 1

CREDITS

Producer, Author, and Instructional Designer
Karen Tucker, Macromedia

Programmer and Author
Mark Castle, Castle Productions

Production
The Holtsberrys at Media Magic

Editors
Judy Ziajka, Loralee Windsor

Indexer
Ty Koontz

Thanks to the following people:
Leslie Alperin, Jay Armstrong, Marvin Avilez, Jennifer Bennett, Tim Bigoness, Monica Dahlen, Jane DeKoven, Ramon de la Paz, Darcy DiNucci, Ken D'Urso, Brian Ellertson, Sherry Flanders-Page, Barbara James, Richard Jenkins, Orson Kellog, Nick Levenstein, Nilson Neushotz, Phil Royer

table of contents

INTRODUCTION   1

LESSON 1   DIRECTOR BASICS   6

Opening Director
Opening the Toolbar
Using the Control Panel
Viewing the Cast
Opening the Score
Opening the Text and Paint Windows
Opening the Script Window
Opening the Debugger

LESSON 2   INTRODUCTION TO ANIMATION   16

Creating a Folder on Your Hard Drive
Starting a New Movie
Creating Text Cast Members
Placing the Text in the Score
Animating the Text with In Between
Repeating the In Between Process
Importing a Background Image and Moving It to the Lowest Layer
Changing the Opacity of the Text with an Ink Effect
Using the Animation Wizard

## LESSON 3 STARTING A PROJECT					42

Opening the File
Setting the Stage Color and Movie Tempo
Importing Media Elements into the Cast
Using Ink Effects and In Between on the Background Image

## LESSON 4 TRANSITIONS AND SOUNDS				52

Using In Between to Animate an Object
Using Reverse Sequence to Reverse the Animation
Exchanging Cast Members to Create a Special Effect
Using a Screen Transition
Adding Sounds to the Score

## LESSON 5 ADDING INTERACTIVITY				66

Building the Menu Screen
Using Ink Effects, Alignment, and Wait
Adding Digital Video
Adding Markers for Navigation
Creating Navigation Scripts
Creating a Projector

## LESSON 6 OTHER ANIMATION TECHNIQUES			84

Setting Movie Properties
Setting Key Frames
Animating with In Between Special
Setting Up the Movie
Animating with Real-time Recording

LESSON 7 KEY FRAMES AND LAYERS   96

Creating a Custom Stage
Importing the Media
Setting the Movie Tempo
Placing the Graphics on the Stage
Copying Sprites to a New Location
Creating the Animation with Key Frames
Playing Selected Frames Only
Layering the Sprites
Exchanging Cast Members
Adding Background Music

LESSON 8 ANIMATION WITH FILM LOOPS   114

Exchanging Cast Members
Creating a Film Loop
Creating Key Frames with a Film Loop
Layering the Sprites

LESSON 9 ADDING BUTTONS FOR NAVIGATION   122

Incorporating Animations from Other Movies
Creating Buttons with the Tool Palette
Pausing the Playback Head
Adding Markers
Adding go to Scripts
Branching to a Menu

LESSON 10 DIRECTOR MULTIMEDIA STUDIO   136

Adding a Glow Effect with xRes
Creating 3D Text with Extreme 3D
Modifying Sounds with SoundEdit 16 or Sound Forge

LESSON 11 SPRITE PROPERTIES AND PALETTES 154

Importing Media Elements
Setting a Movie Palette
Organizing the Cast
Setting the Location of a Sprite
Reducing the File Size of a Bitmap
Finding an Index Color Number
Modifying Sprite Properties
Editing a Cast Member
Snapping to the Grid
Adding Navigational Elements
Adding Sound

LESSON 12 TEXT, BLENDING, AND NAVIGATION 176

Adding Markers
Pausing the Playback Head to Wait for User Input
Adding Sprites to the Stage
Changing the Background Transparent Color
Using Highlights around a Hot Area
Blending Colors
Navigating to a Marker

LESSON 13 COLOR CYCLING 192

Using Relative Markers in Scripts
Setting a Gradient
Animating with Color Cycling

LESSON 14 REUSING YOUR WORK 204

Building a Frame by Exchanging Cast Members
Adding Color Cycling and Highlights
Navigating with Markers

LESSON 15 SHOCKWAVE FOR DIRECTOR 216

Obtaining Shockwave and the Browser Software
Shocking a Movie

APPENDIX A WINDOWS SHORTCUTS 224

Numeric Keypad Shortcuts
Keyboard Shortcuts
Director Window Shortcuts

APPENDIX B MACINTOSH SHORTCUTS 230

Numeric Keypad Shortcuts
Keyboard Shortcuts
Director Window Shortcuts

INDEX 237

introduction

Macromedia's Director Multimedia Studio combines Macromedia Director, the best-selling multimedia authoring program, with professional-level programs for creating and editing sounds, images, and three-dimensional illustrations. The Studio is an all-in-one package for creating interactive media for the World Wide Web, CD-ROM, and interactive TV. Director's easy-to-use interface lets you combine graphics, sound, video, and other media in any sequence and then easily add interactive features with Lingo, the program's powerful scripting language.

This Macromedia Authorized training course introduces you to the major features of the applications in the Director Multimedia Studio and guides you step by step through the development of several real-world Director projects. This 20-hour curriculum includes these lessons:

Lesson 1: Director Basics
Lesson 2: Introduction to Animation
Lesson 3: Starting a Project
Lesson 4: Transitions and Sounds
Lesson 5: Adding Interactivity
Lesson 6: Other Animation Techniques
Lesson 7: Key Frames and Layers
Lesson 8: Animation with Film Loops
Lesson 9: Adding Buttons for Navigation
Lesson 10: Director Multimedia Studio

Lesson 11: Sprite Properties and Palettes
Lesson 12: Text, Blending, and Navigation
Lesson 13: Color Cycling
Lesson 14: Reusing Your Work
Lesson 15: Shockwave for Director

Each lesson begins with an overview of the lesson's content and learning objectives, and each is divided into short tasks that break the skills into bite-size units. Each lesson also includes these special features:

Tips: Shortcuts for carrying out common tasks and ways to use the skills you'll learn to solve common problems.

Shockwave tips: Special considerations for developing Director movies that will be published on the World Wide Web.

Menu commands and keyboard shortcuts: Alternate methods for carrying out commands in the Director Multimedia Studio. Menu commands are shown like this: Menu › Command › Subcommand. Keyboard shortcuts (when available) are shown in parentheses after the step; a plus sign between the names of keys means you press the keys simultaneously.

Appendix A and Appendix B at the end of the book provide a quick reference to shortcuts you can use for Windows and Macintosh (respectively) to give commands in Director.

As you complete these lessons, you'll be building up the skills you need to complete your own Director projects. At the end of the course, you should have mastered all the skills listed under the *What You Will Learn* list at the end of this introduction.

All the files you need for the lessons are included on the enclosed CD-ROM in the Lessons folder. Files for each lesson appear in their own folders, titled with the lesson name. You do not need to copy the Lessons folder to your hard drive. You can complete the lessons by running the files from the CD-ROM.

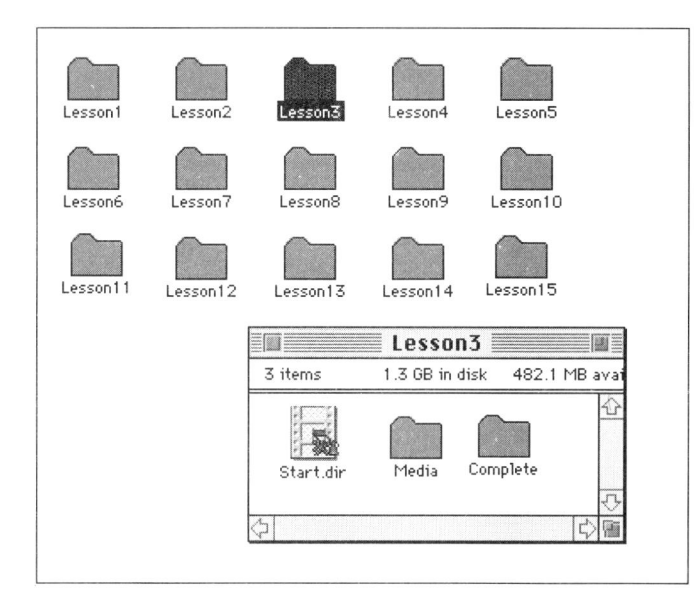

Files for each lesson appear in their own folders, titled with the lesson name. The Complete folder contains completed Director files for each lesson. The Media folder contains the media elements you need to complete each lesson. If a lesson requires a prebuilt file, that file, called Start.dir, will also be in the Lesson folder.

Each Lesson folder contains a Complete folder and a Media folder. The Complete folder contains completed Director files for each lesson, so you can compare your work or see where you're headed. The Media folder contains any media elements you need to complete each lesson. Certain projects require you to use prebuilt files. The prebuilt files you will need are identified at the beginning of each lesson and can be found in the Lesson folder for that lesson.

Each book in the Macromedia Authorized series includes the complete curriculum of a course taught at Macromedia's Authorized Training Centers. The lesson plans were developed by some of Macromedia's most successful trainers and refined through long experience to meet students' needs. We believe that Macromedia Authorized courses offer the best available training for Macromedia programs.

The instructions in this manual are designed for multimedia developers, graphic artists, instructional designers, illustrators, Webmasters, and anyone who wants to become a multimedia developer or Web designer. This course assumes that you're a beginner with Director but assumes that you are familiar with the basic methods of giving commands on a Windows or Macintosh computer, such as choosing items from menus, opening and saving files, and so on. For more information on those basic tasks, see the documentation provided with your computer.

Finally, the instructions in this book assume that you already have the Director 5 software installed on a Windows or Macintosh computer, and that your computer meets the system requirements listed on the next page. This minimum configuration will allow you to run Director 5 and open the training files included on the enclosed CD-ROM. Lesson 10 requires you to use all the products in the Director Multimedia Studio. If you do not own Director 5 or the Director Multimedia Studio, you can use the demo products on the CD-ROM provided with this manual (Windows only: If you use the demo products, you will not be able to complete the sound portion on lesson 10). You will be able to complete all the lessons with the demo products, but you will not be able to save your work. Follow the instructions in the Read Me files on the enclosed CD-ROM to install the demo software.

Welcome to Macromedia Authorized. We hope you enjoy the course.

WHAT YOU WILL LEARN
In this course you will:
Import media types to include in your multimedia presentations
Import, create, and fine-tune text
Animate your movies
Create screen transitions
Play sounds
Create film loops
Add interactive navigation to presentations
Create buttons that provide user feedback
Use Shockwave to produce Director movies for playback on the World Wide Web

MINIMUM SYSTEM REQUIREMENTS

Macintosh
68040 processor or better
   (Power PC 601 or better
   recommended)
16 MB available RAM
25 MB available disk space
640 x 480 screen resolution
8-bit color (256 colors) monitor depth
   Note: To complete the color cycling
   lesson, the monitor must be set
   to 8-bit color.
System 7.1 or higher
QuickTime 2.1
Shockwave, Afterburner, and a browser
   that supports Shockwave
   Note: The preceding requirement
   is for Lesson 15 only.

Windows
486/66 processor or better
   (Pentium recommended)
16 MB available RAM
25 MB available disk space
640 x 480 screen resolution
8-bit color (256 colors) monitor depth
   Note: To complete the color cycling
   lesson, the monitor must be set to
   8-bit color.
Windows 3.1 or higher (Windows 95
   recommended)
   Note: Extreme 3D requires
   Windows 3.1 with Win32s or
   Windows 95.
8-bit SoundBlaster-compatible sound
   card
QuickTime 2.1 for Windows
Shockwave, Afterburner, and a
   browser that supports Shockwave
   Note: The preceding requirement
   is for Lesson 15 only.

director basics

LESSON 1

This lesson is a get-acquainted session, designed to introduce the basic Director components. In this lesson you won't build a project. You'll simply take a guided tour through Director. In later lessons, you'll find out how to use most of the tools introduced here.

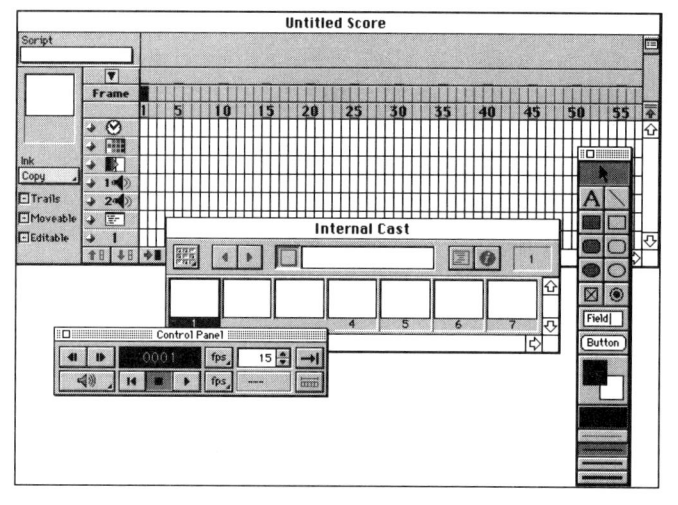

This lesson introduces you to Director's features: the tools you will use to create your own multimedia applications.

WHAT YOU WILL LEARN

In this lesson you will learn to identify the basic Director components used to:

Display images on the screen

Control the playback of movies

Store and organize media elements

Control the timing and position of media elements

Create and modify text

Create and modify graphic images

Create scripts that provide additional functions such as branching and interactivity

Find and fix errors in your scripts

APPROXIMATE TIME
It usually takes about 30 minutes to complete this lesson.

LESSON FILES
None

OPENING DIRECTOR

Director is based on the metaphor of a theater production. That is, Director has a stage, a cast of characters, and a script—the score—that synchronizes cast members and instructs them where to be and when to be there. A Director file is called a *movie*, and a play-only (uneditable) version of a movie is called a *projector*.

1] Double-click the Director icon to open Director 5.

When you open Director, you will see the menu bar and stage. Depending on your Director settings, you may also see the toolbar and Control Panel when you open Director. Each of these is described in this lesson.

The *stage* is where the action occurs. The stage may cover the entire screen or only a portion.

2] Open the menus to see the available commands.

Most of the commands are available through the menus as well as through keyboard shortcuts. The keyboard shortcuts, which you can use to activate a command without using the menus, are listed next to the command name.

The menus you see reflect the *Macromedia User Interface standard*. By making menus and other interface elements consistent from program to program, this new standard makes it easy for you to use different Macromedia applications together. Every application in the Director Multimedia Studio now shares the same basic menu structure and other interface elements (or soon will). With the new standard in place, you should experience the Studio not as a set of separate programs but as a single powerful tool for creating multimedia applications.

OPENING THE TOOLBAR

The buttons on the toolbar provide shortcuts for common commands and functions, such as Open, Save, Print, Rewind, Stop, and Play.

1] Choose Window › Toolbar to display the toolbar (Windows Ctrl+Shift+Alt+B, Macintosh Command+Shift+Option+B).

The toolbar is part of the Macromedia User Interface standard and soon will be found in every Macromedia product.

2] Move the cursor over a tool in the toolbar to see the tool name.

Tooltips are another feature of the Macromedia Interface Standard. If the tooltips don't appear, you may need to turn them on by choosing File › Preferences › General and in the dialog box checking Show Tooltips.

USING THE CONTROL PANEL

Now you will open and use the Control Panel to play versions of the movies you are going to create in this course.

1] Choose Window › Control Panel to open the Control Panel (Windows Ctrl+2, Macintosh Command+2).

The Control Panel controls the playback of a movie with VCR-like controls such as Rewind, Play, and Stop.

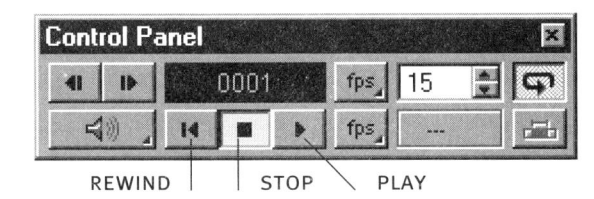

2] Choose File › Open and locate the Complete folder in the Lesson2 folder. Then select Bullet.dir to open it.

You will see the first frame of the movie on the stage.

3] Use the buttons on the Control Panel to play the movie, stop it, and rewind it.

This movie is an animated bullet chart. You will create this movie in the next lesson.

4] When you're done, try playing some of the other movies in the Complete folders.

These are the projects you're going to create in this course.

VIEWING THE CAST

Like a theater production, a Director production needs actors, or a *cast*. In Director's case, the cast members are not people but media elements, also known as *assets*. These elements can be graphics, sounds, digital video, text, or other Director movies and are stored in the *Cast window*. The Cast window is like an off-stage area where the cast members wait until they're called to the stage.

1] Choose Window > Cast to open the cast (Windows Ctrl+3, Macintosh Command+3).
The Cast window displays the *cast members* of the current cast. Each cast member position is identified by a number and, optionally, a name. For every occupied position in the Cast window, a thumbnail image is displayed that represents that cast member's type. A movie's cast can consist of up to 32,000 cast members. You control the row width and the number of visible rows using File > Cast Preferences.

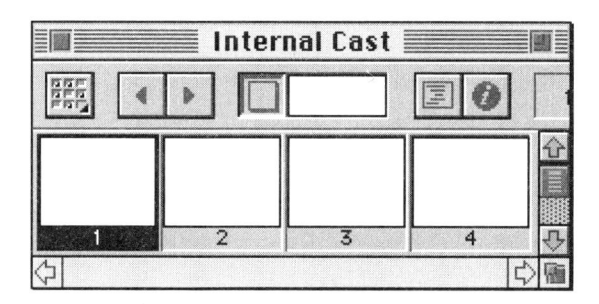

2] Close the cast.

OPENING THE SCORE

For the cast members to know what to do, when to talk, and when to exit, they need a script. In Director, the script is known as the *score*. The score is used to sequence and synchronize the actions of the cast. The score contains *channels*, which run horizontally, that are available for different jobs.

1] Choose Windows > Score to open the score (Windows Ctrl+4, Macintosh Command+4).

Note the different icons at the left of the first few channels. These are reserved for special purposes. (You'll learn how to use these in the next lessons.)

The tempo channel is used to adjust the speed of the movie as it plays.

The palette channel sets the available colors for the movie.

The transition channel allows you to set screen transitions such as fades and wipes.

Two sound channels let you add music, sound effects, and voice-overs.

The script channel is used to write scripts. Scripts provide one way to add interactivity to a movie.

Forty-eight numbered sprite channels are used to assemble and synchronize all the visual media elements such as pictures, backgrounds, buttons, and digital video. A sprite is a representation of a cast member that is on the stage or in the score.

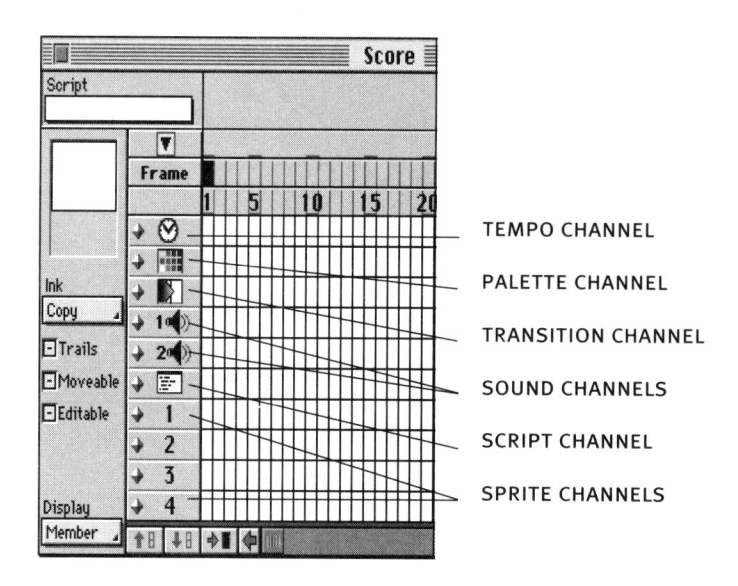

2] Close the score.

OPENING THE TEXT AND PAINT WINDOWS

Director includes tools for creating and editing media: the *Text* and *Paint windows*. You'll take a look at these windows next.

1] Choose Window › Text to open the Text window (Windows Ctrl+6, Macintosh Command+6).

The Text window is used for creating and editing text. Besides changing fonts and point size, you can also adjust the space between lines and between characters.

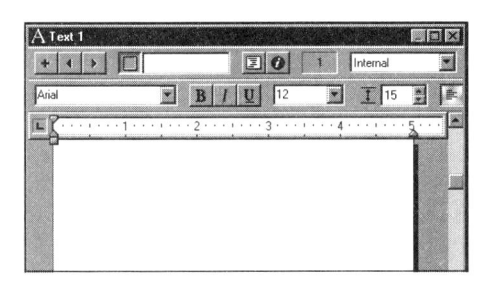

2] Close the Text window by clicking the close box.

3] Choose Window › Paint to open the Paint window (Windows Ctrl+5, Macintosh Command+5).

The Paint window includes a number of tools for creating and editing graphics.

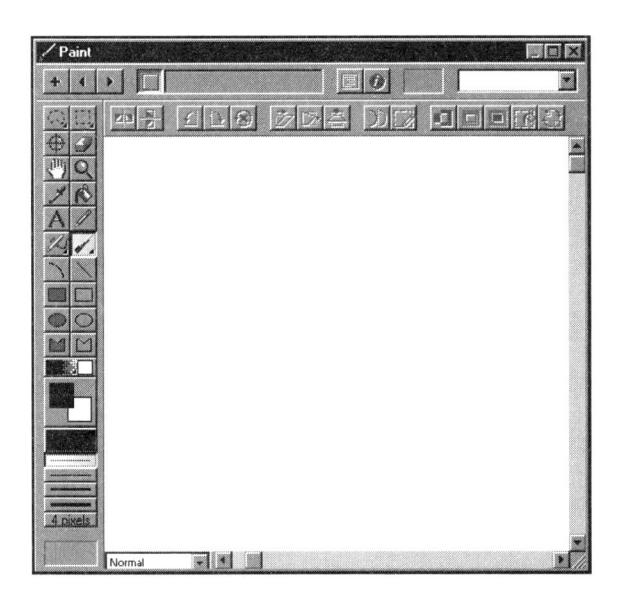

4] Close the Paint window by clicking the close box.

DIRECTOR BASICS

OPENING THE SCRIPT WINDOW

Director movies support an extra dimension that classic theater production does not: nonlinear interactivity. This means a movie can respond to choices that users make by playing an animation, displaying a glossary definition, or branching to another section of the program. To tell Director how to respond, you write *scripts* with Lingo, Director's special scripting language.

1] Choose Window › Script to open the Script window (Windows Ctrl+0, Macintosh Command+0).

You write Lingo scripts in the Script window.

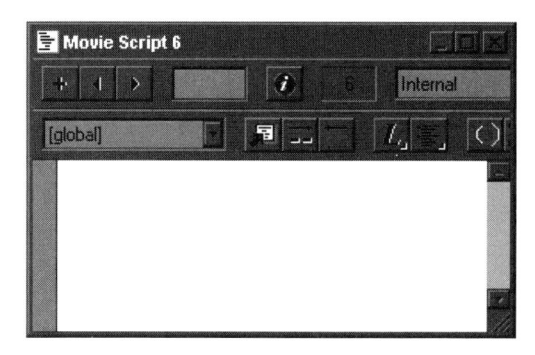

2] Close the Script window.

OPENING THE DEBUGGER

The *Debugger* lets you look at your Lingo scripts while the commands are being executed so you can quickly find and fix Lingo errors.

1] Choose Window › Debugger to open the Debugger (Windows Ctrl+', Macintosh Command+').

The Debugger provides tools so you can set the current line of Lingo, run the current handler line by line, display the value of any variable, and perform many other operations.

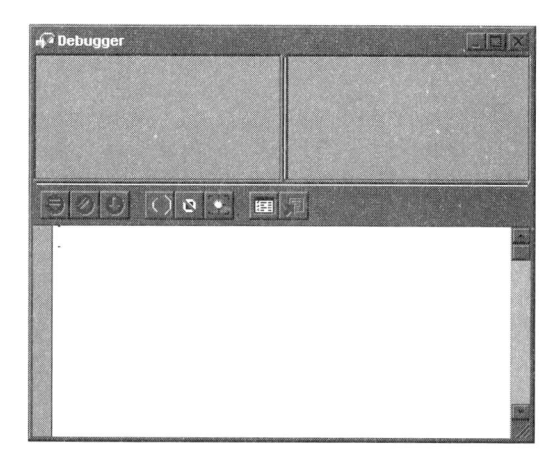

2] Close the Debugger.

WHAT YOU HAVE LEARNED
In this lesson you learned about these basic Director components:

Stage: For displaying objects on the screen [*page* **8**]

Toolbar: For performing shortcuts to common commands and functions [*page* **9**]

Control Panel: For controlling the playback of movies [*page* **9**]

Cast: For storing and organizing media elements [*page* **11**]

Score: For controlling the timing and position of media elements [*page* **11**]

Text window: For creating and modifying text [*page* **13**]

Paint window: For creating and editing graphic images [*page* **13**]

Script window: For creating Lingo scripts that provide additional functions such as branching and interactivity [*page* **14**]

Debugger: For finding and fixing errors in your Lingo scripts [*page* **15**]

introduction to animation

LESSON 2

Animation is the core of Director's power. One simple kind of animation uses the In Between feature to move an object between two positions on the screen. In this lesson you'll create a simple bullet chart that can be used to support an oral presentation, and you'll animate the bullet points so they slide onto the screen from one side.

If you would like to view the final result of this lesson, open the Complete folder in the Lesson2 folder and play Bullet.dir.

Bullet charts are a common form of Director movie, often used to support speaker presentations. In this lesson you will create the text and graphics to build a chart. Then you will animate the chart to create a more engaging presentation.

Here and in the next few lessons, you will be practicing the first two steps of the four-step process that is part of every Director project:

Step 1: Creating and assembling the media elements. Media elements include graphics, digital video movies, sound, text, and animation. You will need to either create new media elements or use ones that have already been developed.

Step 2: Laying out the media elements on the stage and sequencing them in the score. Use the stage to create the look and feel for your production; use the stage and score together to arrange the media elements in space and time.

Step 3: Adding interactivity. Interactivity can include buttons or other navigational elements that branch the user to different parts of the production.

Step 4: Packaging the movie into a projector and distributing it to end-users, or running the movie through Afterburner and embedding it in a World Wide Web page. Projectors are play-only, stand-alone versions of Director movies, so end-users don't need Director on their computers to view your work.

The media you use, how you present media elements, whether or not you add interactivity, and how you package your movie will differ from project to project, but these four steps are a good way to organize any Director project.

WHAT YOU WILL LEARN
In this lesson you will:

Create text

Create a simple animation that moves lines of text across the screen

Import a graphic image

Change the layers on which objects appear

Change the opacity of displayed objects

LESSON FILES
Media Files
Lesson2\Media
Starting Files
None
Completed Project
Lesson2\Complete\Bullet.dir
Lesson2\Complete\Otto.dir

APPROXIMATE TIME
It usually takes about 1 hour to complete this lesson.

INTRODUCTION TO ANIMATION

CREATING A FOLDER ON YOUR HARD DRIVE

Before you begin building anything, you will create a folder to hold all the projects you will create in this course. If you are using the demo version of the Director Multimedia Studio provided on the CD-ROM that came with this book, you do not need to create this folder because you will not be able to save files.

1] Create a folder called MyWork on your hard drive.

You will save all of your work in this folder.

Now you're ready to begin.

STARTING A NEW MOVIE

First you'll create a new movie for this project and set the tempo for the movie.

1] Choose File > New > Movie to start a new movie (Windows Ctrl+N, Macintosh Command+N).

An empty stage appears.

2] Choose Window > Control Panel to open the Control Panel (Windows Ctrl+2, Macintosh Command+2).

The Control Panel provides buttons like those on a VCR for controlling a movie, as well as a tempo display and other controls. For this project, you're only going to set the tempo and then close the Control Panel.

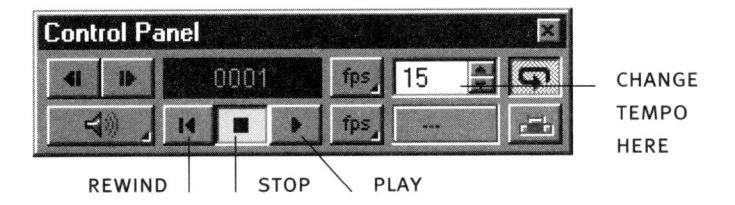

3] Find the tempo display, which shows the tempo of the current frame in frames per second. Make sure the number is 15. Either select the current number and type *15* or click the Up or Down Arrow button to reach 15.

You can change a movie's tempo in the middle of the movie, but for this project you'll just use one tempo, 15 frames per second.

LESSON 2

4] Choose Window > Control Panel to close the Control Panel (Windows Ctrl+2, Macintosh Command+2).

Because three of the most important control buttons—Rewind, Stop, and Play—are duplicated in the toolbar, you won't need the Control Panel for the rest of this project. Closing it gives you more work space on the screen.

CREATING TEXT CAST MEMBERS

To create text that will be animated, start by opening the Text window and typing several lines of text. This begins step 1 of the development process: assembling the cast members.

1] Choose Window > Cast to open the Cast window (Windows Ctrl+3, Macintosh Command+3).

You'll create several lines of text, making each line a separate cast member.

2] Choose Window > Text to open the Text window (Windows Ctrl+6, Macintosh Command+6).

In the Text window you create text and select its font, size, line spacing, and letter spacing.

3] Select a font and size just as you would with a word processor. Select Times and then choose 36 points as the size.

You'll use this font and size for the title.

4] Enter a title. Make up your own or use this one:
Berries Now In Season!

When you enter text in the Text window, it automatically becomes a cast member. The title has become cast member 1. Look in the Cast window to see that cast member 1 now contains the text *Berries Now In Season!*

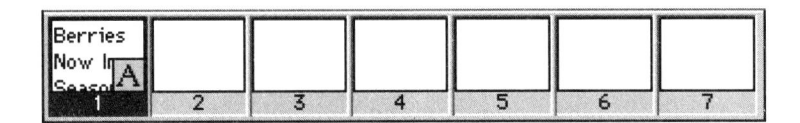

Next you'll create three lines of smaller-size text—the bullet points—each as a separate cast member, because in a few moments you'll animate each line of text separately.

tip *The Text window uses any font installed in the system. If you play the final movie in Director and it does not display the text you intended, the font may not be on the system on which you're running the presentation. If you create a projector, the text becomes a bitmap, so you don't need to be concerned about which system fonts are installed. You will learn how to create a projector later in this course.*

shockwave tip *When you create a projector or run the movie through Afterburner, the text created in the Text window becomes bitmapped. This means the final version will be larger than the original movie. However, you want Shockwave movies to be as small as possible. To resolve this issue, you can create a field cast member using the Field tool in the tool palette instead of creating a text cast member. To create a field cast member, choose Window › Tool Palette, select the Field tool, and then click the stage. The field will be displayed on the stage, and you can type text directly into it.*

5] Click the Plus button on the toolbar of the Text window to add a new text cast member.

CLICK HERE TO ADD
A NEW CAST MEMBER

An empty Text window appears.

6] Change the point size to 24.

For the bullet points, you'll use a smaller point size.

7] Enter a line of text. Make up one or use this:

Lots of tasty varieties

Notice that the text you created is cast member 2.

8] Click the Plus button to create a new text cast member and enter another line:

Low calorie

9] Create one more text cast member, enter another line, and then close the Text window:

Fat-free

The Cast window should look like this:

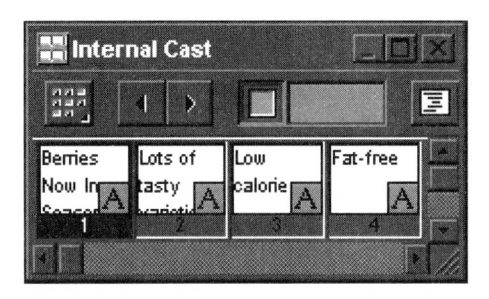

10] Choose File > Save to save your work (Windows Ctrl+S, Macintosh Command+S). Name your file Bullet.dir and save it in the MyWork folder. Remember: If you are using the demo products on the CD-ROM provided with this manual, you will not be able to save your work.

You have finished creating the text. In the next task you'll place sprites representing the text cast members in the score to prepare them for animation.

PLACING THE TEXT IN THE SCORE

To prepare the text for animation, you'll now place *sprites* representing each text cast member on the stage and in the score. This begins step 2 of the development process: sequencing the media.

1] Choose Window > Score to open the score (Windows Ctrl+4, Macintosh Command+4) if the Score window is not already open.

A row in the score is known as a channel. A column in the score is called a frame. There are 48 sprite channels. Frames are numbered across the top from left to right. The smallest unit in the score—a single rectangle—is called a cell.

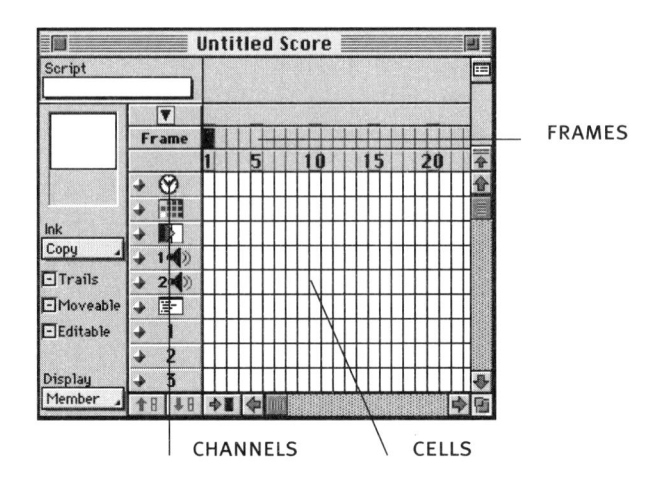

2] In the score, click frame 1 in channel 1 to select it.

Frame 1 will be the starting frame of the movie. Each cast member you place on the stage will automatically be placed in the same frame of the score, but in a different channel.

3] Select cast member 1 in the Cast window and drag it to the stage.

Remember that cast member 1 is the *Berries Now In Season* text that you created earlier. Notice that 01 appears in channel 1, frame 1, of the score. That number corresponds to cast member 1; however, what you see on the stage and what appears in the score is a sprite, which is a representation of the cast member. This is an important distinction. You can modify the sprite you see on the stage in a number of ways, but the changes you make on the stage or in the score will not affect the corresponding cast member itself; they will affect only the sprite on the stage or in the score.

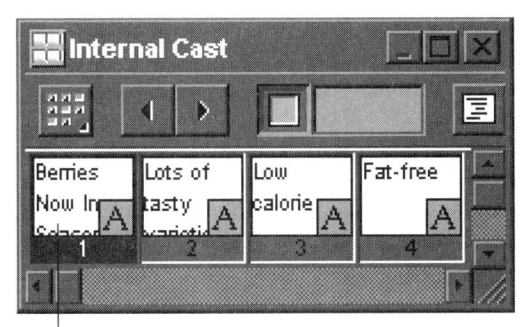

CLICK HERE THEN DRAG TO THE STAGE

4] Click the close box in the score to close it (Windows Ctrl+4, Macintosh Command+4).

Now you can see the full stage.

5] Drag each of the other cast members—2 through 4—from the Cast window to the stage.

23

INTRODUCTION TO ANIMATION

6] On the stage, select each of the lines of text and reposition them to create a bullet chart with the title at the top and the bullet points lined up under the title.

Berries Now In Season!

Lots of tasty varieties

Low calorie

Fat-free

7] Choose Window › Score to open the score.

Notice that the numbers corresponding to each cast member appear in channels 1 through 4, all in frame 1. For each cast member you place on the stage, Director places a cast member number in the score.

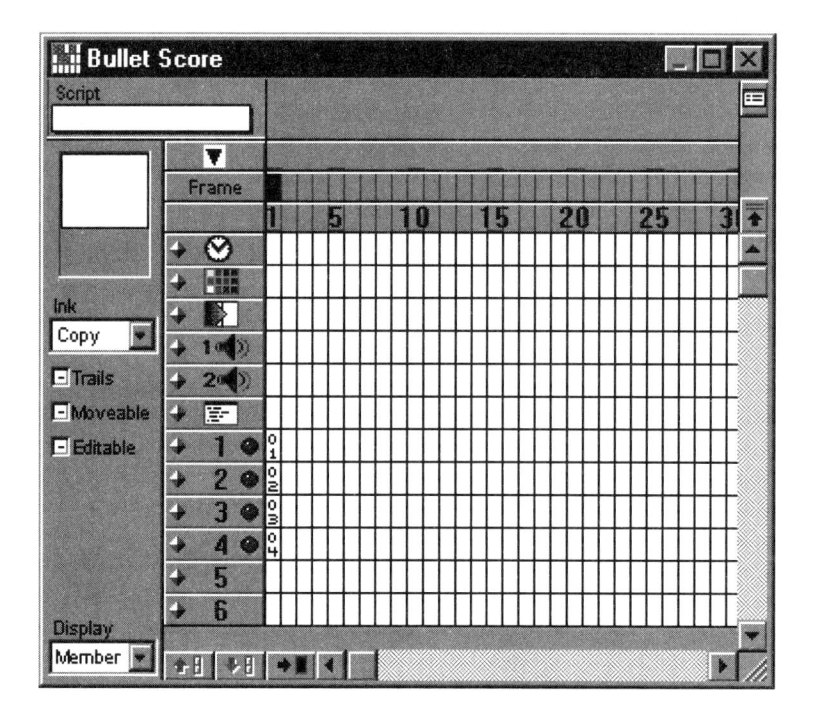

ANIMATING THE TEXT WITH IN BETWEEN

How does Director show animation? Notice the black rectangle at the top of the score. It's the playback head, and it indicates which frame of the movie is currently on the stage. When you play a movie, the playback head moves across the score from left to right, displaying all the sprites in the cells of the particular frame it is in. Quickly displaying sprites from one frame to another makes the sprites look animated.

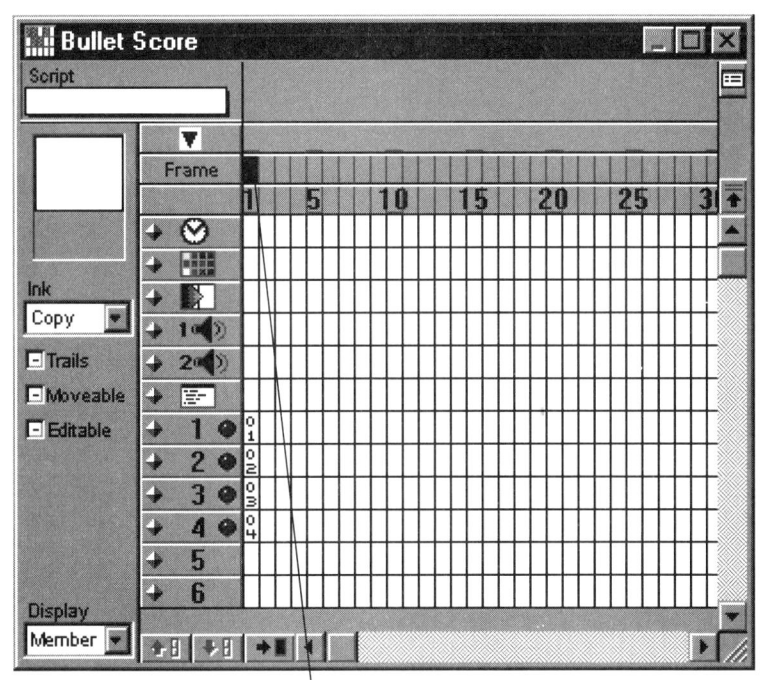

PLAYBACK HEAD

For the task you're about to complete, you'll use In Between for two different functions: to keep stationary images on the screen for a series of frames and to move images across the screen over a series of frames.

1] Select channel 1, frame 1.

You want the title to stay on the screen throughout the movie you're creating. However, right now it's in only one frame. To keep it on screen for every frame of the movie—which in this case will be 60 frames—you'll use In Between.

2] Hold down the Shift key and select channel 1, frame 60.

You've selected all the frames from frame 1 through frame 60 in channel 1.

3] Choose Modify > In Between to place the title in every one of those frames (Windows Ctrl+B, Macintosh Command+B).

The result is that the title stays on screen in one position for 60 frames. The 01 in each cell refers to cast member 1. You could have manually dragged the text to every frame, but having Director do it automatically is much simpler. This is called *in-betweening*, and it is one of the most common operations you perform in Director.

Now you'll position each of the other text sprites in sequence and animate them.

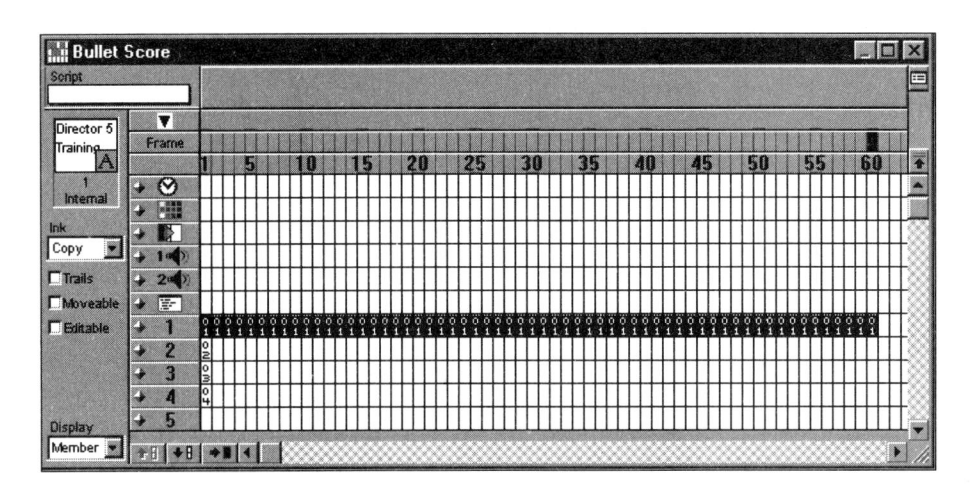

4] Select channel 2, frame 1.

You'll move this sprite a few frames from the start of the movie so the first bullet point appears after the movie starts.

5] Choose Edit > Cut Cells to cut the sprite in channel 2, frame 1 (Windows Ctrl+X, Macintosh Command+X).

Next you'll paste the sprite into two frames of the score.

6] Select channel 2, frame 10, and choose Edit > Paste Cells to paste that sprite into frame 10 (Windows Ctrl+V, Macintosh Command+V).

The animation will begin in this frame.

7] Select channel 2, frame 25, and again choose Edit > Paste Cells to paste the sprite into frame 25.

Frames 10 and 25 are the key frames for the animation of this bullet point. The two cells are key frames because they mark key positions in the animated sequence. You can use the In Between command to fill the positions between the key frames. By in-betweening the two key frames, you show movement. Frame 10 will be the starting position, where the bullet point first appears in the movie. Now comes the primary reason for using In Between for animation: You'll place the sprite in frame 10 in a different position on the stage, and In Between will calculate the appropriate in-between positions.

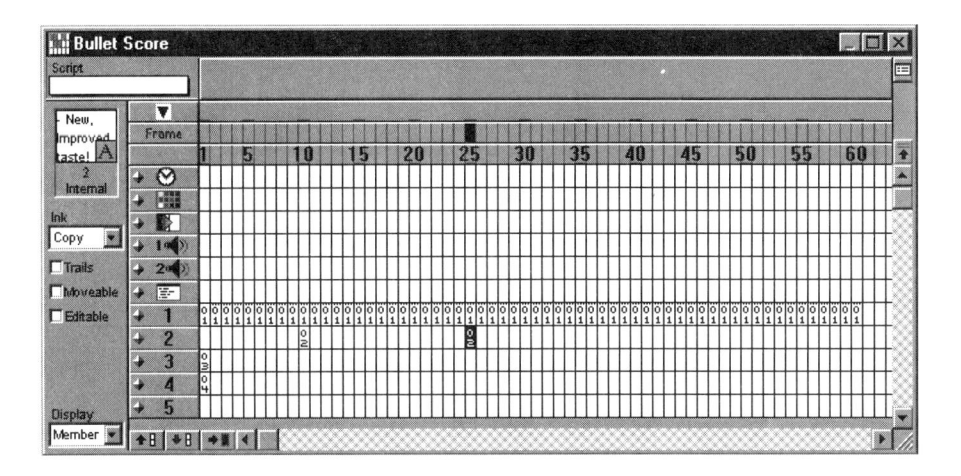

8] Select channel 2, frame 10.

9] On the stage, click to select the bullet point if it's not already selected. Drag the text to the right as far as you can, so the text is not visible on the stage.

tip   *Holding down the Shift key while dragging an object constrains movement vertically or horizontally, depending on which way you move the mouse first.*

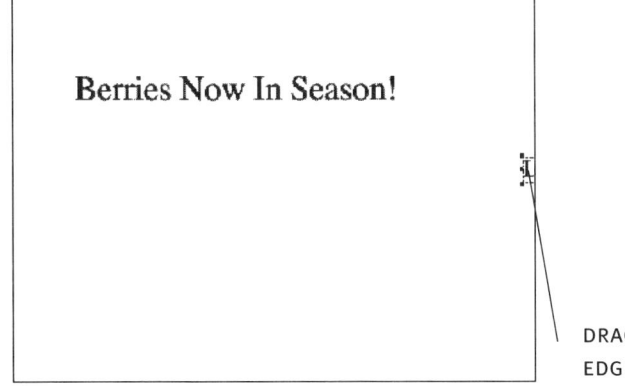

DRAG THE BULLET TO THE
EDGE OF THE STAGE

27

INTRODUCTION TO ANIMATION

10] In the score, hold down the Shift key and click frame 25.

You'll use In Between on this series of cells.

11] Choose Modify › In Between.

Between frame 10 and frame 25 the bullet point will slide onto the screen.

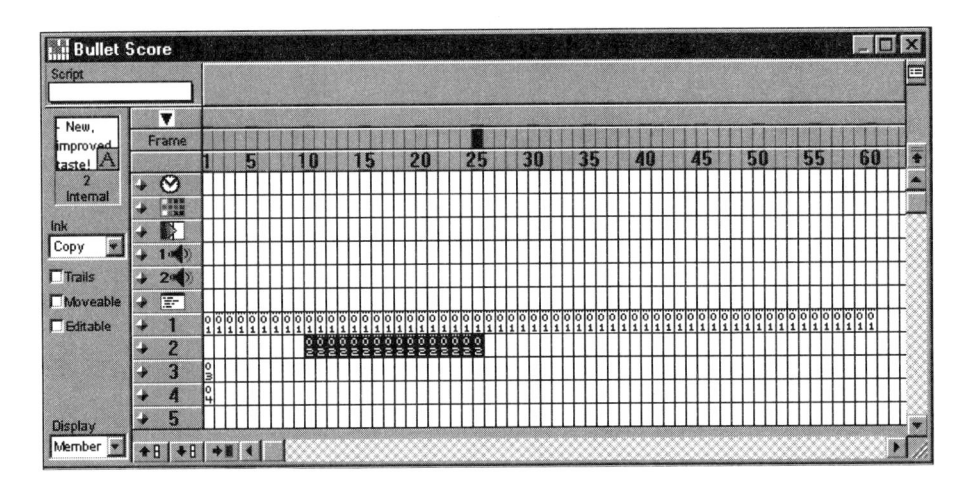

12] Rewind the movie by clicking the Rewind button on the toolbar. Then run the movie by clicking the Play button to see what you've created so far.

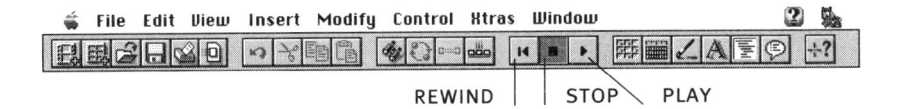

When you play the movie, notice that the playback head moves along the top of the score as the movie plays. The sprites in the current frame (the one where the playback head is located) are displayed. As the playback head moves to the next frame, the sprites in that frame are displayed. The playback head continues moving until it reaches the end of the movie.

How does this affect the bullet point you have in-betweened in the score? Each in-between position of the bullet point that you see is one of the frames between 10 and 25. As the playback head moves across frames 10 through 25, the bullet point animates onto the screen. However, after the bullet point slides on, it vanishes. Why? Because you've only in-betweened it to frame 25, but because frames are filled through frame 60, the playback head continues to move until it reaches frame 60.

LESSON 2

tip *You can drag the playback head to run back and forth over a section of the movie, or you can click the scratch bar, where the playback head moves, to select a frame for viewing.*

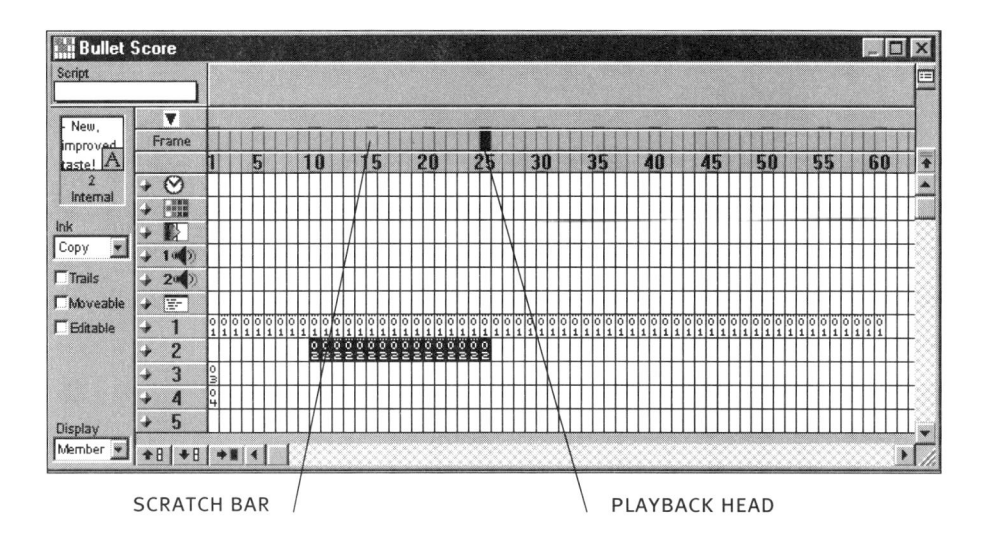

SCRATCH BAR / \ PLAYBACK HEAD

13] In the score, select channel 2, frame 25. Then hold down the Shift key and select channel 2, frame 60.

You'll extend the image of the text at the end of the animation all the way to frame 60.

14] Choose Modify › In Between.

Now you see 02 in all of the cells from frames 25 through 60.

15] Click the Rewind button to rewind the movie. Then run it by clicking the Play button.

The bullet point now slides onto the screen and stays there.

16] Choose File › Save to save your work.

REPEATING THE IN-BETWEEN PROCESS

Now you'll repeat the in-betweening process for the other two bullet points.

1] Select channel 3, frame 1, and choose Edit › Cut Cells to cut the second bullet point.

2] Select channel 3, frame 25, and choose Edit › Paste Cells to paste the bullet point into this cell. Then repeat the process of pasting in channel 3, frame 40.

The key frames for the second animation are channel 3, frames 25 and 40.

3] Select channel 3, frame 25.

4] On the stage, click to select the second bullet point. Drag the text to the right as far as you can, so the text is not visible on the stage.

5] In the score, hold down the Shift key and click channel 3, frame 40.

6] Choose Modify › In Between.

Between frame 25 and frame 40 the bullet point will slide onto the screen. You still need to in-between the text so it stays on the screen until the end of the movie, which is frame 60.

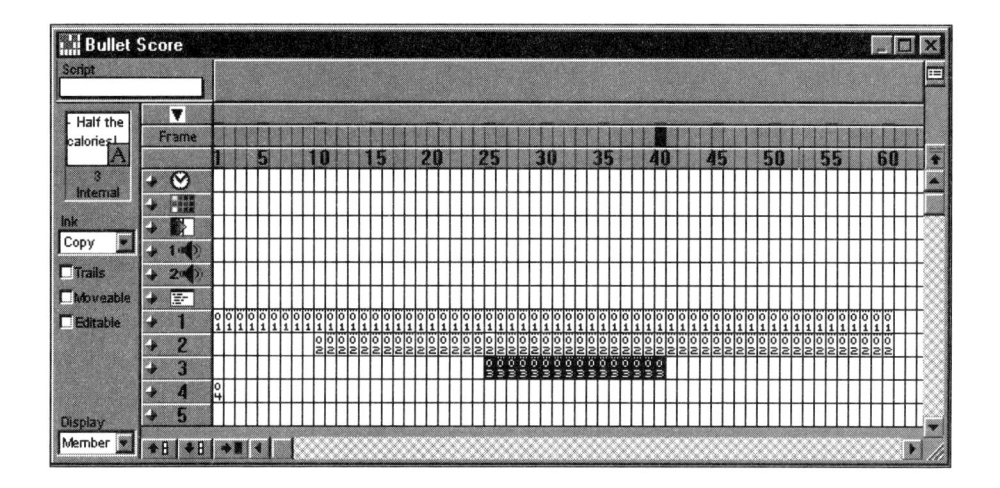

7] Select channel 3, frame 40. Then hold down the Shift key and select channel 3, frame 60.

8] Choose Modify › In Between.

Now you'll animate the final bullet point.

9] Select channel 4, frame 1, and cut the sprite.

10] Select channel 4, frame 40, and paste the sprite. Then also paste the sprite into channel 4, frame 55.

The key frames for the third animation are channel 4, frames 40 and 55.

11] Select channel 4, frame 40.

12] On the stage, click to select the third bullet point. Drag the text to the right as far as you can.

13] In the score, hold down the Shift key and click channel 4, frame 55.

14] Choose Modify › In Between.
Between frames 40 and 55 the bullet point will slide onto the screen.

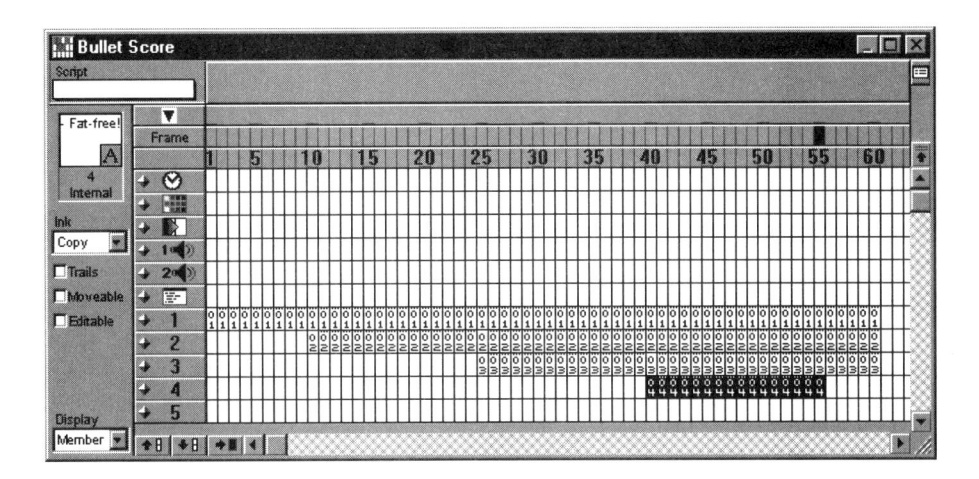

15] Select channel 4, frame 55. Hold down the Shift key and select channel 4, frame 60. Choose Modify › In Between.

16] Rewind and play the movie.
It works!

17] Save your work.

IMPORTING A BACKGROUND IMAGE AND MOVING IT TO THE LOWEST LAYER

Now you're going to import an image to appear behind the text, to give the presentation a little color and depth.

1] Choose File > Import to open the Import dialog box (Windows Ctrl+R, Macintosh Command+R).

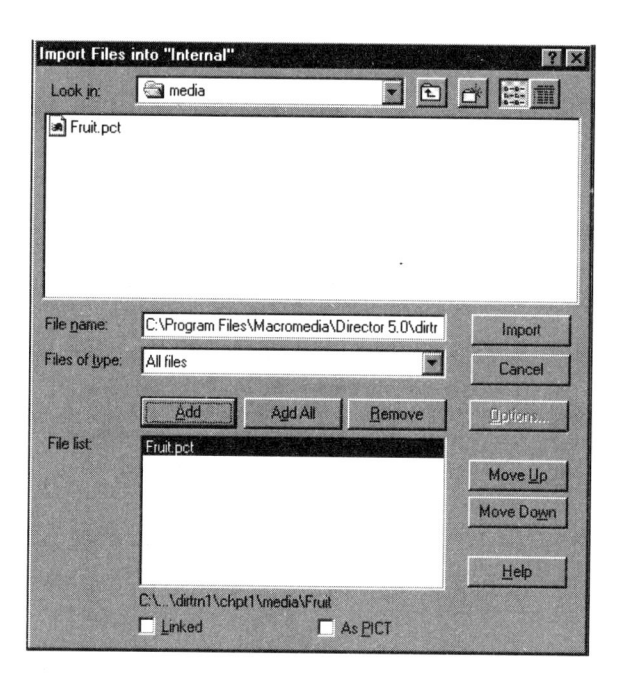

2] Select Fruit.pct from the Media folder, click Add, and then click Import.

3] In the dialog box that appears, click Stage (8 bits), choose Remap to System-Win (if you're using a Windows system) or System-Mac (if you're using a Macintosh), and check the Dither box. Click OK.

This dialog box indicates that the image you are importing is set to a different color depth than the system you're importing it into, and gives you the opportunity to change the color depth to the current stage setting. In the graphic of the dialog box below, you can see that the image is 32 bits and the stage is 8 bits.

In this dialog box you can also reset the palette used to display the image. If you don't select options when you import the graphic, you may get ugly color flashes when the graphic is displayed on stage because of the differences in the color depth of the image, the color depth of the stage, and the palette used to display the image.

This dialog box will not appear if the monitor is set to 32-bit because the image itself is 32-bit. All instructions throughout this course assume the monitor is set to 8-bit.

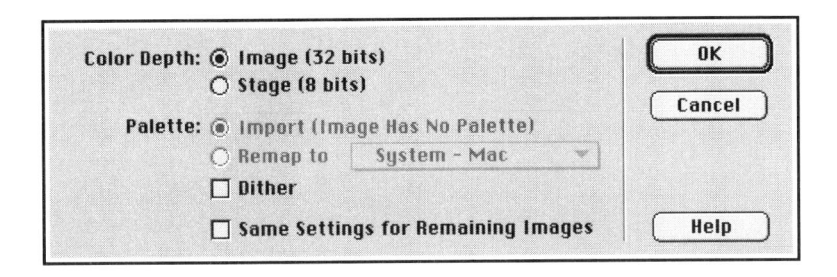

4] Choose Window > Cast to open the Cast window if the Cast window isn't already open.

The new picture is cast member 5, the first available cast position.

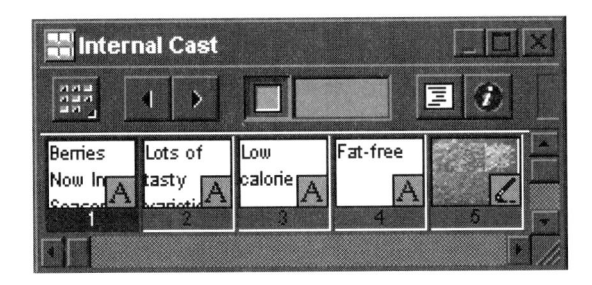

5] Drag the Fruit picture from the Cast window to channel 5, frame 1, in the score.

Next you'll in-between the fruit picture so it's on the screen throughout the movie.

6] Double-click the number 5 in channel 5.

33

INTRODUCTION TO ANIMATION

This selects every frame in channel 5, from frame 1 to the end of the movie—frame 60 in this case.

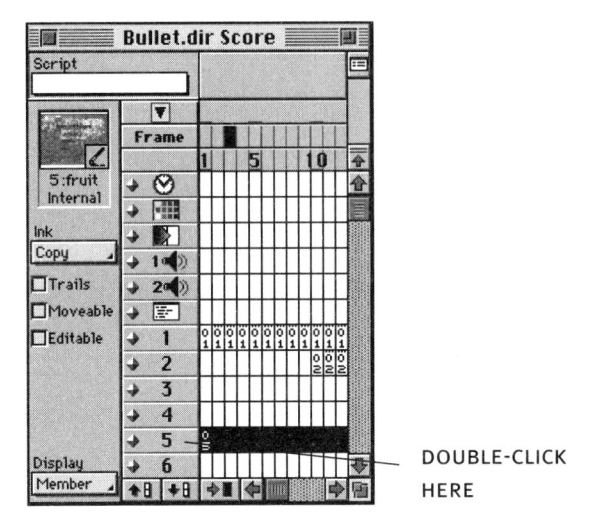

DOUBLE-CLICK HERE

7] Choose Modify > In Between.

8] Rewind and play the movie.

Watch the playback head and notice that it's playing through the frames of the movie. On the stage, however, you'll immediately notice that the text is no longer visible. This is because the fruit image is layered in front of all the text.

Each channel in Director is like a *layer*. You lay down the first, or bottom, layer in channel 1, the second layer in channel 2, and so on. Because the fruit picture is in channel (layer) 5 and it covers the entire stage, nothing else in the lower layers is visible.

However, you want to see the text. The solution is to move the fruit picture to a lower channel—specifically, channel 1—so the picture will always be in the background and the text will be displayed in front of it.

9] Double-click the number 5 in channel 5 to select it.

This selects all the sprites in channel 5.

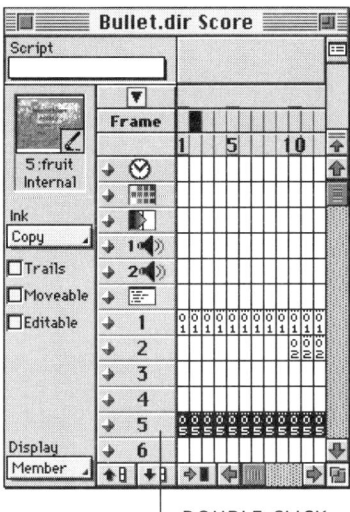

DOUBLE-CLICK HERE

10] Click the Shuffle Up button at the bottom left of the score.

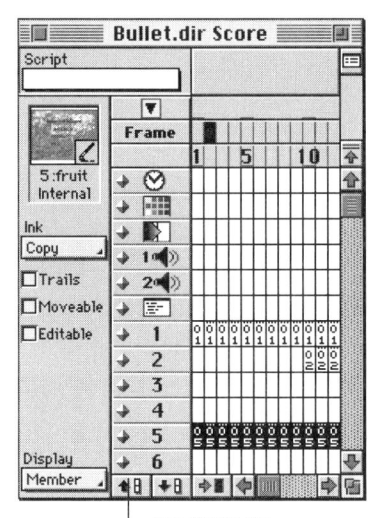

SHUFFLE UP

All the selected sprites in channel 5 are swapped with all the sprites in channel 4. By using the Shuffle Up button, you are reordering the channels. As you shuffle the sprites in channel 5 up, notice that the sprites in the next channel become visible in front of the background graphic.

The Shuffle Down button moves the selected sprites down.

11] Continue clicking the Shuffle Up button until you reach channel 1.

Now the fruit picture is in channel (layer) 1. All the objects in the remaining channels will appear in front of this picture.

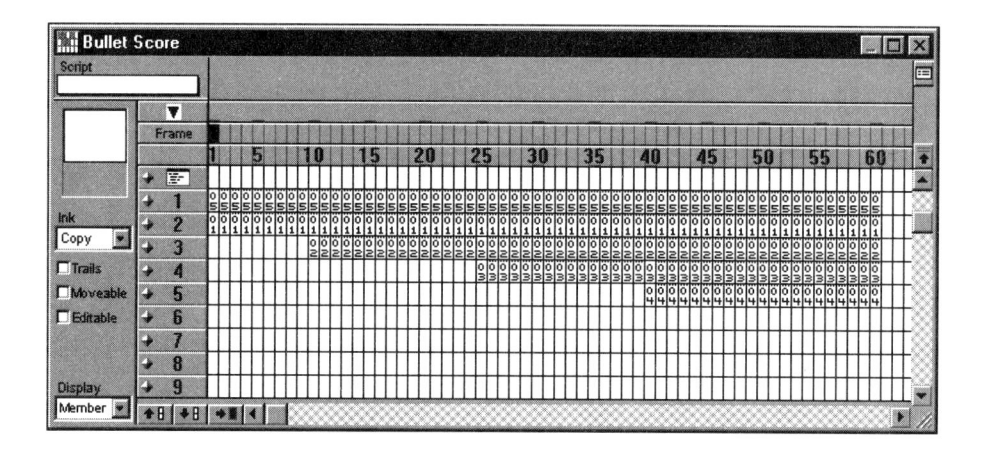

12] Rewind and play the movie.

Although the layering is now correct, there are white boxes surrounding the text. This doesn't look so great against the background image, does it? In the next task, you'll learn how to change this with an ink effect.

CHANGING THE OPACITY OF THE TEXT WITH AN INK EFFECT

Ink effects modify the appearance of a sprite on the stage, affecting how the sprite is displayed against the objects or background behind it. Ink does not affect the cast members themselves. You will often need to apply ink effects to sprites to make them appear exactly the way you want them. Different ink effects do different things. For example, the Bkgnd Transparent ink makes the pixels in the background color of the sprite appear transparent and permits the background to be seen, and the Reverse ink reverses overlapping colors. There are numerous inks to choose from.

1] In the score, double-click channel 2, press and hold the Shift key, and double-click channel 5.

All the cells in channels 2 through 5 are selected. You could also have selected one channel at a time by holding down the Shift key and double-clicking each channel in turn.

2] From the Ink pop-up menu, choose Bkgnd Transparent.

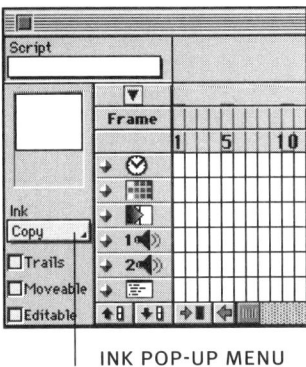

INK POP-UP MENU

All the selected cells now have a transparent background, so you can see the fruit picture behind the text without any white boxes.

3] Rewind and play the movie.

It looks great.

4] Save your work.

INTRODUCTION TO ANIMATION

USING THE ANIMATION WIZARD

You've created an animated bullet chart by creating cast members, placing them in the score, and using In Between. Another way to accomplish the same thing is to use the Animation Wizard, which is a Director Xtra. An Xtra is an add-on tool created by Macromedia or another software developer. An Xtra can either make a common task easier or provide a function that is not available with the standard Director features. Many Xtras are sold separately from Director. However, the Animation Wizard Xtra is included with Director at no charge.

tip *A list of available Xtras is available at Macromedia's Web site: http://www.macromedia.com.*

Using the Animation Wizard, you set the timing and display options and create the text to be displayed. Then the Animation Wizard creates cast members from the text and places sprites representing the cast members in the score in the right sequence. This approach can be a useful alternative to the method you learned earlier in this lesson. To view the final result of the following task, play the Otto.dir movie in the Complete folder.

The first step in the process is to create a new movie and open the Animation Wizard.

1] Choose File > New > Movie to open a new movie.

2] Choose Window > Score to open the score if the score is not already open.

3] Click near the top of the score in frame 2 to set the starting frame of the presentation.

To do this, click just to the right of the 1 in the row that displays the frame numbers. This will move the playback head to frame 2. A blinking vertical line will appear all the way down the score. This line is similar to the insertion point in a word processor.

CLICK HERE

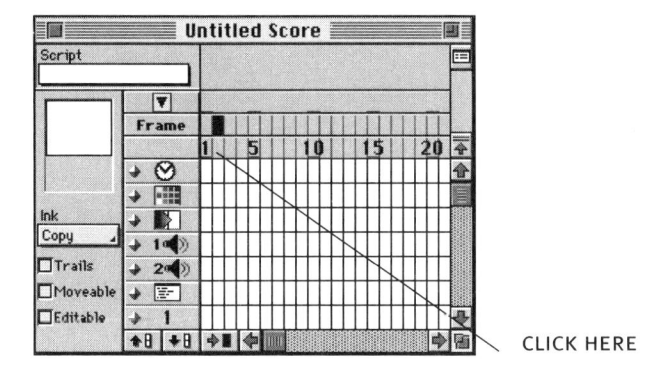

Why are you doing this? The Animation Wizard needs the starting frame for the presentation. In this case, you're setting the presentation to start in frame 2.

4] Choose Xtras › Animwiz (Windows) or Xtras › Animation Wizard (Macintosh).
The Animation Wizard window opens.

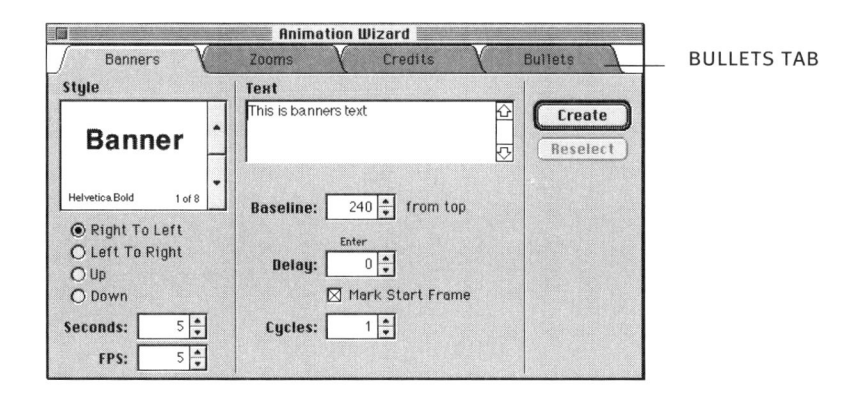

BULLETS TAB

5] Click the Bullets tab at the right of the Animation Wizard window.
You're going to create a simple presentation with animated bullets, so you need to use this section of the Animation Wizard window. Here you can set the text style, motion style (how the bullet animates onto the screen), and timing and create the actual text.

6] Click the Roll button under Style.
This causes the bulleted text to roll onto the screen sequentially, one bullet point after another.

SET FPS   SET SECONDS   CLICK ROLL

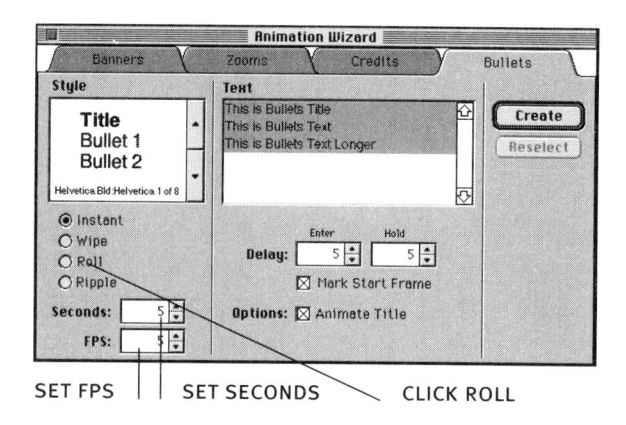

7] Set the speed of the animation by setting Seconds to 2 and FPS to 10.

These settings control the speed of the bullets that animate onto the stage. In this case, the bullets will move at a rate of 10 frames per second and will take 2 seconds to completely animate onto the stage. As you continue working with the Animation Wizard in other projects, you will want to play with these settings and adjust them to fit your needs.

8] Select the text in the Text field and replace it with four lines of text. If you want, you can use the following text:

Berries Now In Season!
Lots of tasty varieties
Low calorie
Fat-free

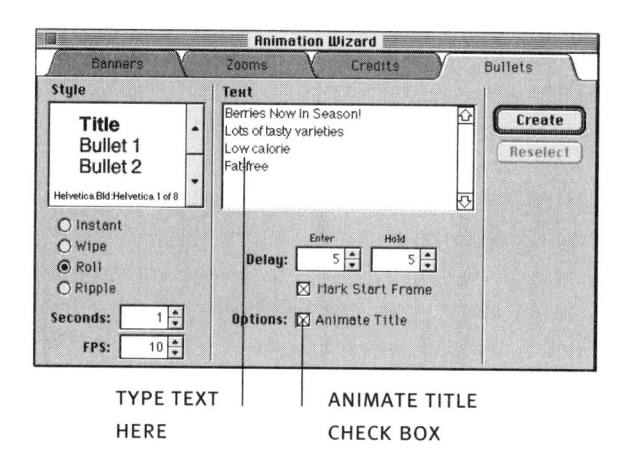

TYPE TEXT HERE   ANIMATE TITLE CHECK BOX

9] Set the Delay times by changing both the Enter and Hold values to 2.

The Enter value is the length of the pause before the bullet point starts animating; the Hold value determines how long the bullet point is displayed before the next action occurs.

10] Uncheck the Animate Title box.

If this box were checked, the title would animate onto the screen just like the bullets. With it unchecked, the title is immediately displayed on the screen. The Animation Wizard will use the first line of text in the text box as the title of the presentation.

11] Click the Create button.

This begins the process of creating the presentation in the score and cast. After a few seconds, you'll see that the Animation Wizard has added items to the score and cast. If you look at the cast, you can see that the Animation Wizard has automatically created cast members from the text you typed. If you look in the score, you can see that channels 1 through 4 contain numbers representing the cast members for each line of text.

Earlier in this lesson, you created a movie by placing sprites that represent cast members in the score. When you use the Animation Wizard, it does automatically most of what you earlier did manually. Check this out by playing the movie.

12] Rewind and play the movie.

Notice that the title is displayed without being animated because you unchecked the Animate Title box in the Animation Wizard.

13] Choose File > Save and save your work as Otto.dir in the MyWork folder.

WHAT YOU HAVE LEARNED
In this lesson you have:
Created text cast members using the Text window [*page* **19**]
Created a simple animation that moves lines of text across the screen by using In Between [*page* **25**]
Imported a graphic image [*page* **32**]
Changed the layer on which the graphic image appears by using the Shuffle Up button [*page* **34**]
Changed the opacity of the text by using ink effects [*page* **36**]

41

INTRODUCTION TO ANIMATION

starting a project

LESSON 3

Over the next three lessons you will build a portion of Macromedia's Showcase CD 5.0. You will bring together sound, graphics, text, animations, video, and interactive branching. In this lesson you will start the project by importing some media elements, setting the color of the stage, and putting a few of the elements into the score.

Macromedia's Showcase CD 5.0 (produced for Macromedia by Xronos, Inc.) is distributed to thousands of people who want to learn more about Macromedia. Because it uses many different animation sequences, video, and other features of Director, it's an ideal project for trying out many effects. In this lesson, you will set up basic movie properties and create a small portion of this project.

If you would like to view the final result of this lesson, open the Complete folder in the Lesson3 folder and play Market.dir.

To give you a jump-start, part of the marketing piece has been prebuilt for you by assembling many of the media elements in the cast and sequencing them in the score. The prebuilt movie, Start.dir, is located in the Lesson3 folder.

WHAT YOU WILL LEARN
In this lesson you will:

Set a background color for a movie

Practice setting a movie tempo

Practice importing graphics and text files

Practice using ink effects

Practice using in-betweening to create animation

APPROXIMATE TIME
It usually takes about 1 hour to complete this lesson.

LESSON FILES
Media Files
Lesson3\Media
Starting Files
Lesson3\Start.dir
Completed Project
Lesson3\Complete\Market.dir

43

STARTING A PROJECT

OPENING THE FILE

Start by opening the prebuilt file.

1] Choose File > Open to open Start.dir in the Lesson3 folder (Windows Ctrl+O, Macintosh Command+O).

Notice that many cells in the score have already been filled in to give you a jump-start on this project, and most of the cast members you need have already been imported.

2] Choose File > Save As. Save the file as Market1.dir in your MyWork folder.

This step preserves the original prebuilt file in case you want to repeat this lesson.

SETTING THE STAGE COLOR AND MOVIE TEMPO

In this task, you perform two steps that are common preliminaries to most projects: applying a color to the stage as the background color for the movie and setting the tempo of the movie in frames per second. Now set the background color and tempo for the movie.

1] Choose Modify > Movie > Properties to open the Movie Properties dialog box (Windows Ctrl+Shift+D, Macintosh Command+Shift+D).

The Movie Properties dialog box lets you specify options such as stage size and color for the currently open movie.

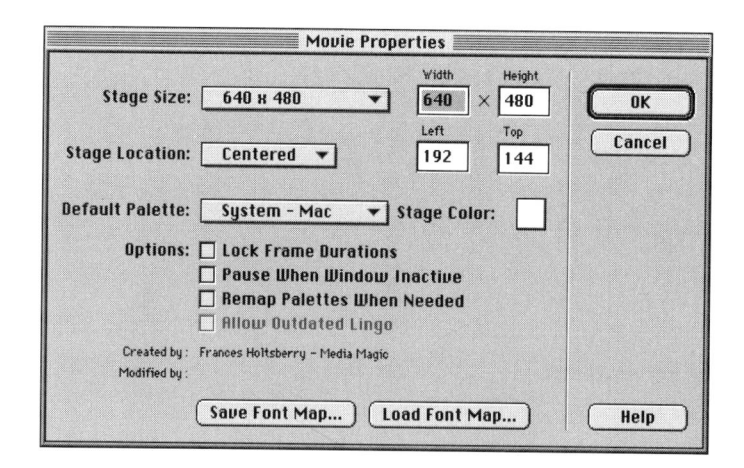

2] Click and hold the mouse button on the Stage Color chip and choose black from the pop-up palette. Click OK to close the dialog box.

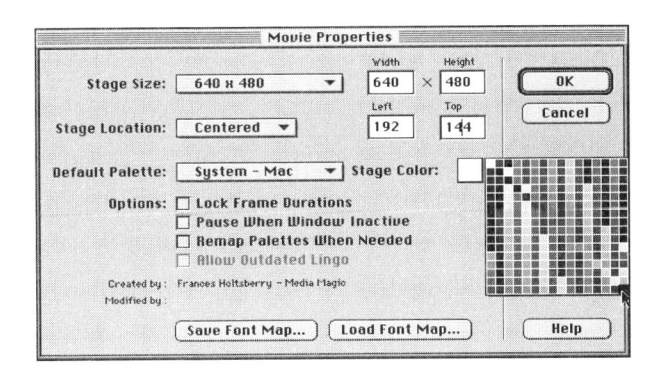

This changes the stage color so the movie is set against a black stage.

3] Click the Score Window icon in the toolbar to open the score if it's not already open (Windows Ctrl+4, Macintosh Command+4).

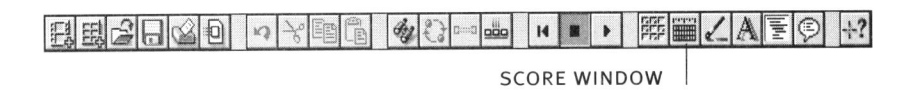

SCORE WINDOW

Now you will set a tempo for the movie: the speed at which the playback head moves from frame to frame.

4] In the tempo channel, double-click frame 1 to display the Tempo dialog box.
You could also select a frame and then choose Modify › Frame › Tempo to set the tempo.

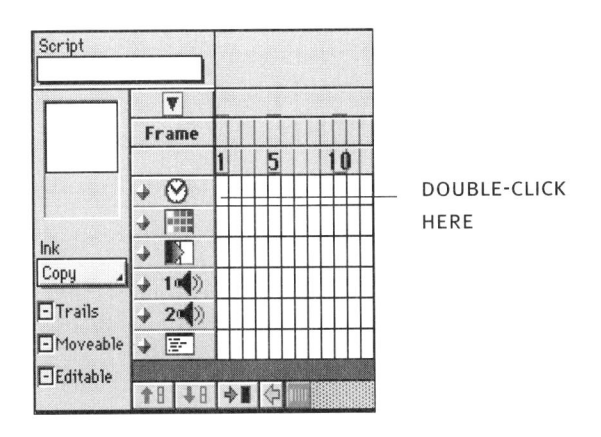

DOUBLE-CLICK HERE

45

STARTING A PROJECT

5] Select Tempo, set the frames per second (fps) to 10 by dragging the slider, and then click OK to close the dialog box.

You should see 10 in frame 1 of the tempo channel. Now the movie will run at 10 fps until Director encounters a new tempo setting in the channel.

CLICK TEMPO AND
DRAG THE SLIDER

tip *Director is frame based. Suppose you have a 60-frame movie set to run at 30 fps. Logically this results in a 2-second movie. However, if the computer is not capable of displaying the information fast enough, Director will show all the frames in the entire movie, no matter how many seconds it takes. QuickTime, on the other hand, will drop frames from the movie in order to play it for exactly 2 seconds.*

IMPORTING MEDIA ELEMENTS INTO THE CAST

To save you the trouble of building this complete presentation from scratch, the cast and score in the prebuilt file are partially filled in. In this task you import additional media elements.

1] Choose Window > Cast to open the Cast window if it isn't already open (Windows Ctrl+3, Macintosh Command+3).

As you can see in the Cast window, many media elements have already been imported for you, but cast member 9 is empty.

2] Select cast member 9, an empty cast position.

Selecting this position tells Director to import media starting at this point in the cast. If you don't select a cast position, Director will import media into the first empty cast member.

46

LESSON 3

3] Choose File › Import (Windows Ctrl+R, Macintosh Command+R), and in the Import dialog box, open the Media folder for Lesson 3.

You'll be importing a graphics file and a text file. Director imports many types of files, as you can see by opening the pop-up list under List Files of Type (Windows) or Show (Macintosh).

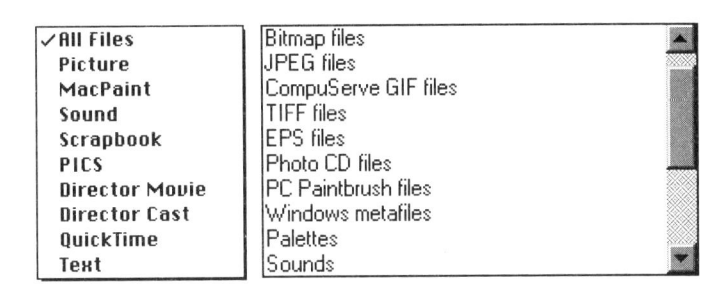

tip *Becoming familiar with the types of files Director can import is important so that you and your colleagues know what file formats to use for program files you may want to import into Director.*

4] Select Ticket.pct and click Add.

Ticket.pct appears in the file list.

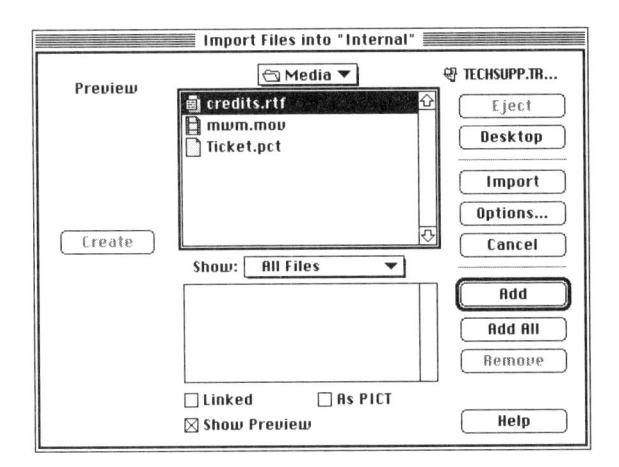

5] Select Credits.rtf, a Rich Text Format file, and click Add.

This adds the Rich Text Format (RTF) file, Credits.rtf, to the import list. An RTF file contains text as well as font information, paragraph information, and other formatting information that makes text look nice on the screen or on a printed page.

47

STARTING A PROJECT

6] Click Import. In the Image Options dialog box, click OK.

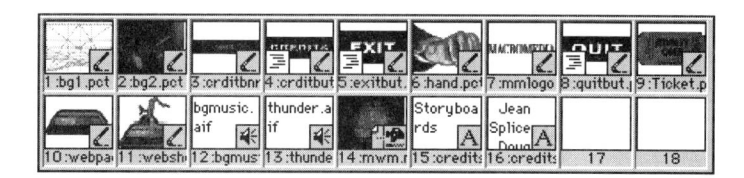

The Ticket.pct file becomes cast member 9. Because there were no empty cast positions after 9, the text file is added at the end of the cast, as cast members 15 and 16.

Why does one text file become two cast members? When Director imports an RTF file, it breaks the file into separate cast members wherever a page break occurs. The advantage of this feature is that you can type text in a word processor and add page breaks where needed. When you import the text into Director, the text will retain its page breaks. The Credits.rtf file has two pages, so it is imported as two cast members.

7] Choose File › Save to save your work (Windows Ctrl+S, Macintosh Command+S).

USING INK EFFECTS AND IN BETWEEN ON THE BACKGROUND IMAGE

In this task you place a background sprite on the stage. Remember that a sprite is only a representation of a cast member that has been placed in the score. Any changes made to a sprite in the score or on the stage do not affect the cast member in the Cast window.

1] In the Cast window, click cast member 1 (Bg1) to select it.

2] Drag cast member 1 to channel 1, frame 2, in the score.
This places the background graphic in the center of the stage.

3] With the same cell selected in the score, choose Bkgnd Transparent from the Ink pop-up menu.
This makes all the white space in the background image transparent, so the black stage shows through. Note that cast member 1 looks just the same as before in the Cast window, and it will appear that way if you drag it onto the stage anywhere else in the movie.

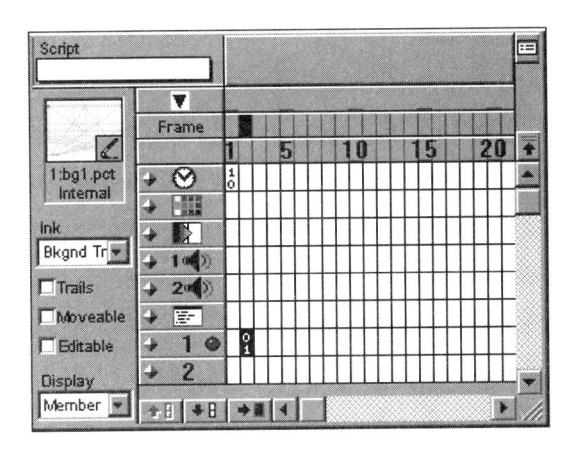

Ink effects modify the appearance of graphics on the stage only. They do not affect the original graphics themselves. You will often need to apply ink effects to graphics to make them appear exactly the way you want them. For example, to make the background pixels transparent on a sprite, you do not need to modify the cast member; you only need to apply the Bkgnd Transparent ink to the sprite.

shockwave tip   *Using ink effects is a great way to alter the appearance of a sprite without having to create new artwork. This also improves the download speed because only a single graphic needs to be downloaded. Note, though, that some ink effects are more memory intensive than others. The ink effects that are the least memory intensive are Copy, Matte, and Background Transparent. These are the first few effects listed in the Ink menu. The ink effects toward the bottom of the menu are the most memory intensive.*

In this movie the background needs to be visible from frame 2 through frame 48 so it is displayed on the stage for a while. You can manually place the background image into each of those frames, or you can have Director do it for you. Having Director place a cast member in a range of consecutive frames is called in-betweening. You used in-betweening in the previous lesson. Frames 2 and 48 are the key frames, and the cast members generated by Director will be the in-between frames. You need to in-between the background so it's displayed during frames 2 through 48.

First you need to modify one of your preferences to make the in-betweening process easier.

4] Choose File > Preferences > Score to open the Score Window Preferences dialog box.

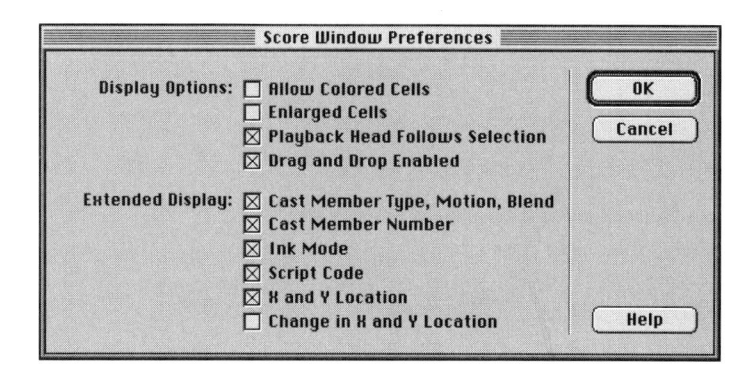

5] In the Display Options section, be sure Drag and Drop Enabled is unchecked. Then click OK to close the dialog box.

When drag and drop is enabled, the pointer in the score is a hand pointer. When you select a cell with the hand pointer and then drag, you move the sprite in the cell. For in-betweening, you want to select a cell and drag across many frames to select those frames. You don't want to move anything. When drag and drop is not checked, a pointer appears in the score instead of the hand. This pointer allows you to select a cell and then drag without moving the sprite in the selected cell. With drag and drop unchecked, it will be easier for you to in-between.

To toggle between the hand and the pointer in the score, press the spacebar.

6] Select channel 1, frame 2, and drag to channel 1, frame 48.

Be sure you drag only in channel 1. Frames 2 through 48 in channel 1 are now highlighted.

7] Choose Modify > In Between (Windows Ctrl+B, Macintosh Command+B).

You should now see 01, representing cast member 1, in all the selected frames. The background graphic has been in-betweened from frames 2 through 48 and will be displayed during those frames.

tip *You can see which cells have been in-betweened by looking at the top of the cell in the score. If three small dots appear, those cells have been in-betweened. Cells without dots have not been in-betweened.*

THE CELLS WITH THE THREE DOTS AT THE
TOP ARE THE IN-BETWEENED CELLS

8] Rewind and play the movie.

You should see the stage color and the background graphic you just incorporated. You also see the Macromedia text and the pointing hand animate onto the stage—the effect that was already in the prebuilt file. As the movie plays, notice the playback head move in the score. You may recall from the previous lesson that as Director plays the movie, what appears on the stage are the sprites in the frame that contains the playback head. As the playback head moves from frame to frame, Director erases the sprites in the frame it is leaving and redraws the stage with the sprites in the frame it enters. This is how the animation effects are created.

tip *With the movie stopped, you can see the animated effects within a range of frames by dragging the playback head back and forth. This is called scrubbing and is a good troubleshooting technique.*

tip *You can also play the movie and temporarily close all open windows by using the keyboard shortcut Alt+Ctrl+Shift+P (Windows) or Option+Command+Shift+P (Macintosh).*

tip *You can also use the numeric keypad to rewind, stop, and play. Press 0 to rewind, the decimal point (.) to stop, and Enter to play. If you press Shift+Enter, all the open windows will close, and you will see only the stage while the movie plays.*

9] Save your work.

WHAT YOU HAVE LEARNED

In this lesson you have:

Used movie properties to set a background stage color for a movie [*page* **44**]
Used the tempo channel to set a movie tempo [*page* **45**]
Imported graphics and text files into the cast [*page* **46**]
Used the Background Transparent ink effect to change the appearance of a sprite without affecting the corresponding cast member [*page* **48**]

transitions and sounds

LESSON 4

In the previous lesson you began building a portion of an interactive marketing piece. In this lesson you continue with the project, creating an animation that reverses, using a screen transition, and importing two files.

With special effects and sound you can capture your audience's attention and keep it! In this lesson you will continue building the Showcase CD by incorporating these effects and learning new techniques.

If you would like to view the final result of this lesson, open the Complete folder in the Lesson4 folder and play Market2.dir.

WHAT YOU WILL LEARN
In this lesson you will:

Create and reverse an animation

Exchange cast members in the score

Use a screen transition

Add sounds, including a sound that plays repeatedly

APPROXIMATE TIME
It usually takes about 1.5 hours to complete this lesson.

LESSON FILES
Media Files
None
Starting Files
Lesson4\Start.dir
Completed Project
Lesson4\Complete\Market2.dir

USING IN BETWEEN TO ANIMATE AN OBJECT

In this task you create an animation that moves the ticket graphic you imported in the last lesson down from the top of the screen.

1] Open Start.dir in the Lesson4 folder and save it as Market2.dir.

Alternatively, you can use the movie you worked on in the previous lesson and save it as Market2.dir in the MyWork folder.

2] Drag cast member 9 (Ticket) from the cast to channel 2, frame 3, in the score.

The ticket is now in the center of the stage.

3] On the stage, select the image of the ticket and drag it to the top center of the stage, so you can just see its bottom edge.

This will be the starting position of the animation.

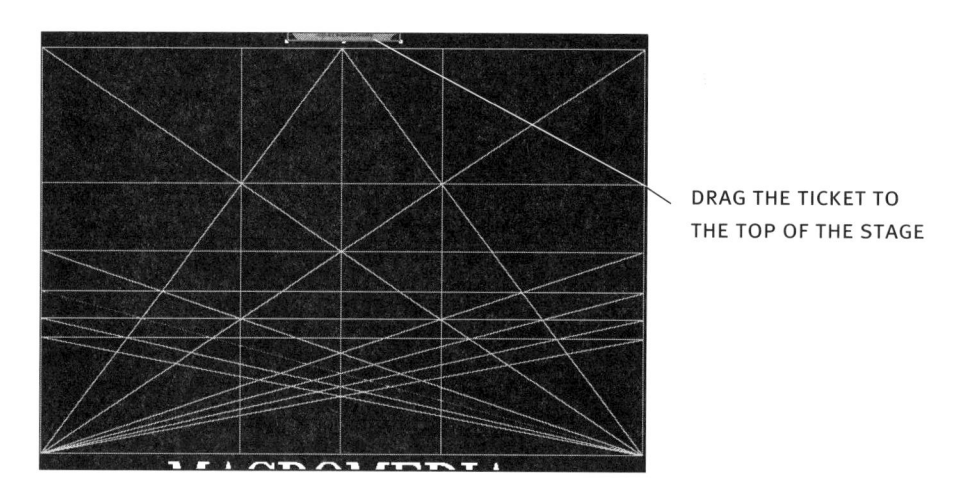

DRAG THE TICKET TO THE TOP OF THE STAGE

tip   *The toolbar takes up 10 pixels of the screen, so 10 pixels of the screen are hidden behind it. If you want to move the sprite completely off the stage, you will need to close the toolbar by choosing Window > Toolbar, and then move the sprite to the top of the stage.*

4] In the score, select channel 2, frame 3, and choose Edit > Copy Cells to copy the image of the ticket (Windows Ctrl+C, Macintosh Command+C).

5] Click channel 2, frame 15, and choose Edit > Paste Cells (Windows Ctrl+V, Macintosh Command+V).

The key frames for this animation will be frames 3 and 15 in channel 2.

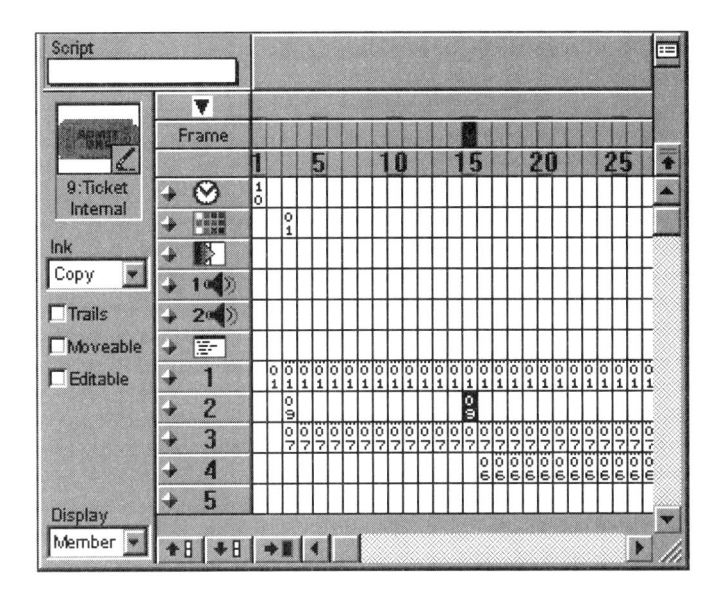

6] On the stage, drag the ticket down the screen while holding down the Shift key. Drag until the ticket is just above the Macromedia text.

tip *The Shift key constrains movement of a sprite on the stage either horizontally or vertically, depending on the direction you initially move the mouse.*

You're going to animate the ticket from the top of the stage to the center of the stage. You now have two copies of the ticket, but in different locations. The ticket in frame 3 is at the top of the stage, and the ticket in frame 15 is in the center of the stage. These two cells are the key frames. You can use the In Between command to fill the positions between the key frames and show movement.

7] Select channel 2, frame 3 through channel 2, frame 15.

8] Choose Modify > In Between (Windows Ctrl+B, Macintosh Command+B).
You've created an animation that moves the ticket from the top of the stage to the middle of the stage.

TRANSITIONS AND SOUNDS

9] Rewind and play the movie to check what you've done.

Next you'll make the ticket stay on the screen in its center-stage location a bit longer. You will do this by extending the number of frames in which the ticket is displayed.

10] In channel 2, click and drag from frame 15 through frame 29. Then apply In Between to the series of cells.

Now the ticket will animate and then stay on the screen for a while.

Did you notice the white edges around the ticket? You can apply an ink effect to the ticket so the white edges don't show.

11] Select channel 2, frames 3 through 29. From the Ink pop-up menu, choose Matte.

The edges around the ticket should now be black.

12] Rewind and then play the movie.

13] Save your work.

The Macromedia text and the pointing hand have already been animated using the same technique as used here. As the movie plays, you should see the ticket, the text, and the hand animate onto the stage. At this point, the stage should look like the image shown here.

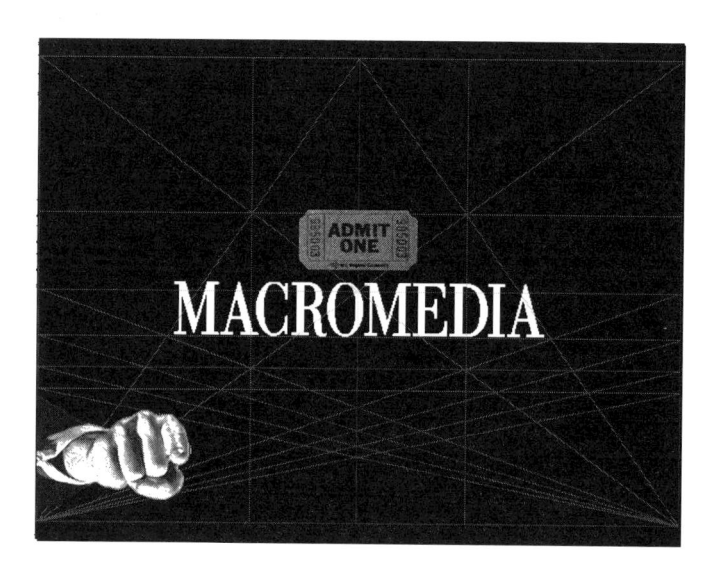

USING REVERSE SEQUENCE TO REVERSE THE ANIMATION

Next you'll animate the ticket off the stage by using the Reverse Sequence feature. This command reverses the selected cells so that the sprites are placed in the exact opposite order.

1] Select channel 2, frames 3 through 15, and copy the selection.

This part of the score animates the ticket down the stage.

2] Select channel 2, frame 30, and paste the selection.

You've pasted in the animation sequence. Now you'll reverse it.

3] Select channel 2, frames 30 through 42, and choose Modify > Reverse Sequence.

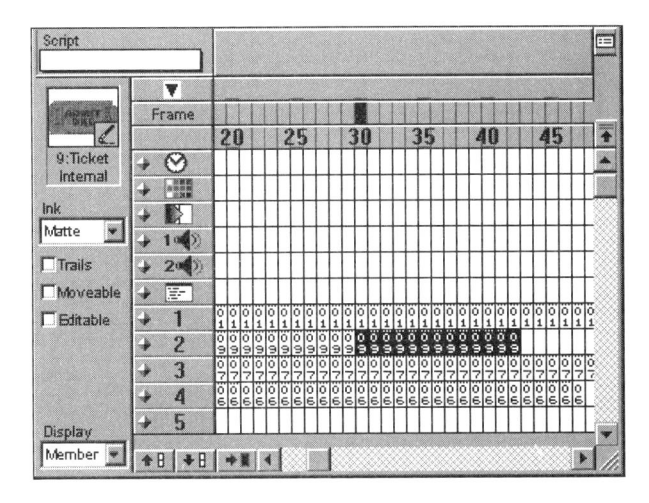

How will this affect the ticket? The ticket will move up on the stage instead of down.

4] Rewind and play the movie to see your progress.

The pointing hand has been animated using the same technique, so both the ticket and the hand animate off the stage.

EXCHANGING CAST MEMBERS TO CREATE A SPECIAL EFFECT

In this section, you'll practice a technique for alternating graphics in frames of the score to create the look and feel of lightning flashes.

1] Drag cast member 10 (Webpage) from the Cast window to channel 1, frame 49, in the score.

2] On the stage, drag the graphic down and left so its bottom is near the bottom center of the stage.

The reason the image of the Web page appeared in the upper-right part of the stage has to do with the image's registration point, which is a fixed reference point on a bitmapped image. When you drag a graphic to the stage, Director automatically centers the registration point on the stage. In this case, the registration point is at the bottom left of the image, so the graphic appeared high on the stage.

Next use an ink effect to remove the white rectangle around the graphic.

3] In the score, choose Matte from the Ink pop-up menu.

This removes the rectangular area around the sprite.

tip *You can also set the ink directly on the stage by first clicking the sprite on the stage, then pressing Ctrl (Windows) or Command (Macintosh), and then clicking the sprite on the stage again. This opens the Ink pop-up menu.*

4] Select channel 1, frames 49 to 54. Then in-between the selection.

Next replace the Web page image in every other frame with an image that's slightly different.

5] In the score, select channel 1, frame 49.

This contains cast member 10 (Webpage).

6] In the Cast window, select cast member 11 (Webshock).

Be sure the Cast window is active and cast member 11 is selected, or the following step won't work.

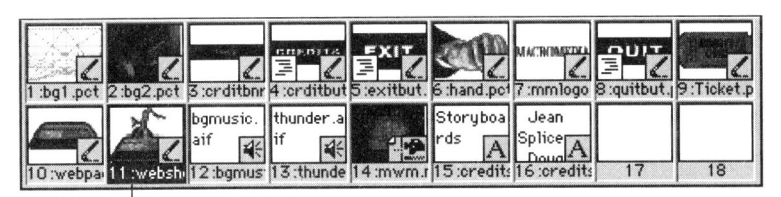

CLICK CAST MEMBER 11

7] In the toolbar at the top of the screen, click the Exchange Cast Members tool (Windows Ctrl+E, Macintosh Command+E).

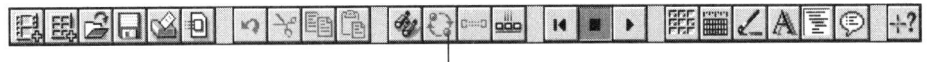

EXCHANGE CAST MEMBERS

The selected sprite in frame 49 (cast member 10) is replaced by the selected cast member in the Cast window (cast member 11). Look at the score and note that cast member 11 is now in the score where cast member 10 was previously.

You do the same for frames 51 and 53.

8] In the score, select channel 1, frame 51; in the Cast window, select cast member 11; and in the toolbar at the top of the screen, click the Exchange Cast Members tool.

The sprite in the score is changed.

9] In the score, select channel 1, frame 53; in the Cast window, select cast member 11; and then click the Exchange Cast Members tool.

The sprite in frame 53 is replaced by cast member 11.

59

TRANSITIONS AND SOUNDS

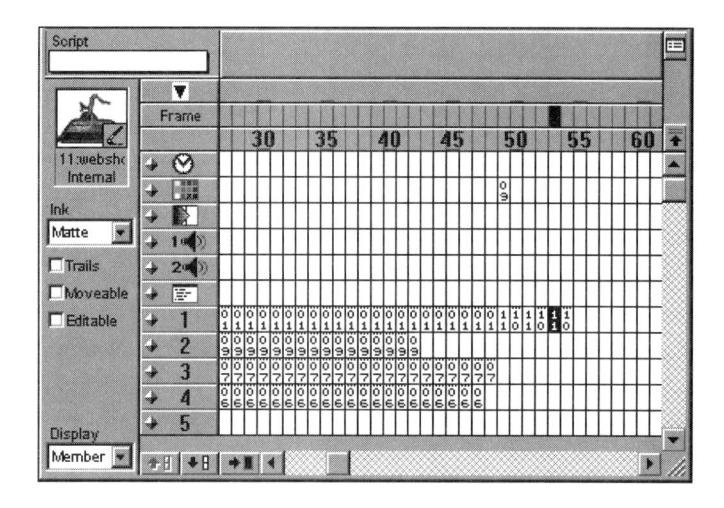

You just used a simple technique to rapidly alternate two graphics to create a flashing effect.

10] Rewind and play the movie.

Note that the image you exchanged with the Web page image appears in exactly the same position on the stage during the sequence. You didn't have to position it. The registration point on each image is in the same location on the art: the lower left. When you exchange cast members, Director aligns the registration points for you.

shockwave tip   As you see, a simple two- or three-frame animation can communicate a concept. Keep graphics and animations as small as possible for faster downloading over the Internet.

11] Save your work.

USING A SCREEN TRANSITION

In this task you use a screen *transition* twice to reveal a new image. Screen transitions are visual effects used to reveal or remove objects on the stage from one frame to another. For example, a Wipe Left transition displays the next frame of the movie by wiping it onto the screen starting from the right side of the stage and moving toward the left side, as if the viewer is opening a curtain. You can make the transition affect the entire stage or only the areas that are changing on the stage, and you can adjust the duration and smoothness of most transitions.

1] In the Transition channel, double-click frame 2 to display the Transition dialog box.

Frame 1 contains the black stage, and frame 2 contains the background sprite that you added earlier. Always place a transition in the frame where the new sprites appear on the stage. In this case, new sprites appear in frame 2. With the transition applied to frame 2, the background sprite will be revealed as the playback head moves from frame 1 (the black stage) to frame 2 (where the background sprite first appears). The transition actually begins to take effect when the playback head begins to exit frame 1.

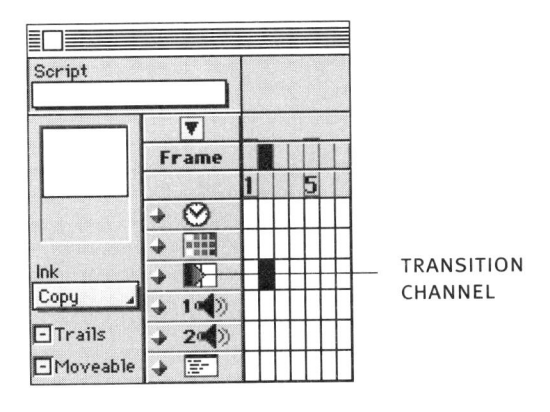

TRANSITION CHANNEL

2] From the Categories box, select All; from the Transitions box, select Center Out, Square; then click OK.

The transition now becomes cast member 17 in the Cast window.

You'll use the same transition in one other part of the piece; you can copy and paste a transition just like any other cast member.

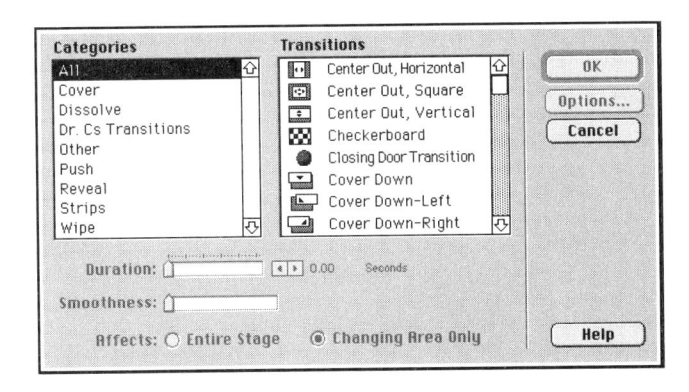

3] Select frame 2 in the transition channel and copy it.

4] Select frame 49 of the transition channel and paste the transition.

5] Rewind and play the movie.

Now you can see how the transition looks in both places.

6] Save your work.

tip *Many transition effects are available as Xtras—extensions that add new capabilities to Macromedia products. Xtras use the Macromedia Open Architecture (MOA) standard to ensure that the same Xtra can work with more than one product. For example, Transition Xtras now available from third parties work in Authorware as well as Director. Go to Macromedia's Web site for information on Transition Xtras now available. Once you have purchased or created an Xtra, you must make it available to Director by copying it to Director's Xtras folder.*

ADDING SOUNDS TO THE SCORE

The next part of this project calls for adding sound in two places in the score. In one case, the sound will loop, or play continuously throughout the movie. In the other case, the sound will play for only a few frames.

1] Drag cast member 12 (Bgmusic) from the Cast window to sound channel 1, frame 1, in the score.

You should see 12 in the cell. This sound will be background throughout the production, so you start it in frame 1.

2] Select cast member 12 in the Cast window and click the Cast Member Properties button in the Cast window.

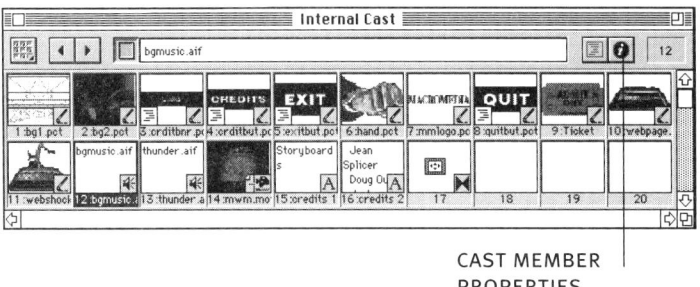

CAST MEMBER PROPERTIES

3] In the dialog box, check the Loop box. Then click OK.

When Director reaches the end of the sound file, it will start again at the beginning.

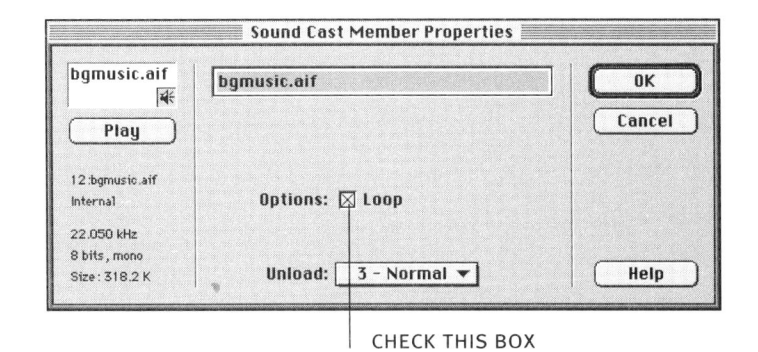

CHECK THIS BOX

Next you'll in-between the sound so it plays through all the frames of the movie.

4] Select Sound channel 1, frames 1 through 73, and choose Modify > In Between.

The sound should now play throughout the movie.

5] Rewind and play the movie.

The sound adds life to this presentation.

Now you will make it more dramatic by adding a thunder sound to sound channel 2 and playing it while the lightning graphics are displayed.

shockwave tip   *Many small sounds add life to movies and can be reused throughout a movie. Sound effects can be sampled at a lower rate than a voice-over and still be acceptable. Digitized speech typically never runs at less than 8-bit 22 kHz, whereas sound effects can run at half that size, at 8-bit 11 kHz.*

6] Drag cast member 13 (Thunder) to Sound channel 2, frame 49, in the score. In-between it from frame 49 to frame 54.

You need to make sure that this new sound finishes playing before leaving the last image. That requires a tempo setting.

7] In the tempo channel, double-click frame 54.

The Tempo dialog box opens.

You can also open this dialog box by selecting the frame and then choosing Modify › Frame › Tempo.

8] Choose Wait for End of Sound in Channel 2 and click OK.

The playback head will not move forward until the sound in channel 2 is finished playing.

CLICK HERE

9] Rewind and play the movie.

Great sound effects! As the movie plays, notice that the playback head pauses a bit when it reaches this second sound. When the sound finishes, the playback head continues. Why did the playback head pause? Because you selected Wait for End of Sound in Channel 2 in the previous steps.

tip *The ability to turn sound on and off will come in handy as you develop a production, when you may tire of hearing the sounds in your movie over and over. When you're ready to view your production in full, you can turn the sound on again.*

10] Click the on/off toggle in sound channel 1 to turn off the looping music.

To hear the music again at any time during this project, click the on/off toggle again. Notice that every channel has an on/off toggle.

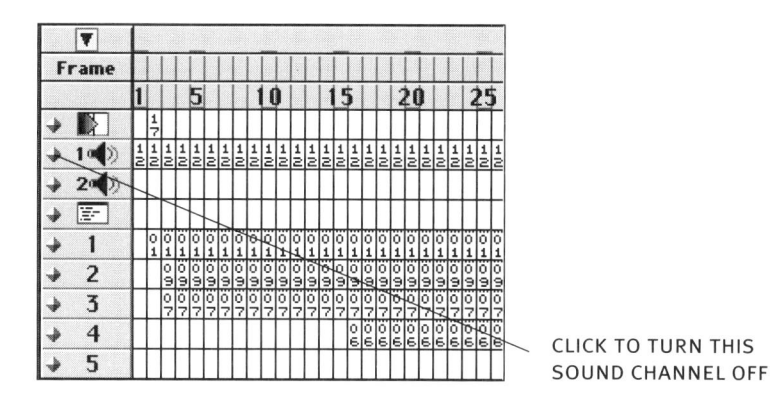

CLICK TO TURN THIS SOUND CHANNEL OFF

tip When you open any movie, all the toggles are turned on. Toggle off states are not saved when you save a movie.

11] Save your work.

WHAT YOU HAVE LEARNED
In this lesson you have:

Used In Between and Reverse Sequence to create and reverse an animation **[page 54]**

Used the Exchange Cast Members command to swap cast members in the score **[page 58]**

Used a screen transition **[page 61]**

Added sounds and used the Loop option make the sound continuous **[page 62]**

TRANSITIONS AND SOUNDS

adding interactivity

LESSON 5

In this lesson you complete the interactive marketing project you've been working on for the past few chapters. This will involve creating new screens, adding interactivity, and importing a digital video file.

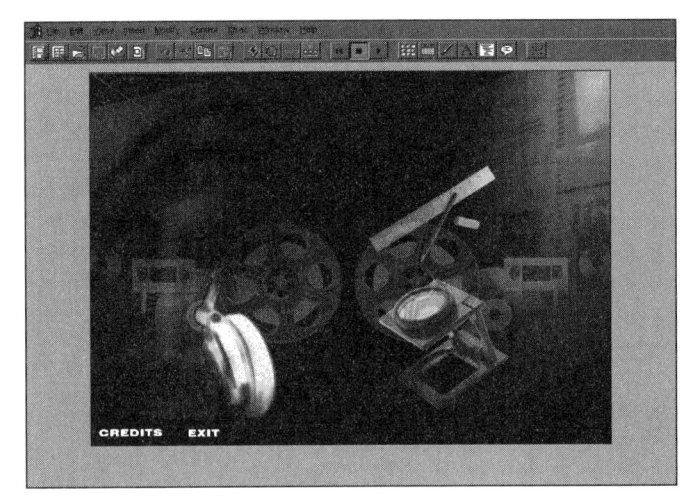

In this lesson you will continue working with the Showcase CD, creating interactive buttons that let users decide what parts of the product to view. You will also incorporate digital video and create a stand-alone projector so users can view the movie without having to install Director.

If you would like to view the final result of this lesson, open the Complete folder in the Lesson5 folder and play Market3.dir.

WHAT YOU WILL LEARN
In this lesson you will:

Align text and other elements on the stage

Insert pauses

Include digital video in a movie

Add navigation markers to the score

Use Lingo commands for navigation

Create a play-only version of a movie to distribute to end-users

APPROXIMATE TIME
It usually takes about 1 hour to complete this lesson.

LESSON FILES
Media Files
None
Starting Files
Lesson5\Start.dir
Completed Project
Lesson5\Complete\Market3.dir

BUILDING THE MENU SCREEN

In this task you create the menu screen with two buttons that allow the user to navigate to a credits screen and to exit the movie.

1] Open Start.dir in the Lesson5 folder and save it as Market3.dir.

This is the prebuilt file. If you completed the previous lesson, you can use the movie you worked on there and save it as Market3.dir in the MyWork folder.

2] Drag cast member 2 (Bg2) from the Cast window to channel 1, frame 55, in the score.

This is the background for the menu screen.

3] Drag cast member 4 (Crditbut) from the Cast window to channel 2, frame 55, in the score.

This is the Credits button users will click to get to the Credits screen.

4] Drag cast member 5 (Exitbut) from the Cast window to channel 3, frame 55.

This is the Exit button users will click to leave the movie.

5] On the stage, position the Credits and Exit buttons side by side at the lower left.

You can use the grid or the alignment palette to help you position the buttons. The alignment palette gives you a variety of horizontal and vertical alignment options. To open the alignment palette, click the Align icon on the toolbar or choose Modify › Align (Windows Ctrl+K, Macintosh Command+K).

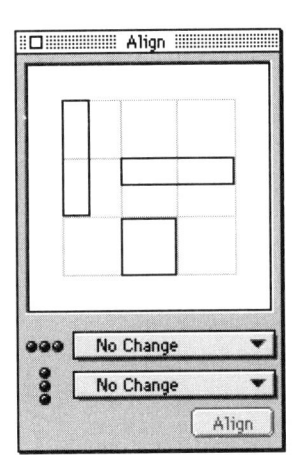

Use the alignment options to align several sprites with a referenced object on the stage. The first sprite you select becomes the reference object.

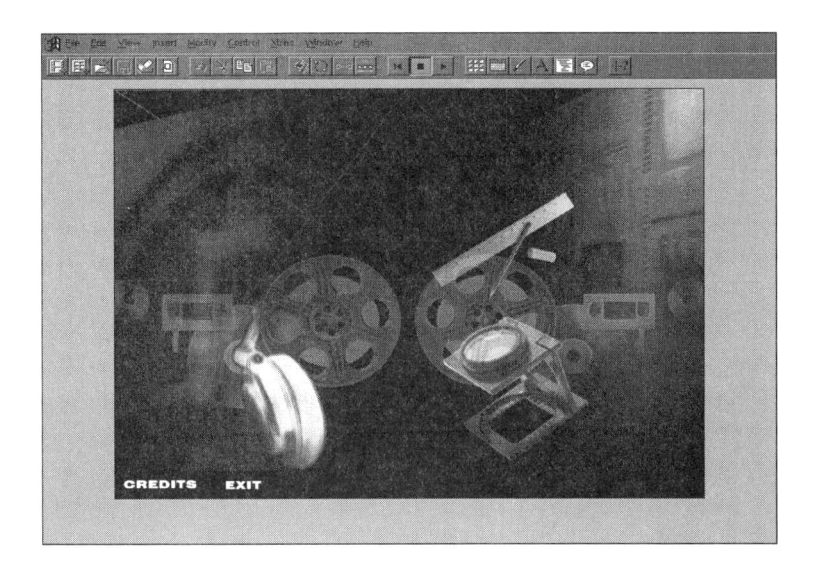

6] In the score, select channels 1, 2, and 3, frame 55, and in-between them to frame 56.

USING INK EFFECTS, ALIGNMENT, AND WAIT

In this task you create the credits screen by bringing text onto the stage and aligning it.

1] Drag cast member 15 to channel 2, frame 65, of the score.

This is a text cast member you imported in a previous lesson.

2] Drag cast member 16 to channel 3, frame 65.

You need to use an ink effect to remove the white rectangles behind the text.

3] Select the two cells (channels 2 and 3, frame 65). Then from the Ink pop-up menu, choose Bkgnd Transparent.

This ink makes the pixels in the background color of the sprites appear transparent, so you can see the background.

4] Drag cast member 3 (Crditbnr) to channel 1, frame 65.

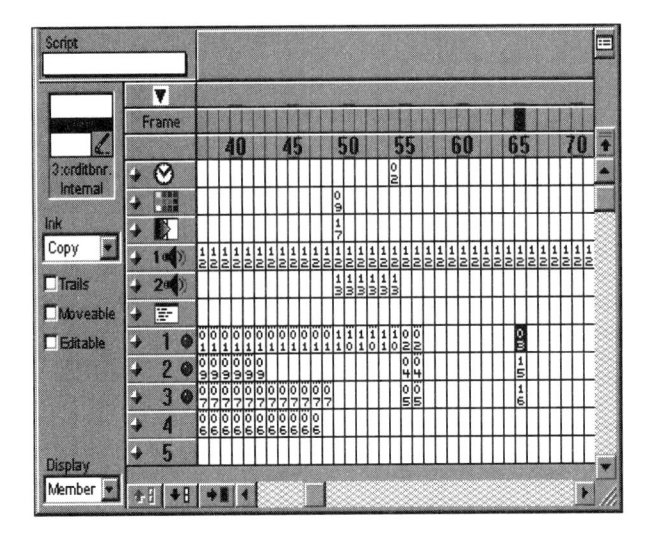

You've brought the elements of the Credits screen onto the stage. It's time to position them so everything looks symmetrical and centered.

5] In the Cast window, double-click cast member 16 to open the Text window.

You'll see the text of the Credits screen. It's already formatted because it was saved from the program that created it as an RTF file, a text format that maintains the colors, fonts, and indents from the imported original file. You can use the Text window to create text from scratch and also to change any of the text attributes.

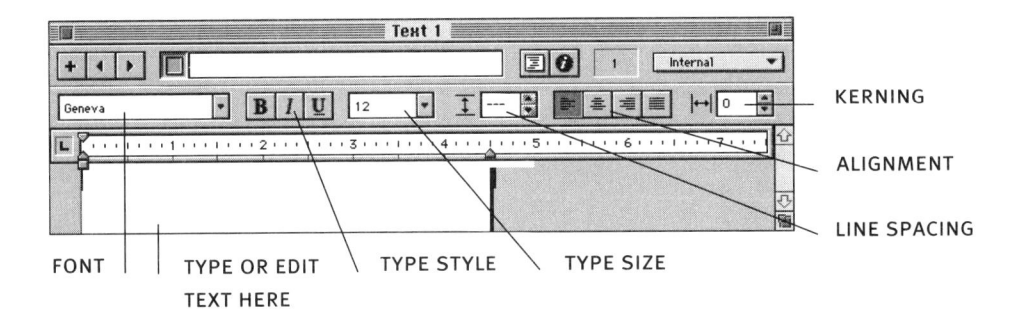

KERNING
ALIGNMENT
LINE SPACING
FONT
TYPE OR EDIT TEXT HERE
TYPE STYLE
TYPE SIZE

6] Select the entire block of text in the window.

To do this, you can either triple-click the text or click in the upper-left corner of the Text window and drag down to the lower-right corner.

7] Click the Align Center button on the Text window toolbar to center the lines of text. Then close the Text window.

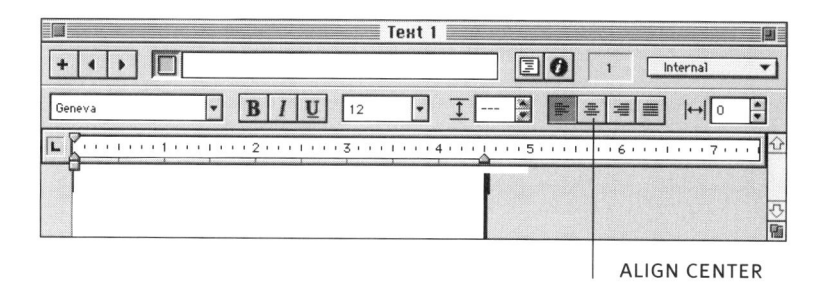

ALIGN CENTER

8] On the stage, align the elements so the screen looks like the following picture.

You may need to resize the boxes around the text by dragging a corner.

tip *Using the grid can make aligning objects on the stage much easier. To use the grid, choose View › Grid › Show (Windows Alt+Ctrl+Shift+G, Macintosh Option+Command+ Shift+G). The same command turns off the grid when you have finished aligning objects. You can set the color and spacing of the grid by choosing View › Grid › Settings.*

9] In the score, select three cells in frame 65: channels 1, 2, and 3. Choose Modify › In Between to in-between them to frame 67.

Next you add a pause so the credits stay on the screen long enough for people to read them. Note that you could in-between the frames over several more frames instead of adding a pause, but the pause gives you more precise control because you can set a specific number of seconds to pause.

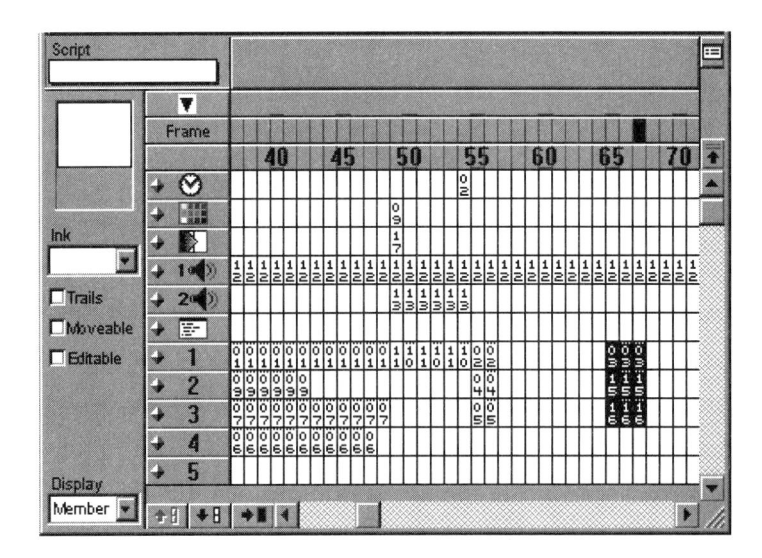

10] Double-click the tempo channel in frame 66 to open the Tempo dialog box.

You're going to set a delay for only this frame. Once the playback head passes this frame, the tempo returns to the one you originally set in the tempo channel.

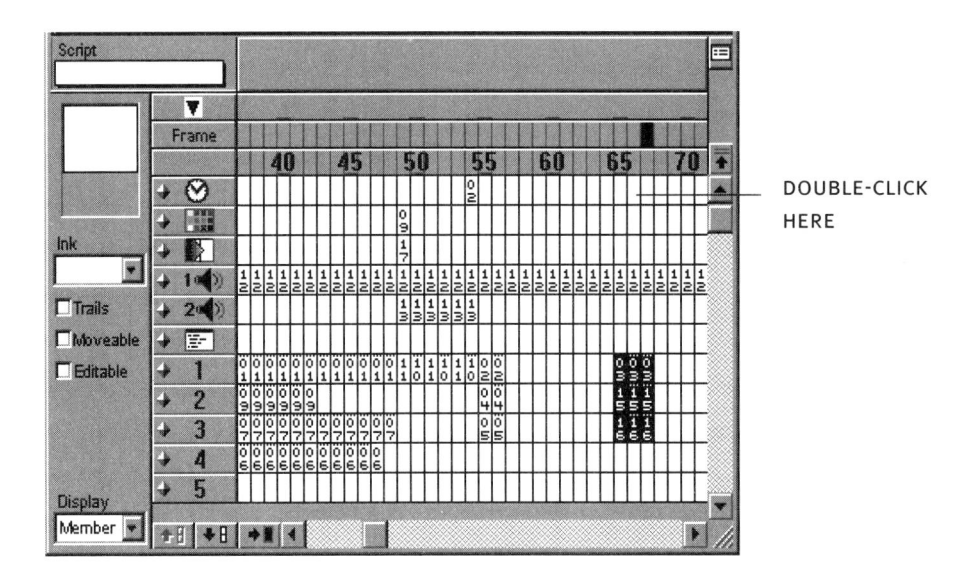

DOUBLE-CLICK HERE

11] Click Wait, set the slider to 2 seconds, and click OK to close the dialog box.

12] Rewind and play the movie to see what you've added.

13] Save your work.

ADDING DIGITAL VIDEO

Now it's time to assemble the ending of the presentation by adding a digital video file.

1] Drag cast member 14 (Mwm.mov) from the Cast window to channel 1, frame 70, of the score and in-between it from frame 70 through frame 73.

This file is a QuickTime movie of a "Made with Macromedia" logo.

2] Double-click frame 71 in the tempo channel. In the Tempo dialog box, click Wait for End of Digital Video in Channel. Type *1* in the Channel field. Click OK to close the dialog box.

Before the playback head continues, it will wait until the digital video in channel 1 is finished playing.

3] Double-click frame 72 in the tempo channel, click Wait, set the slider to 2 seconds, and click OK to close the dialog box.

After the movie finishes playing, the last frame of the movie will stay on the stage for 2 more seconds because the playback head will stay on this frame for 2 seconds.

4] Save your work.

ADDING MARKERS FOR NAVIGATION

Now that you've learned several ways of sequencing the media for a Director movie, it's time to learn the last two steps of the four-step process described in Lesson 2: adding interaction and creating a projector—one way of packaging the movie for distribution. In this task, you begin to create the interaction by adding buttons that users can click to navigate to different parts of the movie. So far, you've created linear movies only—they play from start to end without any user interaction. With Lingo, you can provide a way for users to control how they view the movie.

You've already built a credits screen and a menu screen. In preparation for scripting the navigation between these screens, you will add markers to the score. These triangular markers are used to identify frames of the movie. After you drag a marker in the score, you can type a label next to it. The marker label is used to branch to a location in a movie. The Lingo script included in the prebuilt file relies on the marker label, so be sure you type the label exactly as described in the following steps.

1] Drag a marker from the upper left of the score to frame 55 and type *Menu* next to it.

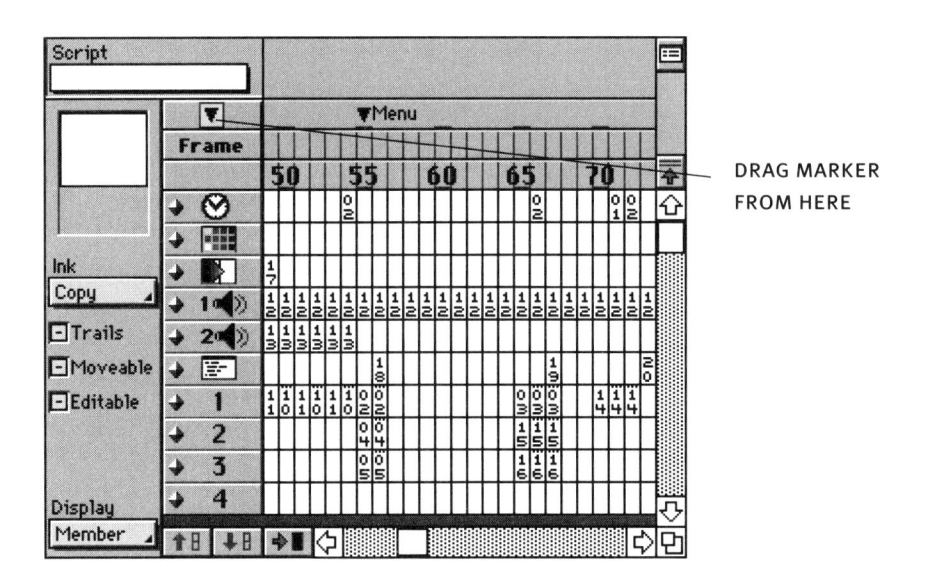

DRAG MARKER FROM HERE

Remember: The prebuilt movie relies on the marker label, so be sure you type the label exactly as it is shown here.

2] Drag a marker from the upper left of the score to frame 65 and type *Credits* next to it.

Again, be sure to type the label accurately.

3] Drag another marker to frame 70 and type *Exit* next to it.

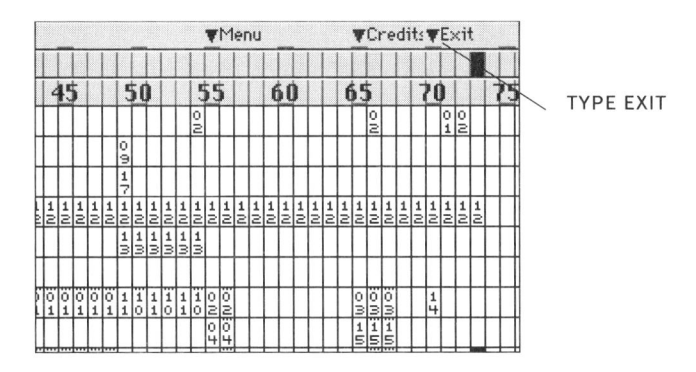

TYPE EXIT

CREATING NAVIGATION SCRIPTS

In this task you create simple navigation scripts that use the markers you just inserted in the score.

Scripts are combinations of words that convey instructions and information to Director. Scripts are written in Lingo, a language very similar to English. A set of Lingo statements is called a *handler;* handlers "handle" events such as mouse clicks and keyboard commands. A handler is a set of instructions, grouped like sentences in a paragraph, and has a beginning and an end.

Here you'll create a statement that causes the menu screen to remain on the stage while Director waits for a button to be clicked.

1] In the script channel, double-click frame 56.

The Script window opens.

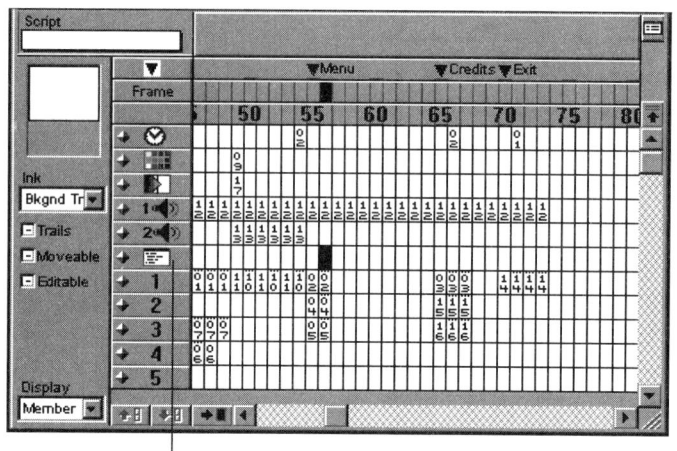

SCRIPT CHANNEL

The two statements *on exitFrame* and *end* are already in the Script window, and the insertion point is indented under the first line. Whenever you double-click the script channel, the Script window opens and contains these two statements.

2] Type *go to the frame* in the Script window below *on exitFrame*.

```
on exitFrame
   go to the frame
end
```

Recall that handlers handle events. In this case, this handler will handle the *exitFrame* event, which occurs when the playback head exits a frame. Typing *go to the frame* will make the playback head go to the frame in which it's already located. In other words, the playback head stays in the same frame, and all sprites in that frame remain displayed on the stage.

The phrase *the frame* is a built-in Lingo function that returns the frame where the playback head is currently located. If the playback head is on frame 50, 50 is returned. If it's on 10, 10 is returned. The value returned is completely dependent on the current location of the playback head.

The *on exitFrame* statement tells Director to follow the instructions in the handler as soon as the playback head leaves the frame. In this case, of course, upon leaving the frame the playback head is sent right back to that same frame. The result is that the playback head never leaves the frame.

> **tip** *Never loop on a frame with a transition because the transition will play over and over, and you won't be able to see the mouse pointer.*

3] Close the Script window. Then rewind and play the movie.

The movie plays and then pauses at the menu screen. Look at the playback head and notice that it's paused on this frame. It pauses here because of the script you added in the previous step.

Next you will create a script to return users to the menu screen after the credits screen is displayed.

> **tip** *You can press Enter on the numeric keypad to close the Script window.*

4] Double-click frame 67 in the script channel.

The Script window opens.

5] Type *go to frame "Menu"* below *on exitFrame*. Then close the Script window.

```
on exitFrame
  go to frame "Menu"
end
```

Remember that earlier you created a marker called Menu. Now you're using Lingo to find that marker and branch to it. After the credits screen is displayed for 2 seconds, the playback head will move immediately to the Menu marker, and the menu screen will reappear.

Note that there's a big difference between the expression *go to the frame*—which basically means stay in the current frame—and the expression *go to frame "marker"*—which requires you to specify a destination frame for the playback head to branch there. In scripting Lingo, one word can make a big difference.

77

ADDING INTERACTIVITY

6] Rewind and play the movie. When you get to the menu screen, click the Credits button.

The credits screen should be displayed for 2 seconds, and then the menu screen should reappear.

The prebuilt file already contains the scripts for the Credits and Exit buttons so they branch to the markers you created in this lesson. These buttons contain *go to* scripts like the ones you just added.

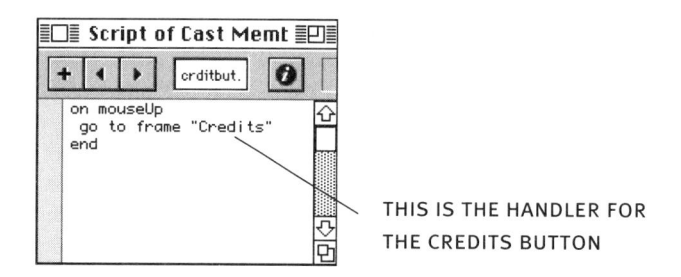

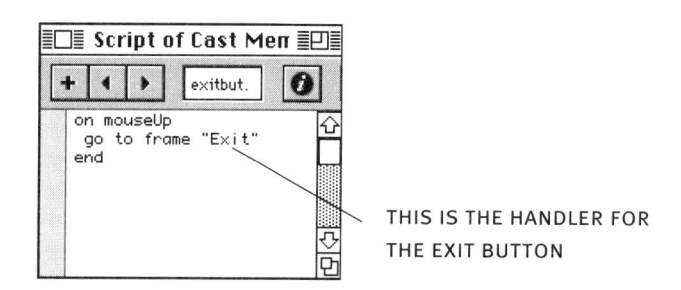

```
on mouseUp
  go to frame "Credits"
end
```

THIS IS THE HANDLER FOR THE CREDITS BUTTON

```
on mouseUp
  go to frame "Exit"
end
```

THIS IS THE HANDLER FOR THE EXIT BUTTON

tip Marker labels are not case-sensitive, but spelling is important. If you spell a label one way and then refer to it later with a different spelling, Director will not be able to locate the marker and will return an error message.

7] Click the Stop button on the toolbar to stop the movie (Windows Ctrl+. (period), Macintosh Command+. (period)).

Next you'll create a script to exit the movie after the "Made with Macromedia" video finishes. Recall that in the previous steps, you added a 2-second wait period so that after the video finishes playing, the last frame of the video stays on the stage for 2 more seconds.

8] Double-click the script channel in frame 73, the last frame of the movie.

The Script window opens.

9] Type *quit* below *on exitFrame* and close the Script window.

```
on exitFrame
    quit
end
```

The *quit* command closes Director and displays the desktop. In this case, Director will close after the last frame of the "Made with Macromedia" video stays on the screen for 2 seconds (because of the 2-second wait period).

> **tip** *The* quit *command closes the Director program itself, not just the movie that is open. You should be sure to save your work before clicking the Quit button.*

10] Save your work.

11] Rewind and play the movie.

The movie should pause at the menu screen.

12] Click Credits.

The credits screen is displayed for 2 seconds, and then the menu screen is displayed again.

13] When you're ready to quit, click Exit.

After you click Exit, the "Made with Macromedia" video plays, a 2-second pause occurs, and then Director quits. Remember that this button works because the prebuilt file already contains the scripts for the Exit button.

CREATING A PROJECTOR

You're almost finished. To distribute a movie to users who don't own Director, you can either "shock" the movie for playback on the World Wide Web or create a projector, which is a play-only version of a movie. Shocking a movie is discussed in Lesson 15. In this lesson you create a projector.

You can use the same Director movie to create a projector for either the Macintosh or Windows platform. To create a projector for Windows, you must use the Windows version of Director. To create a projector for the Macintosh, you need the Macintosh version of Director.

tip *Why do you need both Windows and Macintosh versions of Director to create projectors for both platforms? There are significant differences between these two platforms that require you to view, edit, and tweak a movie on the platform on which it will play. You may have to make changes to such things as color palettes, fonts, window locations, and Xtras.*
If you use Xtras that come from developers other than Macromedia, be sure to check the documentation for each Xtra for any restrictions on distribution (some may not allow you to distribute work created with them unless you pay a fee). So that Xtras always work in the projector, create a folder and put the projector in it. In the same folder place an Xtras folder that contains any Xtras the projector uses. When the end-user runs the projector from this folder, Director will be able to locate and use the Xtras needed for the projector.

1] Open Director if it isn't already open.

2] Choose File > Create Projector.

The Create Projector dialog box appears.

3] Open the MyWork folder and double-click Market3.dir.

This is the movie you have been working on in this lesson.

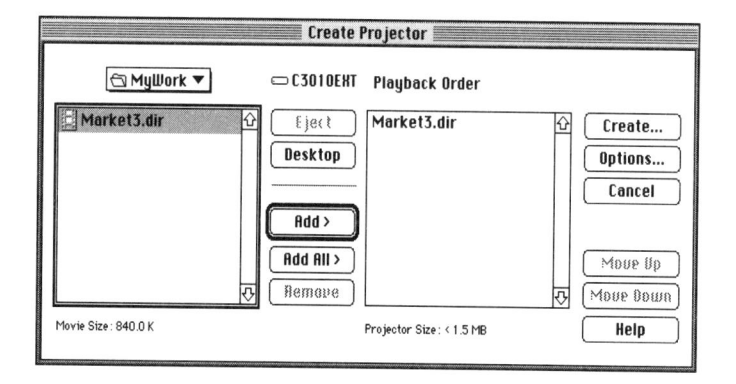

4] **Click Options. In the Create for pop-up list at the top of the Projection Options dialog box, select the type of computer on which the projector will run—in this case, the computer you're using right now. Click OK to close the dialog box and return to the Create Projector dialog box.**

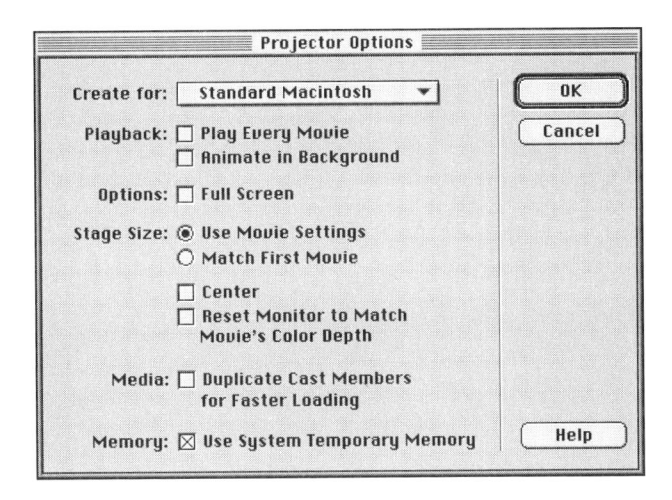

5] **Click Create.**
A Save dialog box appears.

6] **Select the MyWork folder and name the file MyMrktng. Then click Save.**
A status dialog box appears while Director builds the projector. When the process is finished, look in the MyWork folder. You should see a projector icon titled MyMrkting. On Windows machines, the name will have an .exe extension.

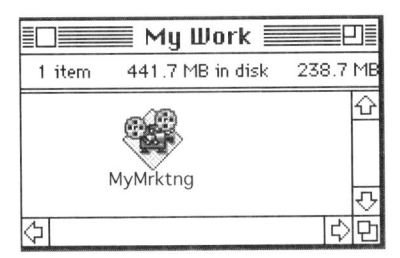

7] When Director finishes building the projector, quit Director.

8] Locate the projector you just created and play it.

To play the projector, double-click it. This launches the play-only version of Director, which plays the movie or movies embedded in it and then quits Director automatically.

You've created a mini-version of the opening scene of Macromedia's Showcase CD in a short period of time. Of course, if you were to develop a complete interactive marketing piece, you would add product facts and data, company information, and so forth.

Before distributing any projector, check your licensing agreements with any other companies whose products you may need to distribute with the projector.

tip *On the Macintosh, you can easily create a custom icon for your projector. The following are instructions for System 7.x.x. To replace the projector icon, copy the image you want to use onto the clipboard. Select the projector icon in the Finder and choose File › Get Info. In the Information window, select the image of the icon and choose Edit › Paste to paste the icon from the clipboard. After you close the Information window, the new image will appear in place of the projector icon.*

tip *Macromedia's royalty-free licensing policy means that you can distribute applications created with Director or Authorware to millions of end-users on multiple platforms—free. The requirements are that you include the "Made with Macromedia" logo on your product's packaging and credit screen, complete the run-time distribution agreement, and register your product with Macromedia. Refer to the Made with Macromedia (MwM) folder on your Director Multimedia Studio CD for the run-time distribution agreement, logos, and logo usage guidelines. Before distributing any projector, check your licensing agreements with any other companies whose products you may need to distribute with the projector.*

WHAT YOU HAVE LEARNED
In this lesson you have:

Aligned text and other elements on the stage while building a menu screen [*page* **71**]

Inserted pauses using the Wait setting in the tempo channel of the score [*page* **72**]

Added digital video to a movie [*page* **73**]

Added navigation markers to the score [*page* **74**]

Used the Lingo commands *go to the frame*, *go to frame "marker"*, and *quit* for navigation [*page* **75**]

Created a projector to distribute to end-users [*page* **79**]

techniques

other animation

In this lesson you will create special effects using two animation techniques: In Between Special and real-time recording.

In Between Special is like In Between in that it automatically creates sprites for each cell between key frames in the score. In Between Special, though, enables Director to interpolate more than a simple change in position. You use it when you want a sprite to move in a curved path, to accelerate or decelerate across the stage, or to change color or blend.

Real-time recording can be used to replay the actions you use to create an effect on stage. In this lesson, you will use it to animate the dotted lines in this graphic.

LESSON 6

You use real-time recording to move a sprite around the stage with the mouse. When you use real-time recording, Director automatically records the movements in the score.

In Between Special can create appropriate in-between sprites for animations that move in special patterns such as circles. You'll use it to make the sun travel in an arc in this lesson.

If you would like to view the final result of this lesson, open the Complete folder in the Lesson6 folder and play Sun.dir and Skater.dir.

WHAT YOU WILL LEARN

In this lesson you will:

Set movie properties

Create a circular animation with a special type of in-betweening

Record mouse movements in real-time

Leave a trail of sprites on the stage

LESSON FILES
Media Files
Lesson6\Media
Starting Files
None
Completed Project
Lesson6\Complete\Sun.dir
Lesson6\Complete\Skater.dir

APPROXIMATE TIME
It usually takes about 1 hour to complete this lesson.

OTHER ANIMATION TECHNIQUES

SETTING MOVIE PROPERTIES

In this lesson you use In Between Special to create animation along a circular path to make a sun move in a circle. Your first task is to import the media and set the background color.

1] Choose File > New > Movie to open a new movie (Windows Ctrl+N, Macintosh Command +N).

2] Choose File > Save and save the movie as Sun.dir (Windows Ctrl+S, Macintosh Command+S).

3] Choose File > Import and select the Smallsun.pct file in the Media folder (Windows Ctrl+R, Macintosh Command+R). Click Add and then click Import.

Because the graphic is a 32-bit image and the stage is set to 8-bit color depth, the Image Options dialog box is displayed.

4] In the Image Options dialog box, click Stage (8 bits), then click OK.

Now you have a picture of a sun in the cast.

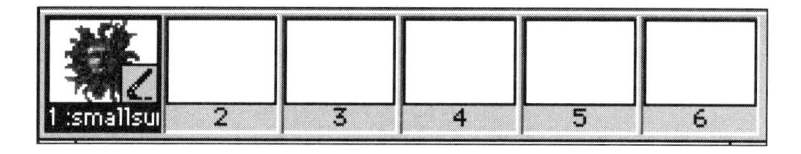

5] Choose Modify > Movie > Properties and click the Stage Color chip in the dialog box that appears.

The color palette opens.

6] Click the black square in the lower-right corner of the palette and close the Movie Properties dialog box.

You now have a black stage.

SETTING KEY FRAMES

Now you'll set the key frames for the sun's movement.

1] Drag the sun from the Cast window to channel 1, frame 1, and set the ink to Matte.
As you can see, the Matte ink removes the bounding box (rectangular area) around the sprite. Artwork within the boundaries is opaque. Matte functions much like the lasso in the Paint window, in that the artwork is outlined rather than enclosed in a rectangle.

You know by now that a key frame is a key position in an animation, where a change takes place. You're going to animate the sun in this task by moving it around the stage, creating key frames, and in-betweening the key frames. To make your sprite follow a curved path, you must set the sprite in at least three positions on the stage in different frames.

2] Place the sun in the upper-left area of the stage.
This is the first key frame of the animation you're about to create.

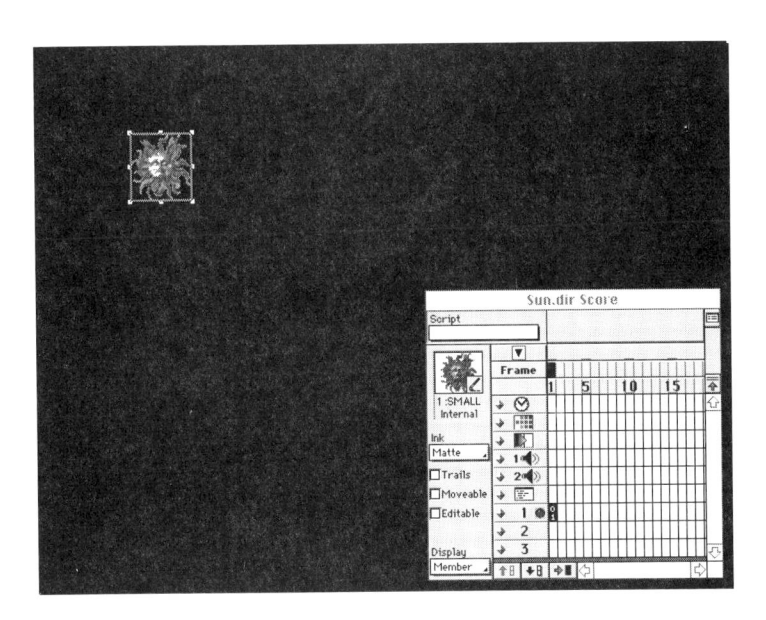

3] In the score, copy the frame and paste it into frame 15. Then drag the sun to the upper-right corner of the stage.

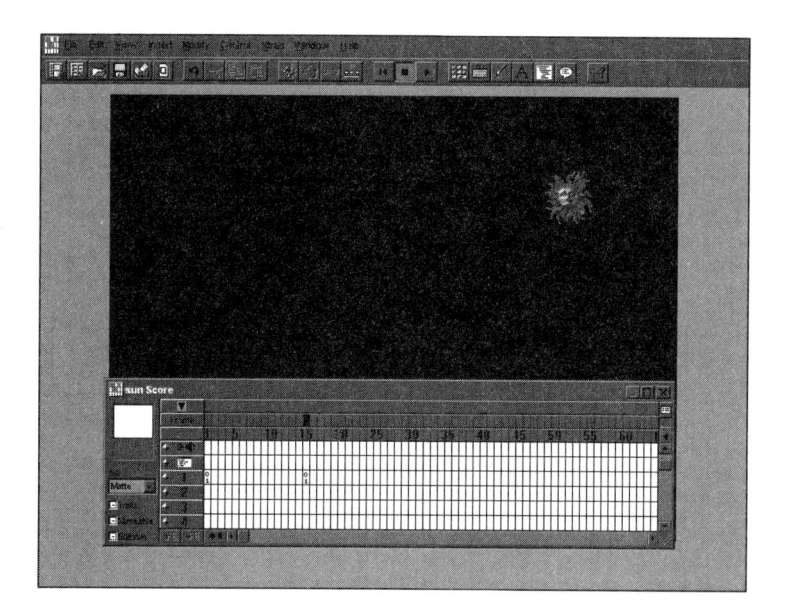

4] Next, copy frame 15 in the score and paste it into frame 30. Drag the sun to the bottom-right corner of the stage.

5] In the score, copy frame 30 and paste it into frame 45. Drag the sun to the bottom-left corner of the stage.

6] In the score, copy frame 1 and paste it into frame 60.

Copying the sprite at the beginning position to the ending position ensures that the sun ends up in the same position at which it started. You now have defined the circular path of the sun animation.

ANIMATING WITH IN BETWEEN SPECIAL

Next you'll use In Between Special to fill in the score.

1] Select channel 1, frames 1 through 60. Then choose Modify › In Between Special (Windows Ctrl+Shift+B, Macintosh Command+Shift+B).

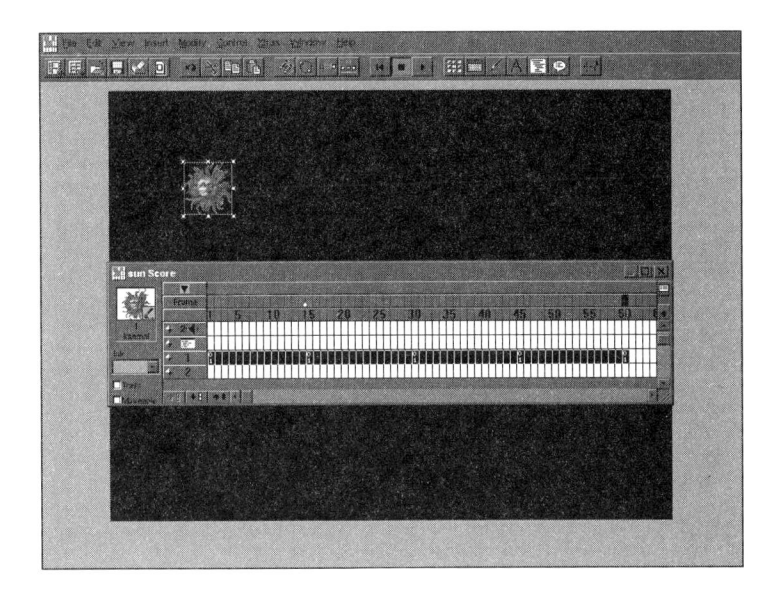

A dialog box appears.

2] Check the Circular box, check the Position box, and slide the slider toward the left side of the scale.

Circular affects sprites that begin and end at the same point. If Circular is checked, the sprite will circle around the stage. Notice as you slide the slider that the circle in the upper left of the dialog box changes: It becomes rounder.

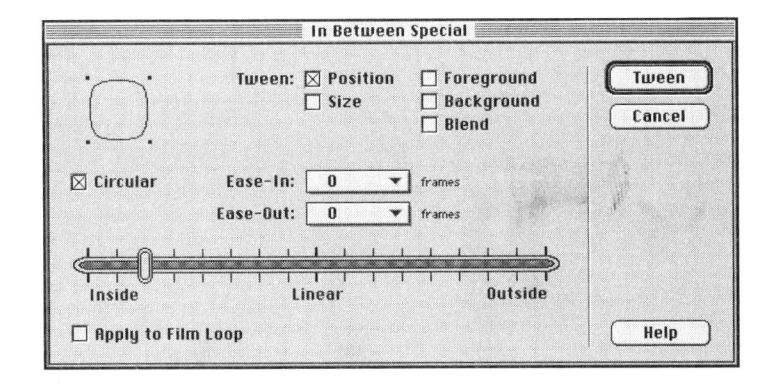

3] Click Tween to complete the process and close the dialog box.

The selected cells in the score are now filled in with the in-between positions of the sprite.

4] Play the movie.

That's pretty neat. Try using this same cast member and vary your selections in the dialog box. If you leave the cells selected, you can redo the In Between Special operation with slightly different parameters. Experiment to see which effect you like best. Then rewind and play the movie to see your results.

5] Save your work.

SETTING UP THE MOVIE

Next you will learn another way of creating animation. Real-time recording creates animation by recording the movement of a sprite as you drag it across the stage. Here you'll create an animation on top of a graphic by recording your mouse movements.

tip *This real-time recording technique is especially good for simulating the movement of a cursor. For example, you can use it to move a cursor across the screen as part of a demonstration or training program.*

1] Choose File > New > Movie to open a new movie. Then save this movie as Skater.dir.

2] Choose File > Import and select Skater.pct in the Media folder. Click Add and then click Import. In the Image Options dialog box, click Stage (8 bits) and OK.

Now you have a picture of a robot skater in the cast.

3] Choose Modify > Movie > Properties and click the Stage Color chip.

The color palette opens. If you completed the previous task, you will already have a black stage. If not, change the stage color using the next step.

4] Click the black square in the lower-right corner of the palette and then close the Movie Properties dialog box.

You now have a black stage.

ANIMATING WITH REAL-TIME RECORDING

Now you will record your mouse movements.

1] Drag the skater from the Cast window to channel 1, frame 1, in the score.

Now the skater is in the center of the stage.

2] Click channel 2, frame 2.

You're going to create a sprite here.

3] Choose Window > Tool Palette to open the tool palette and then select the Filled Ellipse tool.

FILLED ELLIPSE TOOL

4] On the stage, draw a very small circle by clicking and dragging with the Filled Ellipse tool.

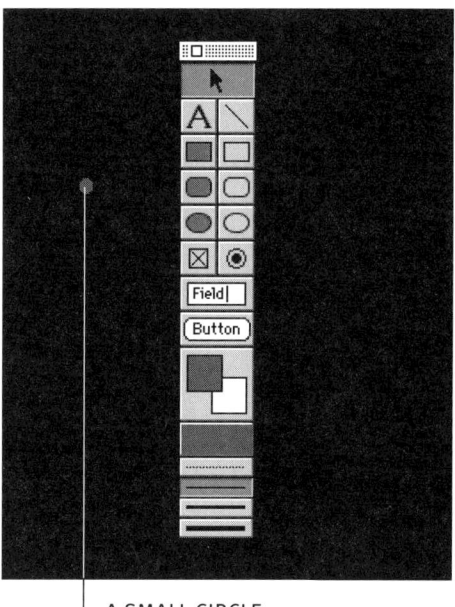

A SMALL CIRCLE

5] Click the foreground color on the tool palette to open the color palette and select a bright color for the circle, so you will be able to see it against the skater graphic.

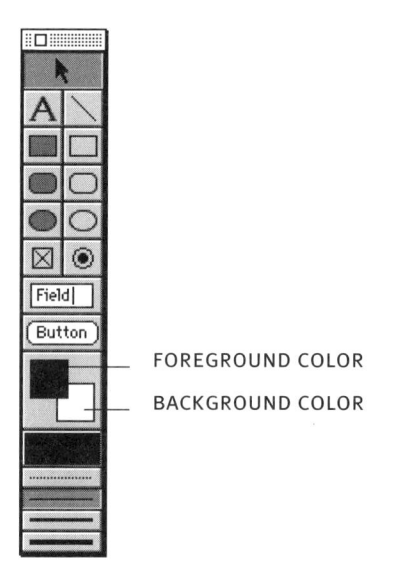

FOREGROUND COLOR
BACKGROUND COLOR

This circle will be used as a brush when you draw on the skater graphic. Look in the Cast window and notice that the circle is now cast member 2.

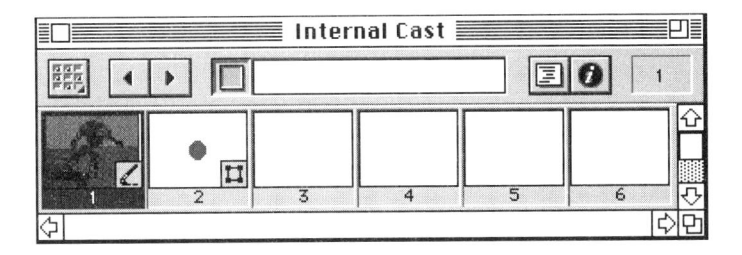

Look in the score and notice that channel 2, frame 2, contains cast member 2.

6] Delete the sprite from channel 2.
In this case, you don't want the sprite here—yet. This sprite will be placed in the score when you perform the real-time recording. Notice that when you delete a sprite from the score, the cast member still remains in the Cast window, so the bright circle is still in the cast.

7] Be sure the circle cast member is selected in the Cast window.

8] In the score, select channel 2, frame 1.
This is where you want to place the first new sprites created by real-time recording.

9] Position the cursor anywhere over the picture on the stage and hold down the Control key and spacebar simultaneously. Click and drag the mouse while holding the keys. Do this two or three times to get a good visual effect.
As you drag, you will see the sprite move across the picture. The cast member and its movements will be recorded in the score.

This procedure is known as real-time recording because Director is recording your mouse movements directly into the score, as you work. Look in the score and notice that several new channels and frames have been filled.

OTHER ANIMATION TECHNIQUES

10] Select all the cells in the score by choosing Edit > Select All (Windows Ctrl+A, Macintosh Command+A).

All the cells in the score should be highlighted now.

11] With all the cells in the score selected, check the Trails box.

This will cause all the motions to leave trails behind them and look like a drawing taking place in real time.

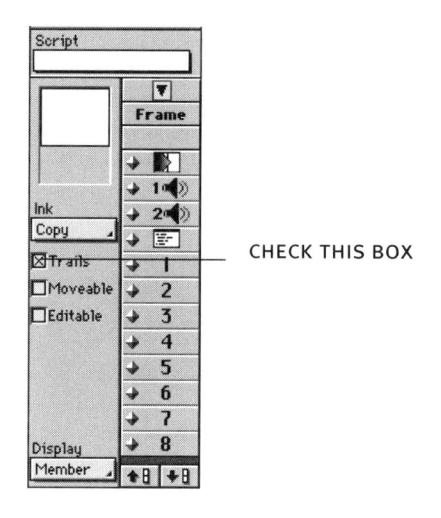

CHECK THIS BOX

tip Using Trails is a great way to simulate handwriting.

12] Rewind and play the movie to see your work.

Great effect! With real-time recording and the Trails option, you can create many animated special effects.

13] Save your work.

WHAT YOU HAVE LEARNED

In this lesson you have:

Set the background color of a movie [*page* **86**]

Created a circular animation with In Between Special [*page* **88**]

Used real-time recording to record mouse movements [*page* **91**]

Used the Trails option to leave a trail of sprites on the stage [*page* **94**]

OTHER ANIMATION TECHNIQUES

key frames and layers

LESSON 7

As you know, one basic method of creating animation is to define the key frames of an animation and then in-between the key frames to show movement. In this lesson you will practice in-betweening by building an animation of a piece of paper floating from one folder to another. As you build the animation, you will practice layering techniques to make the paper appear to come out of a folder and move into another folder.

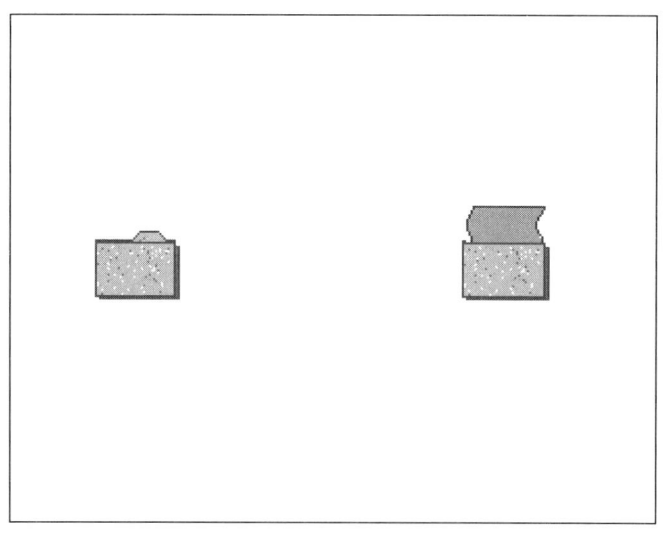

Establishing the key frames of an animation and then in-betweening them is a common method of creating animation in Director. In this lesson you will use shuffling, create a custom stage size, and add sound for further impact.

If you would like to view the final result of this lesson, open the Complete folder in the Lesson7 folder and play Paper.dir.

WHAT YOU WILL LEARN
In this lesson you will:

Create a custom stage size

Practice importing media elements

Practice setting a tempo for a movie

Practice applying ink effects to sprites

Practice creating key positions for an animation

Practice In-betweening key frames to show movement

Practice constraining the movement of sprites horizontally and vertically

Copy and move cells simultaneously in the score

Practice layering sprites below and above each other

Play selected frames only

Practice swapping cast members

Make a sound file play continuously

APPROXIMATE TIME
It usually takes about 1 hour to complete this lesson.

LESSON FILES
Media Files
Lesson7\Media
Starting Files
None
Completed Project
Lesson7\Complete\Paper.dir

KEY FRAMES AND LAYERS

CREATING A CUSTOM STAGE

First you will set a custom stage size by using the Movie Properties dialog box. This stage size is smaller than the one Director uses by default.

1] Choose File > New > Movie to open a new movie (Windows Ctrl+N, Macintosh Command+N).

An empty stage appears.

2] Choose Modify > Movie > Properties to open the Movie Properties dialog box.

This is where you can set a custom stage size.

3] In the Stage Size menu, choose Custom, type *304* in the Width field, type *230* in the Height field, and click OK to close the dialog box.

You now have a custom-sized stage, 304 by 230 pixels.

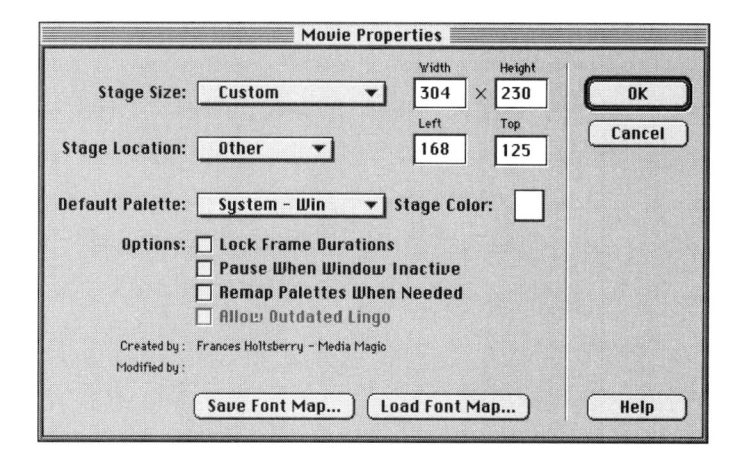

4] Save your work as Paper.dir in your MyWork folder (Windows Ctrl+S, Macintosh Command+S).

IMPORTING THE MEDIA

Next you need to import the media you'll be using in this animation.

1] Choose File > Import (Windows Ctrl+R, Macintosh Command+R).

The Import dialog box opens.

2] In the Files of Type menu (Windows), choose Macintosh PICTs. In the Show menu (Macintosh), choose Picture.

Choosing this filter causes Director to display only graphics files in the list box.

3] Locate the Media folder in the Lesson7 folder, click Add All, and click Import.

This adds all the graphics files in the Media folder to the list and begins the import process.

If you are using a Windows machine, the Image Options dialog box opens.

4] Windows only: In the Image Options dialog box, choose Stage (8 bits) and Remap to System-Mac. Then check the Same Setting for Remaining Images box at the bottom of the dialog box. Click OK to close the dialog box.

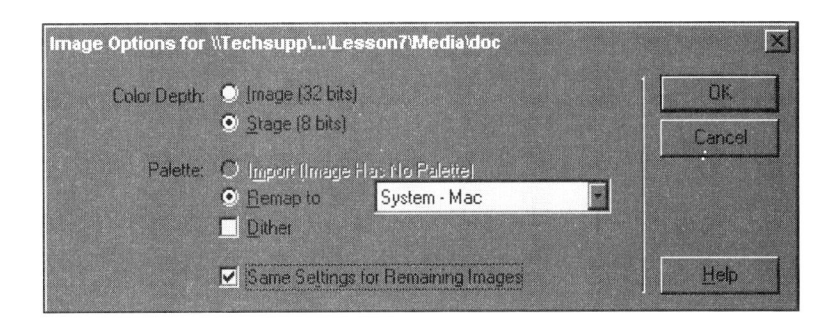

You need to remap all the images to the Macintosh system palette because all the graphics were created using the Macintosh system palette but Windows automatically sets the palette to the Windows system palette, which uses different colors. You must remap to the Macintosh system palette so that all the graphics will be displayed with the correct colors.

By checking Same Setting for Remaining Images, you ensure that all the graphics will be imported with this same setting and that this dialog box won't be displayed as each graphic is imported.

After you click OK in the dialog box, you'll notice the Director elements, such as the tool bar and score, are black and white. This indicates that the movie contains a palette other than the Windows system palette. This affects the Director user interface only and does not affect the movie itself.

99

KEY FRAMES AND LAYERS

SETTING THE MOVIE TEMPO

Now you will set the speed of the movie by setting its tempo.

1] Open the score (Windows Ctrl+4, Macintosh Command+4).

2] Double-click frame 1 of the tempo channel to open the Tempo dialog box and drag the tempo slider to 10 fps.

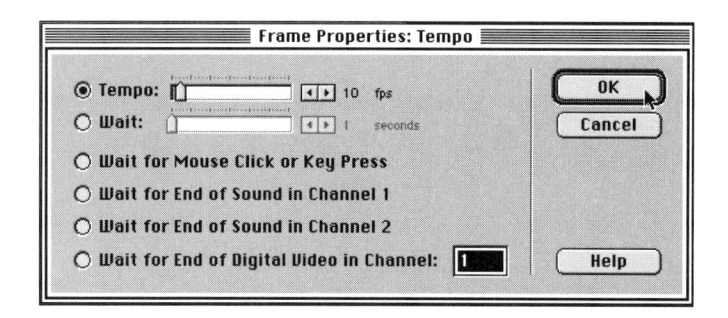

This frame rate is a requested rate only, not an absolute rate. If the machine is capable of yielding the requested rate, it will, but slower machines may not be able to achieve the faster tempo settings that can be specified in the Tempo dialog box.

PLACING THE GRAPHICS ON THE STAGE

Now that the movie basics are set up, you'll place the graphics on the stage.

1] Drag cast member 5 (folder) from the Cast window to channel 1, frame 1, in the score.

Whenever you drag a cast member from the Cast window to the score, it is automatically centered on the stage.

2] Choose Copy from the Ink menu in the score.

Copy is probably already selected because it's the default ink. If the sprite were not rectangular and the background were not white, a white box would appear around the sprite. In this case, because the background is white, you cannot see the white box around the sprite, so this ink works well. Sprites with Copy ink animate faster than sprites with any other ink.

3] Drag the folder to the left side of the stage.

This sprite will be the folder from which the paper flies.

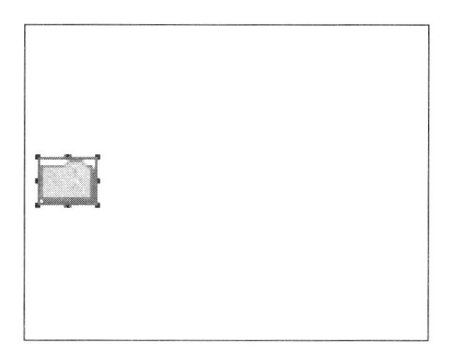

4] Drag cast member 1 (doc) to the stage so it covers the folder.

Because Director automatically places each new sprite in the next available channel, the paper is in channel 2, frame 1.

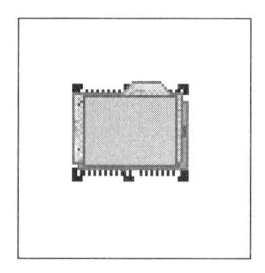

tip *When a sprite is selected in the score and the Score window is active, you can use the arrow keys on the keyboard to nudge the sprite one pixel at a time on the stage.*

5] With the paper selected, choose Copy from the Ink menu in the score.

6] Drag cast member 6 (folder2) to the stage and place it on top of the folder and paper sprites.

This is the top flap of the folder. Director automatically places this cast member in channel 3, frame 1, the next available channel.

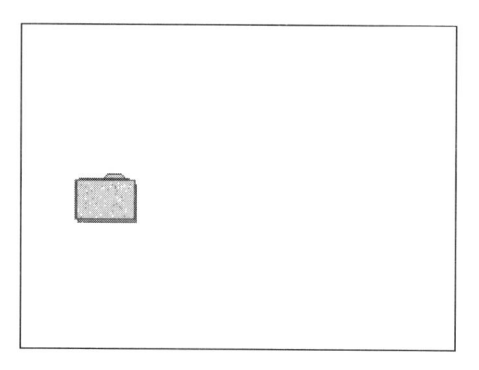

7] Save your work.

COPYING SPRITES TO A NEW LOCATION

In this task, you will create a copy of the layered sprites, creating the folder to which the paper will fly.

Before, you copied and pasted sprites to new locations using the Edit menu. Here, you'll learn a quicker method.

1] Select channels 1 through 3 with the arrow pointer. Press the spacebar to toggle the arrow pointer to a hand. Then press Alt (Windows) or Option (Macintosh) at the same time.

2] While holding these keys down, drag to channel 4 and then release the mouse.

When you drag, the arrow pointer becomes a hand with a plus sign (+) in it. This indicates that you will be copying instead of just moving the sprites.

The sprites should be copied to the new location: channels 4, 5, and 6.

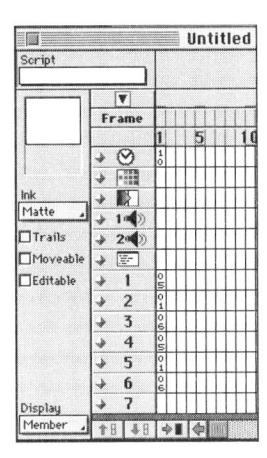

3] With the duplicate folder and paper still selected, drag them to the right side of the stage.

If the duplicate folder and paper are not selected, in the score select frame 1, channels 4 through 6. This selects the sprites on the stage.

As you drag to the right, hold down the Shift key to constrain movement of the sprites horizontally. If you hold down the Shift key and drag vertically instead of horizontally, the sprite movement will be constrained vertically.

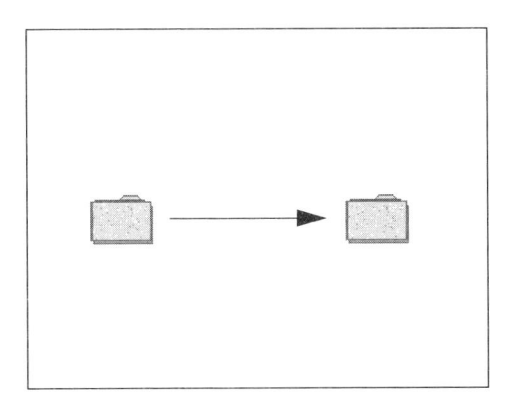

tip *The movement of the sprite will be constrained either vertically or horizontally, depending on which direction you first drag the sprite.*

KEY FRAMES AND LAYERS

4] Select channel 5, frame 1, and delete it.

This is the second piece of paper in the second folder. You don't need it because you're going to work with the piece of paper in channel 2.

5] In-between channels 1, 3, 4, and 6 from frames 1 through 30 (Windows Ctrl+B, Macintosh Command+B).

This keeps the folder on the stage through all 30 frames. Do not in-between channel 2 at this time because channel 2 contains the paper, which will animate to different locations on the stage.

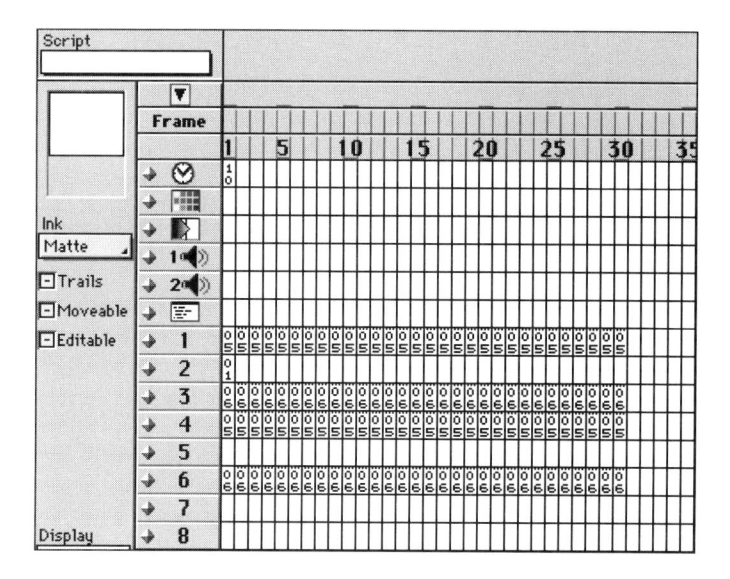

tip *To select the same range of frames in some channels but not others, select the frames in the first channel and then Ctrl+click (Windows) or Command+click (Macintosh) the other channel numbers you want to select.*

CREATING THE ANIMATION WITH KEY FRAMES

In this section you create the paper animation.

1] Copy channel 2, frame 1 (the paper), to channel 2, frame 10.

This will be the first key frame of the paper animation.

2] Select channel 2, frame 10.

On the stage, you will see a selection box. The selected object is the paper, but you can't see the paper because it's layered below the top of the folder.

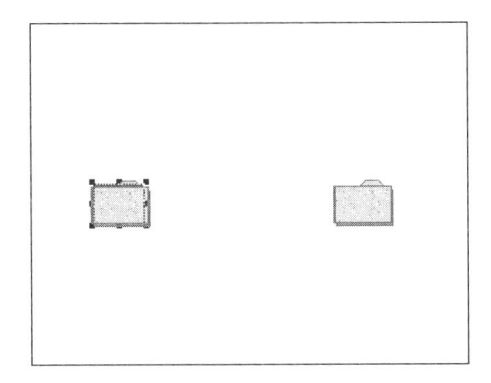

The paper is in channel 2, and the top of the folder is in channel 3. Sprites in lower-numbered channels are behind sprites in higher-numbered channels, so you cannot see the paper sprite because it is behind the top of the folder.

3] Drag the selection up the stage so the paper is completely out of the folder.

As you drag, hold down the Shift key to constrain movement vertically. You'll see the paper sprite come out of the folder.

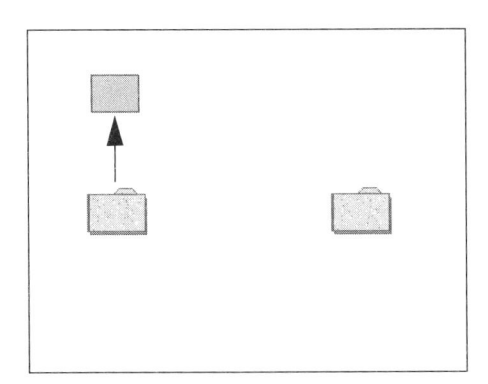

KEY FRAMES AND LAYERS

4] In the score, copy channel 2, frame 10, to channel 2, frame 20. On the stage, drag the sprite above the second folder.

Again, hold down the Shift key to constrain the sprite's movement.

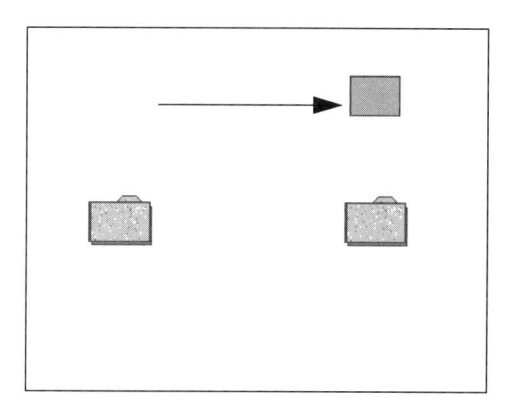

5] In the score, copy channel 2, frame 20, to channel 2, frame 30, and drag the sprite into the second folder to complete the key frames.

The frames you've established in channel 2 (frames 10, 20, and 30) are the key positions of the paper motion.

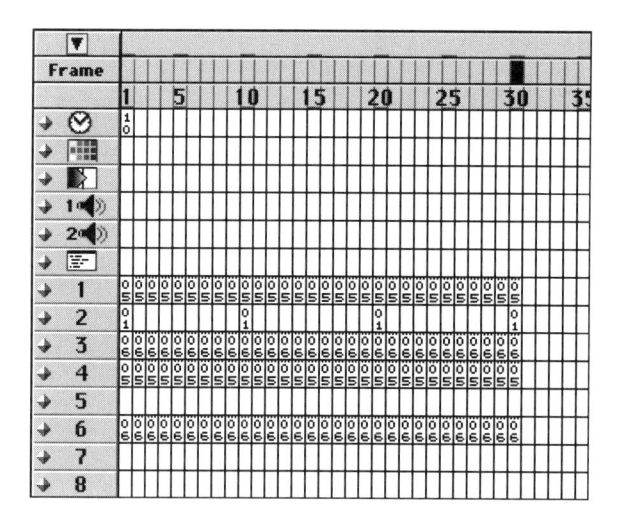

6] In-between channel 2 from frames 1 through 30.

7] Save your work.

PLAYING SELECTED FRAMES ONLY

On the Control Panel, you can click the Selected Frames Only icon to play back only frames you have selected in the score. You can also click Loop Playback, which causes the playback head to automatically loop back to the beginning once it gets to the last frame.

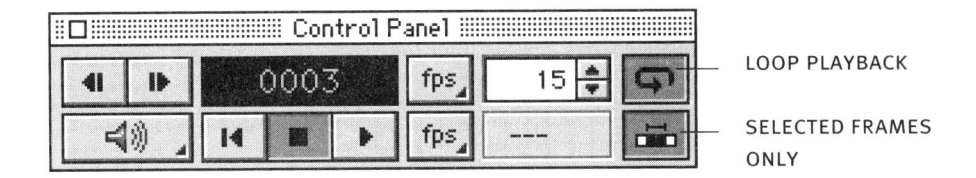

LOOP PLAYBACK

SELECTED FRAMES ONLY

1] Select channel 2, frames 1 through 15, open the Control Panel (Windows Ctrl+2, Macintosh Command+2), and click the Selected Frames Only button and the Loop Playback button.

A green line appears below the frame numbers at the top of the score to indicate the selected frames.

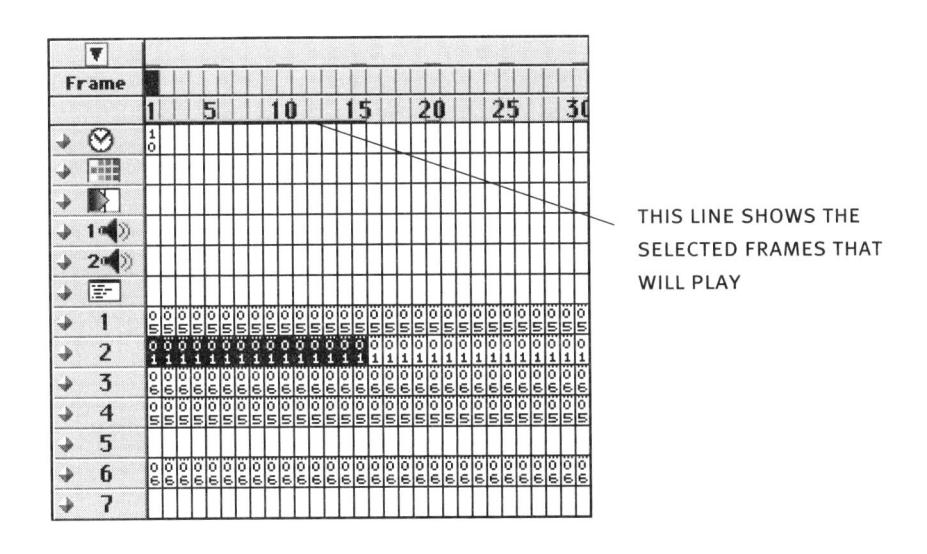

THIS LINE SHOWS THE SELECTED FRAMES THAT WILL PLAY

2] Click Play on the Control Panel.

Only part of the animation plays because you chose Selected Frames Only. In addition, because you chose the Loop Playback option, the selected frames play over and over.

KEY FRAMES AND LAYERS

3] Click the Selected Frames Only button to remove the green line. Then click Play on the Control Panel.

Great! Establishing key frames and in-betweening them makes the animation work.

Did you notice a problem? When the paper animates to the second folder, it goes behind the folder entirely, not between the folder flaps. There is a problem with the layers: The paper is in channel 2, but the top of the second folder is in channel 6, and the bottom of the folder is in channel 4. Because both folder sprites are in higher-numbered channels than the paper, the paper looks as though it is going completely behind the folder. You need to shuffle some of the sprites to different channels.

If you cannot see the problem clearly, click the Selected Frames Only button to turn this option off. Then select frames 20 through 30, click the Selected Frames Only button to turn this option on, and play the movie. You should be able to see that the paper falls entirely behind the folder.

4] Stop the movie.

You need to make some changes to the layers.

LAYERING THE SPRITES

In Lesson 2, you learned that sprites in higher-numbered channels appear to be in front of sprites in lower-numbered channels. Conversely, sprites in lower-numbered channels appear behind sprites in higher-numbered channels. Therefore, a sprite in channel 48 would appear at the very front of the stage, and a sprite in channel 1 would appear at the very back. In this animation, the paper should look as though it falls between the two folder flaps. To create this effect, you need to shuffle the paper sprites.

1] Select channel 2, frames 20 through 30. Then click the Shuffle Down button until the sprites are in channel 5.

2] Click Play on the Control Panel again.

The paper is layered correctly and falls into the folder as it should.

You can see the importance of using channel order to affect the way sprites are layered. By placing the last part of the paper animation in channel 5 instead of keeping it in channel 2, you make the paper appear to fall in between the top and bottom parts of the folder.

Did you notice that as you shuffle the sprites down, the sprites in the next channel move up? This did not affect your animation, but it's always a good idea to keep things tidy, so you should move the other sprites back to their original locations.

3] Select channels 2 and 3, frames 20 through 30, and move them to channels 3 and 4, frames 20 through 30, with the Shuffle Down button.

Now everything should be back to its original position.

4] Save your work.

EXCHANGING CAST MEMBERS

This animation could be improved by adding different versions of the paper so that it looks like it's flapping as it animates across the stage. You'll exchange cast members to add this enhancement.

1] Select channel 2, frame 3, and then select cast member 2 in the Cast window. Click Exchange Cast Members on the toolbar.

EXCHANGE CAST MEMBERS

Now cast member 1 has been replaced with cast member 2 in this cell. You should see 02 in channel 2, frame 3.

2] Select channel 2, frame 4, select cast member 3 in the Cast window, and click Exchange Cast Members.

You should see 03 in channel 2, frame 4.

3] Select channel 2, frame 5, select cast member 4 in the Cast window, and click Exchange Cast Members.

Do this several times, for all the sprites in channel 2, using all the versions of the paper (cast members 1 through 4, in order). Don't forget to swap the cast members in channel 5, frames 20 through 30; these are the last parts of the paper animation.

4] Rewind and play the animation.

You should now see the paper flap and animate from one folder to another.

5] Save your work.

ADDING BACKGROUND MUSIC

Sound can add a great deal to your animation, setting a soothing mood or generating excitement. In this task you will add background music that will play while the animation runs.

1] Choose File › Import, select Files of Type: All files (Windows) or Show: All files (Macintosh). Select Boiling.aif in the Media folder, click Add and then click Import to import the sound.

The sound becomes a cast member in the Cast window.

2] Select the sound cast member and click the Cast Member Properties button in the Cast window.

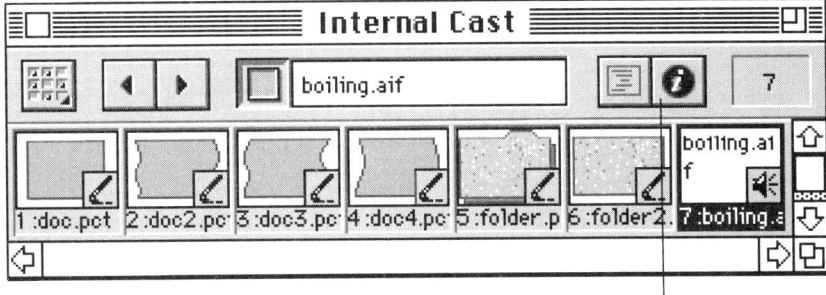

CAST MEMBER PROPERTIES

3] In the dialog box that appears, check the Options: Loop box and then click OK to close the dialog box.

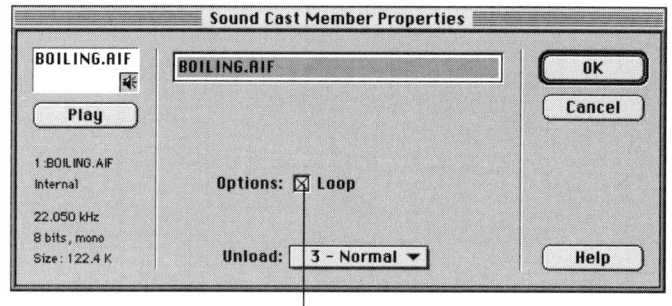

CHECK THIS BOX

This makes the sound loop back to the beginning when it reaches the end of the sound file. Looping sounds gives the impression of a longer, continuous sound. This is a great option, especially if you need to keep file size to a minimum. Also, if you are developing custom music, you can spend less time and money on shorter sound files. Then you can loop them to make them seem longer.

shockwave tip *Keep sounds small and loop them to give the impression of longer sounds. This helps reduce download time.*

4] Drag the sound cast member to sound channel 1, frame 1, and in-between it from frames 1 though 31.

Now the sound is available throughout the animation.

tip *Notice how you in-betweened the sound to frame 31, one frame past the end of the movie. This ensures that Director won't cut off the sound as it reaches the end of the movie.*

5] Save your work. Then rewind and play the movie.

What a difference a sound makes!

WHAT YOU HAVE LEARNED
In this lesson you have:

Created a custom stage [*page* **98**]

Imported media elements into the Cast window [*page* **98**]

Set a movie tempo [*page* **100**]

Applied ink effects to graphics [*page* **101**]

Copied and moved cells with the drag/copy method [*page* **102**]

Created key frames [*page* **105**]

Constrained the movement of sprites horizontally and vertically [*page* **105**]

In-betweened key frames to show movement [*page* **106**]

Used the Control Panel to play selected frames only [*page* **107**]

Layered sprites [*page* **108**]

Exchanged cast members [*page* **110**]

Added and looped a sound file [*page* **111**]

animation with film loops

LESSON 8

In the previous lesson you created animation by defining key frames and then in-betweening the key frames to show movement. As part of that lesson, you exchanged cast members numerous times to display different versions of the paper. That procedure was time consuming! In this lesson you will build the same animation using a different technique: a *film loop*. A film loop encapsulates several cast members in one. You can then in-between this single cast member to create motion.

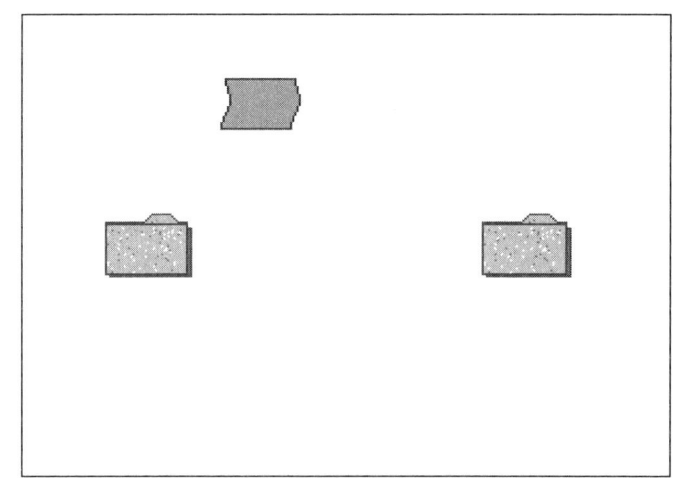

Film loops encapsulate several cast members in one cast member, making it easier for you to create motion with multiple cast members. You will use this technique along with In Between to quickly create the same animation you developed in the previous lesson.

If you would like to view the final result of this lesson, open the Complete folder in the Lesson8 folder and play Loop.dir.

To give you a jump-start, the media elements have been assembled in the cast and sequenced in the score in Start.dir. You completed this same task in the previous lesson, so you don't need to repeat it here.

WHAT YOU WILL LEARN
In this lesson you will:
Encapsulate several cast members in one cast member
Create key frames with a film loop cast member
Practice in-betweening key frames to show movement
Practice layering sprites

APPROXIMATE TIME
It usually takes about 1 hour to complete this lesson.

LESSON FILES
Media Files
Lesson8\Media
Starting Files
Lesson8\Start.dir
Completed Project
Lesson8\Complete\Loop.dir

115

ANIMATION WITH FILM LOOPS

EXCHANGING CAST MEMBERS

First you need to open the start file. Then you will incorporate the alternative versions of the paper cast members.

1] Open Start.dir in the Lesson8 folder and save it as Loop.dir in your MyWork folder.

The folders and paper are already set up on the stage and in the score.

Windows only: You'll notice the Director elements, such as the tool bar and score, are black and white, indicating that the movie contains a palette other than the Windows system palette. Remember that this affects the Director user interface only and does not affect the movie itself.

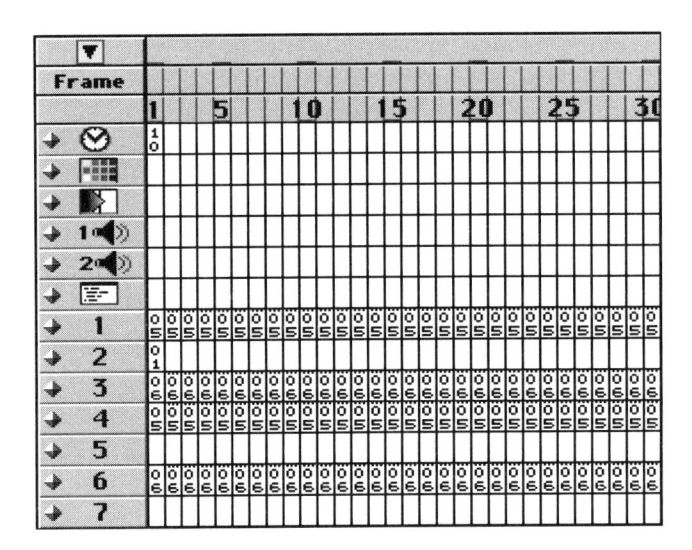

Next you will in-between channel 2 and then exchange the paper cast members. This is different than what you did in the previous lesson, where you exchanged cast members after you in-betweened the key frames. In this task, you will exchange cast members before you create the key frames.

2] In-between channel 2, frame 1, to frame 5.

You should see 01 in channel 2, frames 1 through 5.

3] Select channel 2, frame 2, in the score, select cast member 2 in the cast, and click Exchange Cast Members on the toolbar (Windows Ctrl+E, Macintosh Command+E).

EXCHANGE CAST MEMBERS

116

LESSON 8

This is an alternative version of the paper. You should see 02 in channel 2, frame 2.

4] Select channel 2 frame 3, select cast member 3, and click Exchange Cast Members on the toolbar.

This is another version of the paper. You should see 03 in channel 2, frame 3.

5] Select channel 2, frame 4, select cast member 4, and click Exchange Cast Members on the toolbar.

You should see 04 in channel 2, frame 4; 01 should remain in channel 2, frame 5.

6] Save your work.

CREATING A FILM LOOP

A film loop is created by using both the score and the Cast window. This film loop will contain the four alternative versions of the paper, encapsulated in one cast member.

1] In the score, select channel 2, frames 1 through 5, and choose Edit > Copy.

These cells will make up the pieces of the film loop.

2] In the Cast window, select cast member 7, an empty cast member, and choose Edit > Paste.

A dialog box will appear prompting you to name the film loop.

3] Type *Paper Loop* and click OK to close the dialog box.

Now the film loop is a new cast member in the Cast window.

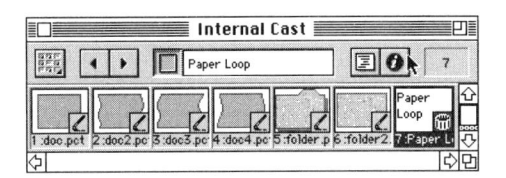

4] Click the Cast Member Properties button, uncheck the Options: Play Sound box, and click OK to close the dialog box.

Director has two sound channels in the score. When Director reaches a film loop and the Play Sound box is checked, Director reserves the first sound channel and attempts to play a film loop sound for the duration of the film loop, even if the film loop has no sound in it. If the Play Sound box is checked and the film loop does not have a sound, you will hear only silence while the film loop is playing. As a precaution, then, it's wise to uncheck this box in the first place and enable sound in the film loop only when you have a sound in the film loop you want to play.

5] Delete channel 2, frames 1 through 5.

You no longer need them because they've been encapsulated in the film loop as cast member 7.

CREATING KEY FRAMES WITH A FILM LOOP

In this task, you will use the film loop to define the key frames of the animation.

1] Drag the Paper Loop (cast member 7) from the Cast window to channel 2, frame 1, in the score.

This is the starting point of the animation.

2] On the stage, drag the paper so it covers the left folder.

Because the paper is in channel 2, it will look as though it's inside the folder.

3] Copy channel 2, frame 1 (the paper film loop), to channel 2, frame 10.

This is the first key frame of the paper animation.

4] Select channel 2, frame 10.

On the stage, you will see a selection box. The selection object is the paper film loop, but you can't see the paper because it's layered below the top folder flap.

5] Drag the selection box up the stage so the paper is completely out of the folder.

As you drag, hold down the Shift key to constrain movement vertically. You'll see the paper sprite come out of the folder.

6] In the score, copy channel 2, frame 10, to channel 2, frame 20. On the stage, drag the sprite above the second folder.

Again, hold down the Shift key to constrain movement.

7] Copy channel 2, frame 20, to channel 2, frame 30, and drag the sprite within the second folder to complete the animation.

8] In-between channel 2 from frames 1 through 30.

9] Rewind and play the movie.

The animation plays. It's the same animation you created in the previous lesson, but you didn't need to exchange the cast members over 30 frames to incorporate the different versions of the paper. By creating a film loop, you encapsulated four different cast members in a single cast member and then in-betweened that one cast member to create movement. This procedure is a great time saver.

10] Save your work.

LAYERING THE SPRITES

Did you notice that the paper falls behind both of the folder flaps, just as it did in the previous lesson? You need to shuffle the last part of the paper sprites down.

1] Select channel 2, frames 20 through 30, and then click the Shuffle Down button until the sprites are in channel 5.

2] Play the movie again.

The paper is layered correctly and falls into the folder as it should.

3] Select channels 2 and 3, frames 20 through 30, and move them back to channels 3 and 4, frames 20 through 30.

Now everything should be back to its original position. Remember: You don't need to move the sprites back, but it's good to keep the score well organized so you can find things easily.

4] Rewind and play the animation.

5] Save your work.

ON YOUR OWN

Add the sound file Boiling.aif. so it plays throughout the entire animation. Go back to the previous lesson if you need help. Don't forget to add an additional frame to the movie (frame 31) so the sound is not cut off before the movie ends.

WHAT YOU HAVE LEARNED
In this lesson you have:

Created a film loop [*page* **117**]

Created key frames using a film loop [*page* **119**]

In-betweened key frames to show movement [*page* **120**]

adding buttons for navigation

In the previous two lessons you created an animation by defining key frames, in-betweening the key frames, and creating a film loop of the same animation. In this lesson you will create a menu screen with two buttons that will branch to either of the two animations. For variety, you will also reverse the sequence of one of the animations so the paper flies from right to left instead of left to right.

Buttons are commonly used to present users with choices for navigating through a program. In this lesson you will create buttons and add scripts for branching to other sections of the movie.

LESSON 9

If you would like to view the final result of this lesson, open the Complete folder in the Lesson9 folder and play Branch.dir.

WHAT YOU WILL LEARN
In this lesson you will:

Copy animations from one movie to another

Practice reversing the direction of an animation

Create buttons

Set button text style and color

Pause the movie to wait for user input

Add markers to the score

Branch to different parts of the movie

APPROXIMATE TIME
It usually takes about 1 hour to complete this lesson.

LESSON FILES
Media Files:
None
Starting Files:
Lesson9\Paper.dir
Lesson9\Loop.dir
Completed Project:
Lesson9\Complete\Branch.dir

INCORPORATING ANIMATIONS FROM OTHER MOVIES

First you will open a new movie and add the animations you created in the previous lessons.

1] Open a new movie and save it as Branch.dir (Windows Ctrl+N, Macintosh Command+N).

You'll copy all the cells from the previous lessons into this movie.

2] Open Paper.dir in the Lesson9 folder. Then select all the cells in the score (Windows Ctrl+A, Macintosh Command+A) and copy them (Windows Ctrl+C, Macintosh Command+C).

This is the first floating-paper animation you created.

Windows only: You'll notice the Director elements, such as the tool bar and score, are black and white, indicating that the movie contains a palette other than the Windows system palette. Remember that this affects the Director user interface only and does not affect the movie itself.

3] Open Branch.dir, select frame 10 in the tempo channel, and paste the cells you copied (Windows Ctrl+V, Macintosh Command+V).

You should see all the frames you copied pasted into the score starting in frame 10. Note that the cast members referred to in the score are also pasted into the cast.

You created this animation in a previous lesson so that the paper floats from left to right. You will modify this animation so the paper floats from right to left.

124

LESSON 9

4] Select all the frames in channel 2. Then choose Modify › Reverse Sequence.

These frames contain part of the floating-paper animation. By reversing the sequence, you will make the paper fly from right to left instead of left to right.

The last part of the animation is in channel 5, so you need to reverse the frames in that channel as well.

5] Select all the frames in channel 5. Then choose Modify › Reverse Sequence.

Now all the channels and frames that contain the floating-paper animation have been reversed from their original sequence, so the paper will fly from right to left instead of left to right.

6] Rewind and play the movie to see the result.

The paper floats from right to left now.

7] Save your work (Windows Ctrl+S, Macintosh Command+S).

Next you will incorporate the film loop you created in a previous lesson. This animation shows the paper floating from left to right.

8] Open Loop.dir in the Lesson9 folder, select all the cells in the score, and copy them.

This is the second floating-paper animation (the film loop) you created.

9] Open Branch.dir, select frame 50 in the tempo channel, and then paste the cells you copied.

You now have both animations in one score.

CREATING BUTTONS WITH THE TOOL PALETTE

Now you'll create two buttons that will be used to branch to the animations.

1] Select the entire frame 10 and drag/copy it to frame 1.

Remember: To drag/copy, select the cells you want to copy with the arrow pointer. Toggle the arrow to a hand pointer by pressing the spacebar and at the same time press Alt (Windows) or Option (Macintosh). While holding these keys down, drag to the new location in the score. Then release the mouse.

This will be the main menu frame where the buttons will be located. You've copied this channel so that the frame contains all the elements of the animation.

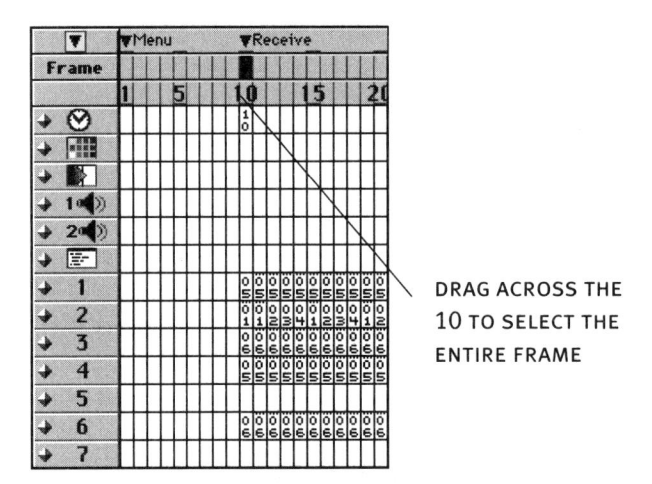

DRAG ACROSS THE 10 TO SELECT THE ENTIRE FRAME

2] Delete frame 1, channel 2.

The paper sprite is in mid-air here, so you should delete it so it's not visible on this menu frame.

Next you will create the buttons.

3] Select channel 7, frame 1.

You'll place a button in this cell.

4] Open the tool palette (Windows Ctrl+7, Macintosh Command+7) and choose the Button tool.

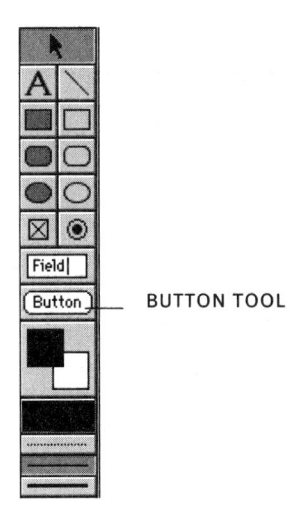

BUTTON TOOL

5] Click the stage to create the button and then type *Receive the Document* within the button.

Modify the font, style, and text color as you like by selecting the text, choosing Modify › Font, and making selections in the Font dialog box. To resize the button, click the button on the stage to select it and then drag a handle.

shockwave tip   *Any sprite can be a button. However, using the tool palette to create a button is an especially good technique in shocked movies because buttons created this way are smaller than buttons created with graphics.*

6] Drag the button below the two folders on the stage.

7] Create another button, typing *Send the Document* as the button text.

This button should be in channel 8, frame 1.

8] On the stage, drag the Send the Document button below the Receive the Document button.

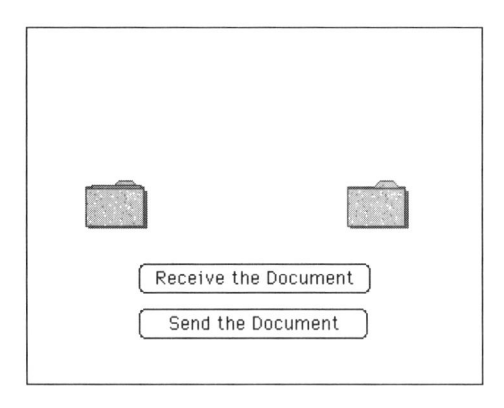

9] Save your work.

PAUSING THE PLAYBACK HEAD

In Lesson 5 you learned that scripts are combinations of words that convey instructions to Director. A set of Lingo statements attached to an object is called a handler. Handlers are used to determine how to deal with specific events, such as a mouse click or a keyboard command.

This time you'll use Lingo's *pause* command to cause the playback head to halt. The *pause* command is useful for halting the movie while a menu is displayed or for letting users look at a screen as long as they want.

How does Director use your commands? As the playback head moves from left to right across the score, various event messages are being sent to Director about the events that are happening, including *exitFrame*, *enterFrame*, *mouseUp*, and *mouseDown* events. For example, suppose the playback head is in frame 1 and is leaving frame 1 to go to frame 2. As the playback head moves out of frame 1, it sends an *exitFrame* event message, meaning "I'm leaving frame 1." As the playback head moves into frame 2, it sends the *enterFrame* event message, meaning "I'm entering frame 2." You can control what Director will do with those event messages. You can pause the playback head, make the system beep, branch to another area in the movie, and so on. You'll be creating some simple scripts next that will control the playback head and make the movie work as you want it to.

> **tip** *The* pause *command physically stops the playback head, which means any sound, digital video, or film loops will stop. When you use* go to the frame, *the playback head is still active, so sound, digital video, or film loops do not stop. Since this is a static screen*, pause *works fine here. In many cases, using* pause *is recommended over looping on the same frame (with* go to the frame*), or looping between two frames. This is because pausing uses much less processor time than repeatedly moving the playback head to the beginning of the frame.*

1] Double-click frame 1 in script channel 1 to open the Script window.

You'll add the pause here.

The Script window contains *on exitFrame* and *end* already. These two lines are displayed by default whenever you open a new script in the script channel. As you learned in Lesson 5, this handler will handle the *exitFrame* event, which occurs when the playback head exits a frame.

2] Type *pause* below *on exitFrame*. Then close the window.

```
on exitFrame
   pause
end
```

You've just written a script that instructs Director to pause the playback head when it receives the *exitFrame* event message in frame 1.

3] Rewind and play the movie.

Look at the playback head as the movie plays and notice that it stays in frame 1.

4] Stop the movie.

ADDING MARKERS

In Lesson 5, you used markers for navigation purposes. Here, too, you will add markers that will be referred to in the button scripts you're going to create.

1] Drag a marker to frame 1 and label it *Menu*.

Be sure to type the marker label exactly as it is shown here. Lingo finds these markers by their spelling (capitalization does not matter).

2] Drag another marker to frame 10 and label it *Receive*.

This marker indicates the starting frame of the Receive document animation.

ADDING BUTTONS FOR NAVIGATION

3] Drag a marker to frame 50 and label it *Send*

This marker indicates the starting frame of the Send document animation.

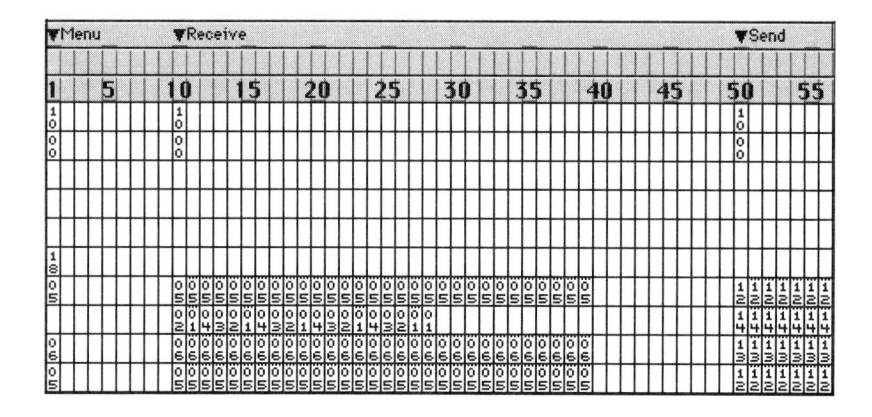

4] Save your work.

Now that the markers are in place, you can add the scripts that refer to them.

ADDING GO TO SCRIPTS

Next you'll add scripts for the buttons so they navigate to the markers you just created.

1] Select channel 7, frame 1 (the button called Receive the Document), and from the Script pop-up menu, choose New Script to open the Script window.

You are going to create a script for this button.

The Script window already contains *on mouseUp* and *end*. These two lines are displayed by default whenever you open a new script in a sprite channel. (By contrast, when you open a new script in the script channel, *on exitFrame* and *end* are displayed by default.) In this case, the event that is being handled is a *mouseUp* event, which occurs when the mouse is clicked on a sprite.

2] Type *go to frame "Receive"* below *on mouseUp*. Then close the window.

Be sure you type the marker label exactly as you spelled it earlier.

```
on mouseUp
   go to frame "Receive"
end
```

When the Receive the Document button is clicked (and the mouse button is released), a *mouseUp* event message is sent to Director. This tells Director that the mouse was clicked on this button. Director looks for scripts that tell it what to do when it receives this message. In this particular case, you've written a script that instructs Director to branch to the Receive marker when this button is clicked.

3] Select channel 8, frame 1 (the button called Send the Document), and from the Script pop-up menu, choose New Script to open the Script window.

You are going to create a script for the Send the Document button. Again, the Script window already contains *on mouseUp* and *end*.

4] Type *go to frame "Send"* below *on mouseUp* and close the window.

```
on mouseUp
   go to frame "Send"
end
```

Be sure you type the marker label exactly as you spelled it earlier.

When this button is clicked, the *mouseUp* event message is sent. Director looks for scripts that tell it what to do when it receives this message. In this case, you've written a script that instructs Director to branch to the Send marker when this button is clicked.

5] Save your work and rewind and play the movie. Click the Receive the Document button.

Watch the playback head. The playback head branches to the Receive marker and plays the animation. Notice that the paper now floats from right to left because you reversed the sequence.

6] Stop the movie.

Oops! Did you notice that the playback head continued through the rest of the score? The script you added branched the playback head to a marker labeled Receive, and the playback head then continued to move through the score, through the Send section, and then to the end of the movie. So the viewer can stay on the Receive screen for as long as he or she likes, you can prevent the playback head from continuing by adding another script.

7] Select the script channel, frame 39, the last frame of the first animation.

This is where you'll want the playback head to loop back to the beginning of the Receive animation.

8] From the Script pop-up menu, choose New Script to open the Script window. Type *go to frame "Receive"* **below** *on exitFrame* **and close the window.**

Because this is a new script in the script channel, the Script window contains *on exitFrame* and *end*.

```
on exitFrame
  go to frame "Receive"
end
```

This will branch the playback head to the Receive marker.

THE PLAYBACK HEAD
WILL BRANCH BACK HERE

THIS SCRIPT BRANCHES THE
PLAYBACK HEAD TO THE
RECEIVE MARKER

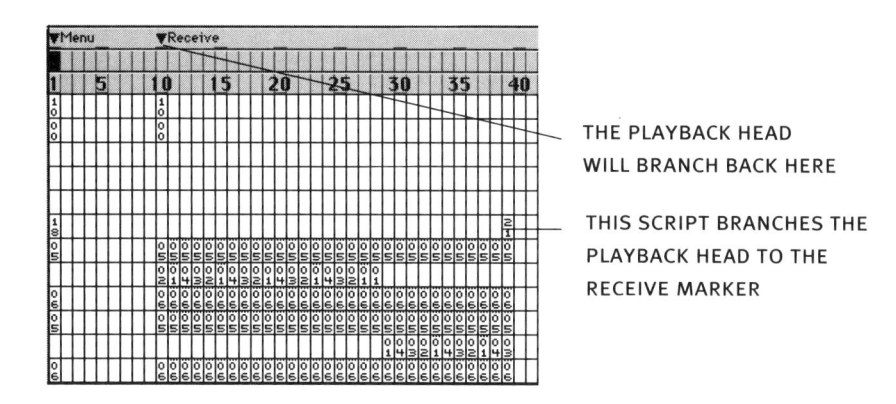

9] Save your work and rewind and play the movie. Click the Receive the Document button.

The playback head branches to the Receive marker and plays the animation. Notice that the animation continues to loop because of the script you just added. Watch the playback head when you click the button. When it reaches frame 39, it goes back to the Receive marker.

10] Stop the movie and rewind and play it again. Click the Send the Document button.

The playback head branches to the Send marker and plays the animation. If you later decide to add to the score, you will have the same problem as you did before—the playback head will continue through the movie. You know how to fix that now!

11] Select the script channel, frame 79, the last frame of the Send animation.

This is where you'll want the playback head to loop back to the beginning of the Send animation.

12] From the Script pop-up menu, choose New Script to open the Script window. Type *go to frame "Send"* below *on exitFrame*.

Because this is a new script in the script channel, *on exitFrame* and *end* are displayed by default in the Script window.

```
on exitFrame
  go to frame "Send"
end
```

133

ADDING BUTTONS FOR NAVIGATION

This will send the playback head back to the Send marker as soon as it exits frame 79.

13] Rewind and play the movie. Click the buttons and watch the playback head.

Great! You now have two buttons that branch to different parts of the movie—but it would be even better if you had a Menu button to return to the menu from each section, right? You'll add that next.

14] Save your work.

BRANCHING TO A MENU

1] Select channel 9, frame 10 (the first frame of the first animation), open the tool palette, and select the Button tool.

You're going to create a Menu button.

2] Create a button on the stage and title it *Menu*.

Place this button near the bottom of the stage, like the other two buttons.

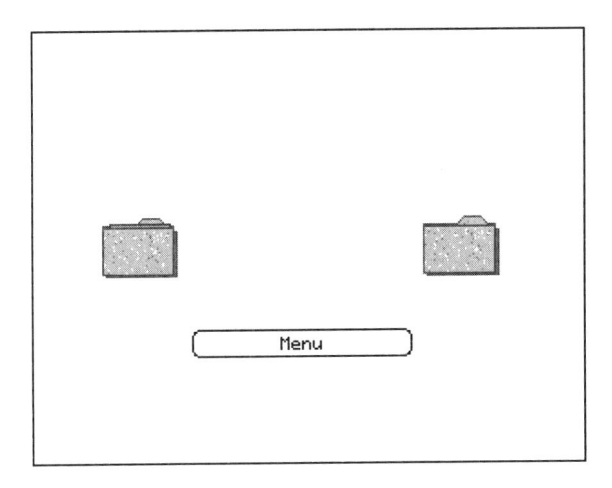

3] With the cell still selected in the score, from the Script pop-up menu choose New Script to open the Script window. Type *go to frame "Menu"* below *on mouseUp* and close the window.

Because this is a new script in a sprite channel, *on mouseUp* and *end* are displayed by default in the Script window.

```
on mouseUp
  go to frame "Menu"
end
```

Recall that earlier you created a marker and labeled it Menu. When the user clicks this button, the *mouseUp* event message will be sent to Director, and your script will branch to the Menu marker.

4] In-between channel 9, frames 10 through 39.
The regular animation goes from frames 10 through 39, and the Menu button should be available throughout the entire animation.

5] Copy channel 9, frame 10, and paste it into channel 9, frame 50. Then in-between that cell through frame 79.
The film loop animation goes from frame 50 through frame 79, and the Menu button should be available throughout the entire animation.

6] Rewind the movie and play it. Test all the buttons and watch the playback head.
They work! Using markers and a *go to frame "marker"* command is a very simple and basic method of branching to different parts of a movie.

7] Save your work.

WHAT YOU HAVE LEARNED
In this lesson you have:
Copied animations from one movie to another [*page* **124**]
Created buttons and applied button text style and color [*page* **125**]
Used the *pause* command to halt the movie [*page* **128**]
Added markers to the score and labeled them [*page* **129**]
Used *go to frame "marker"* to branch to different parts of the movie [*page* **130**]

director multimedia studio

LESSON 10

When creating multimedia, you first need to create the graphics, text, sound, and other elements that will be incorporated into the project. The Director Multimedia Studio provides everything you need to create dynamic multimedia from the ground up, including Macromedia xRes, a tool for image editing; Extreme 3D, a tool for creating 3D graphics; SoundEdit 16 version 2 plus DECK II, a tool for audio production with the Macintosh, or Sound Forge XP, a general-purpose sound editor for Windows; and Director, which brings all the elements together into an interactive application.

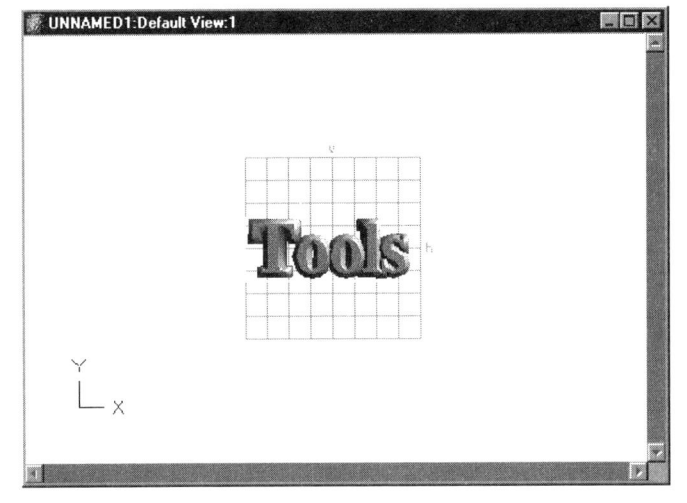

In addition to Director, the Director Multimedia Studio includes professional tools for creating and editing various types of media. In this lesson you'll learn to use the Director Multimedia Studio software.

In this lesson, you will use the products in the Director Multimedia Studio to create new media and modify existing media. These media will be incorporated into a multimedia production in the next lesson. This lesson is not intended to give you a full overview of each product, but it should give you a brief experience with each one.

If you would like to view the final results of this lesson, open the Complete folder in the Lesson10 folder and view Hammer.pct, Leader.aif, and Text.pct.

WHAT YOU WILL LEARN
In this lesson you will:
Add a glow effect to a graphic
Create 3D text
Fade a sound file

APPROXIMATE TIME
It usually takes about 1.5 hours to complete this lesson.

LESSON FILES
Media Files
Lesson10\Media
Starting Files
None
Completed Project
Lesson10\Complete\Hammer.pct
Lesson10\Complete\Leader.aif
Lesson10\Complete\Text.pct

tip   *If you do not have your own versions of these products, you can use the demo versions on the CD-ROM included with this book. Windows only: If you use the demo versions, you will not be able to complete the sound portion of this lesson.*

ADDING A GLOW EFFECT WITH XRES

Macromedia xRes is a powerful creative tool for editing images, painting naturalistic textures, and creating composite graphics. Macromedia xRes enables you to create and manipulate graphics and anti-aliased text, which can be used in your multimedia productions. In this task, you will add a glow around a graphic for use in the speaker support application you will create in the next lesson.

1] Open Macromedia xRes.

xRes opens, and you see an empty window.

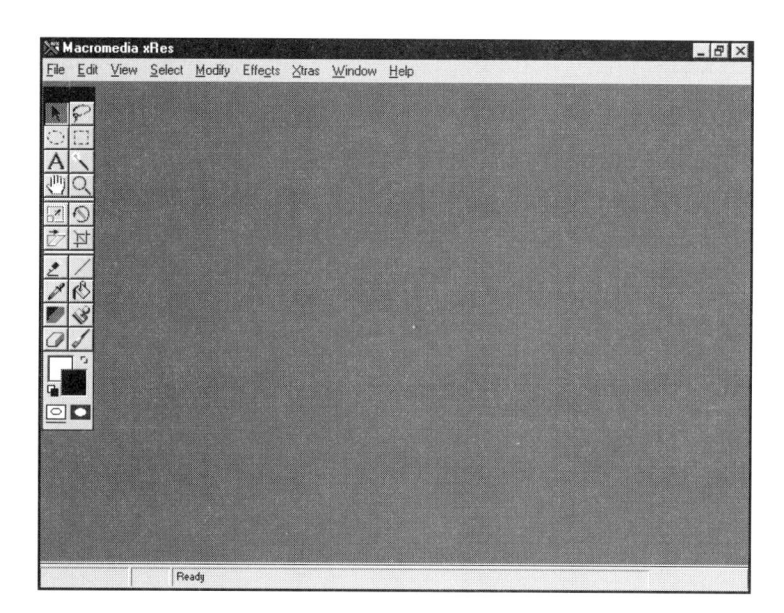

2] Choose File > Open and select Hammer.pct in the Media folder.

The hammer image appears in a window.

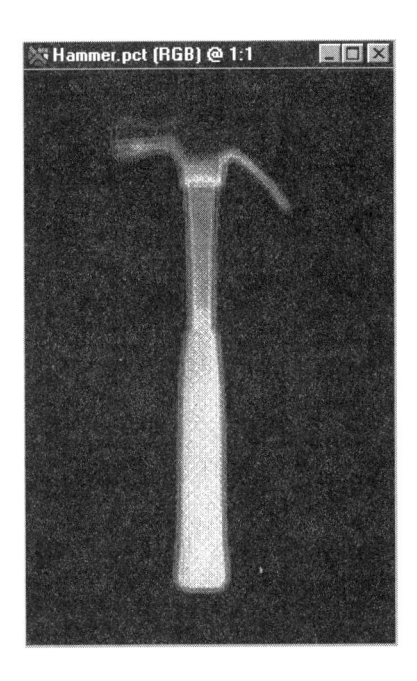

3] Select the Magic Wand tool in the toolbar and click the black background area of the image.

The Magic Wand selects all the contiguous pixels of the chosen color (black) anywhere in the image. In this image, this selects everything but the hammer, allowing you to adjust the background.

MAGIC WAND

4] Choose Select > Inverse or click the Invert Selection button on the toolbar to select only the hammer.

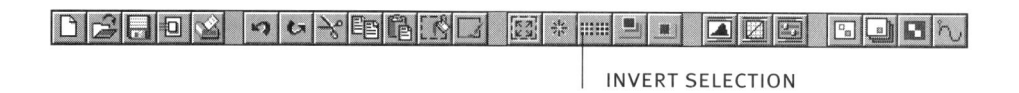

INVERT SELECTION

The hammer should be the only object selected now. Look at the top part of the hammer—it's not fully enclosed by the selection. You're going to apply a blur around the edge of the hammer, so you will need the edge to be fully defined at the top, so that the blur is evenly applied. You will smooth out the top part of the hammer next.

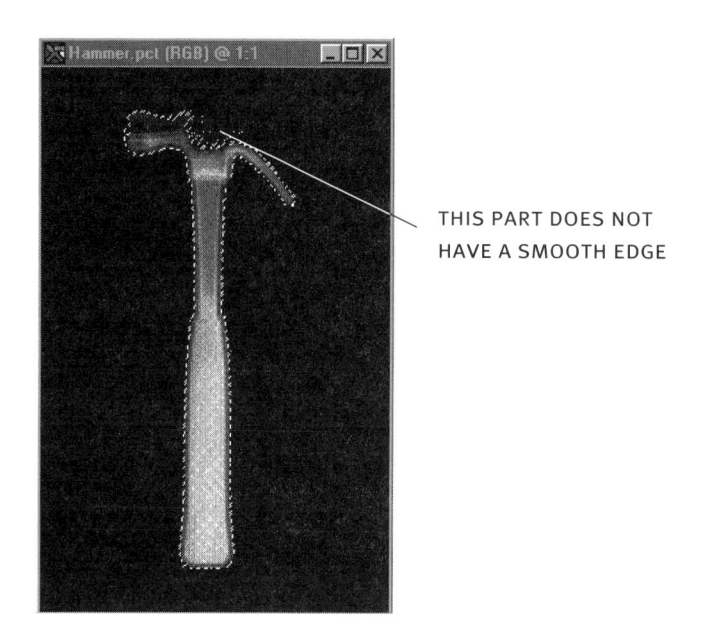

THIS PART DOES NOT
HAVE A SMOOTH EDGE

5] Select the Zoom tool from the Tools Palette and then click the top part of the hammer.

You should now have a closer view of the hammer.

6] Select the Lasso tool.

It looks like this:

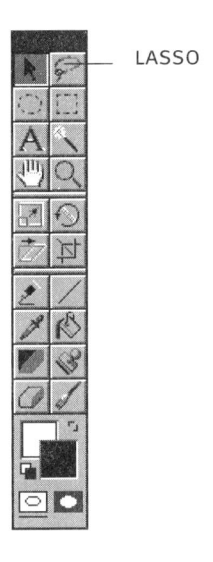

LASSO

7] Press and hold down the Shift key while you drag the lasso around the top part of the hammer.

Using the Lasso tool plus the Shift key tells the program to include the section you lasso as part of the selected image. This will smooth out the top part of the hammer and create an even edge. The screen should look like this:

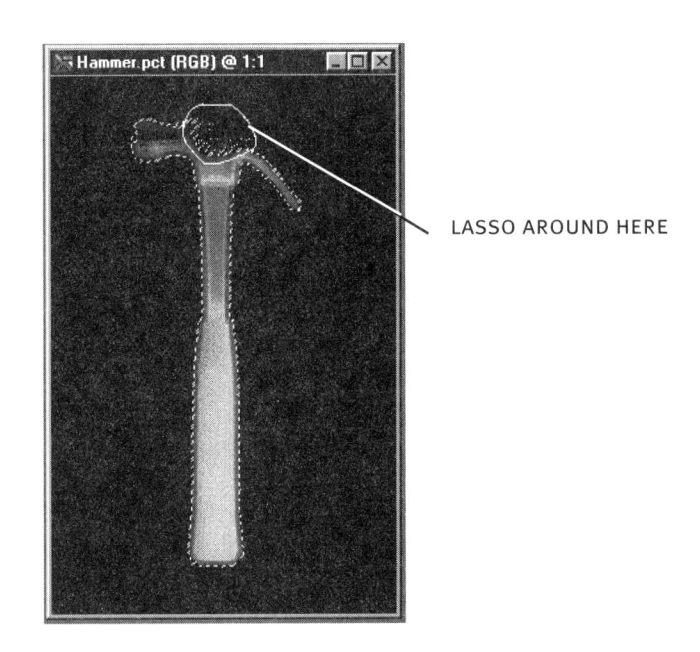

LASSO AROUND HERE

8] Choose Select > Inverse or click the Invert Selection button on the toolbar.

As you can see, the top of the hammer is smooth and fully enclosed now. When you choose Select > Inverse, the fully enclosed hammer is selected. You're going to apply a glow around the hammer, so you need to have the image selected now.

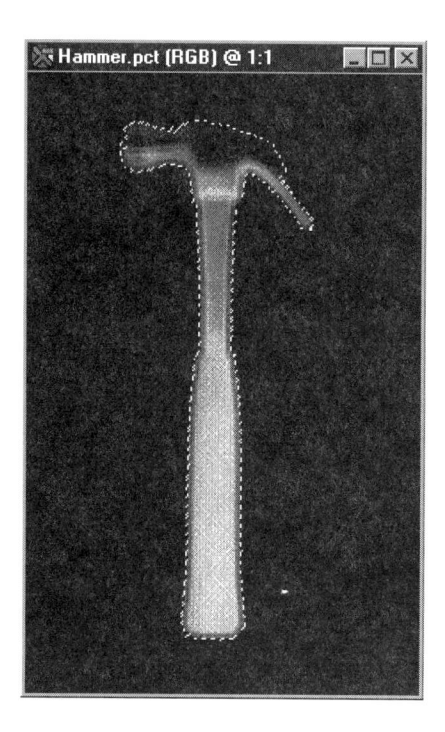

9] Choose Window > Palettes > Picker to open the Color window. Then click the Picker tab to display the Color Picker.

You select colors from here.

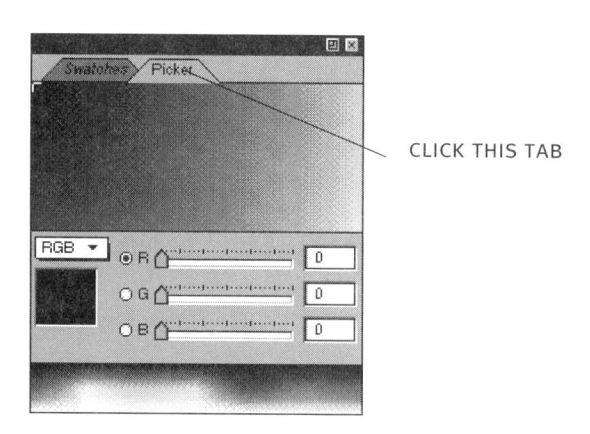

CLICK THIS TAB

10] Click a blue color.

Notice that the foreground color chip in the tools palette is blue. You will use this color as the glow around the hammer, but first you need to move the color to the background color chip.

11] On the keyboard, press X.

This sets the background color chip in the tools palette to blue.

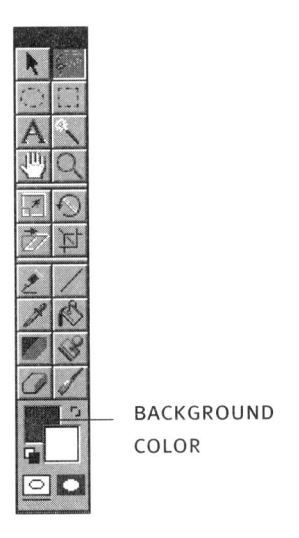

BACKGROUND COLOR

12] Press the Delete key to fill the background with the blue color.

Be sure you press the Delete key and not the Backspace key or any other key. Pressing Delete changes the background to blue.

13] Choose Select › Inverse.

Only the hammer is selected now.

14] Choose Window › Channels to open the Channels window.

Images can be saved in various color modes, such as RGB, gray scale, or CMYK. The hammer was saved in RGB mode. For all objects saved in RGB mode, there are four channels: RGB, Red, Green, and Blue. Each channel allows you to see different views of the image, such as the red colors or blue colors.

DIRECTOR MULTIMEDIA STUDIO

You are going to create a new channel that will hold the view of the hammer outline.

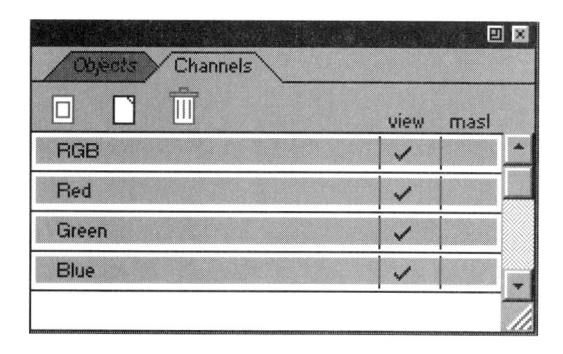

15] Store the selection in a new channel by choosing Select › Store › New.

In the Channels window you'll see a new channel, channel 4. This channel now holds the shape of the hammer. The blur needs to be in the shape of the hammer, so you need to store the hammer as a separate channel.

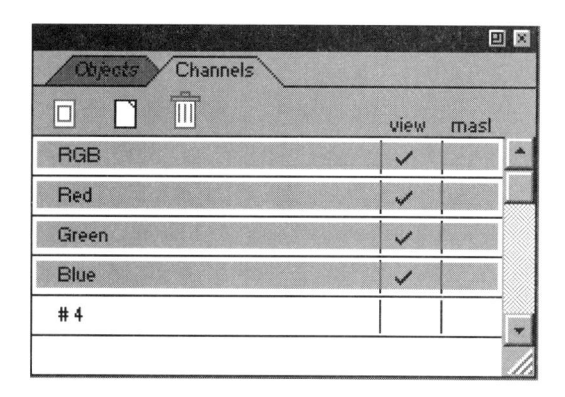

16] Choose Select › None (Windows Ctrl+D, Macintosh Command+D).

This deselects the image.

17] In the Channels window, click channel 4.

Selecting channel 4 (the hammer shape) enables you to edit it.

18] Drag channel 4 to the Select from Channel icon in the Channels window.

The Select from Channel icon is the first icon on the left in the Channels window. This step turns channel 4 into a selection, so all the other channels are not selected. The hammer is now white because it's masked (the screen looks like a black piece of paper with the hammer shape punched out of it).

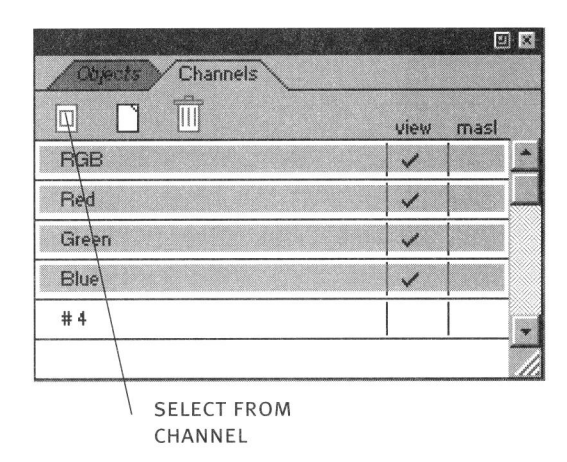

SELECT FROM CHANNEL

19] Click the Invert Selection button on the toolbar.

This selects the outer part of the hammer image so you can apply the blur to the edges of the hammer only, and not to the inside of the hammer shape.

20] Choose Effects > Blur > Gaussian to open a dialog box.

This effect creates a blur on an image.

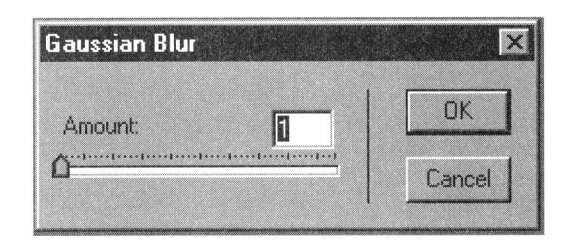

21] Type *15* in the Amount box and click OK.

You won't see anything on the screen because all the other channels are not selected.

22] Choose Select > None.

Nothing should be selected now.

145

DIRECTOR MULTIMEDIA STUDIO

23] In the Channels window, click the RGB channel.

All the boxes in the View column will be checked. This turns on all the channels so you can now see blue in the background.

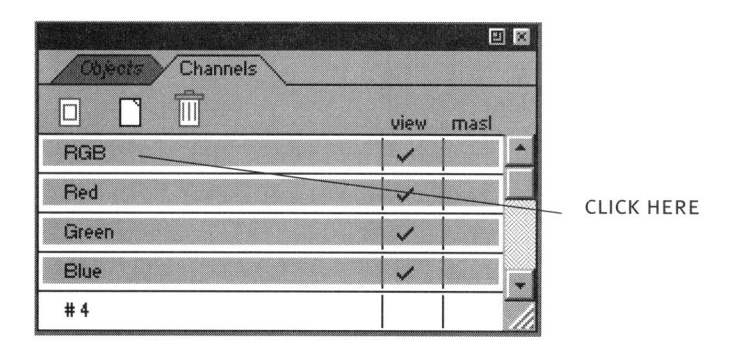

CLICK HERE

24] Check the box in the Mask column for channel 4 only.

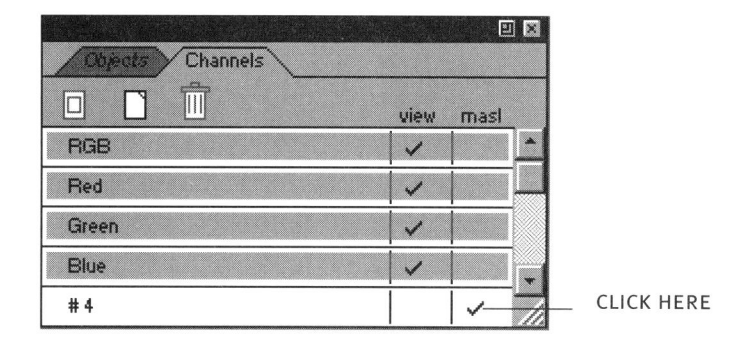

CLICK HERE

This shows the area where the mask was applied. Now you can clearly see the results: The hammer has a blue glow around it.

25] Choose File > Export > PICT to export the image as a PICT file. Save your work as Hammer.pct in the MyWork folder.

Director can import PICT files, so this is a good choice. You are now ready to use your new graphic in a multimedia application.

26] Choose File > Exit (Windows Ctrl+Q) or File > Quit (Macintosh Command+Q) to close xRes.

CREATING 3D TEXT WITH EXTREME 3D

In this task, you will create 3D text for use in the product information screen you're going to create in the next lesson.

1] Open Extreme 3D.

A window, called Untitled 1: Default View: 1, opens, displaying the work area and the working plane, the grid on which you can develop your work.

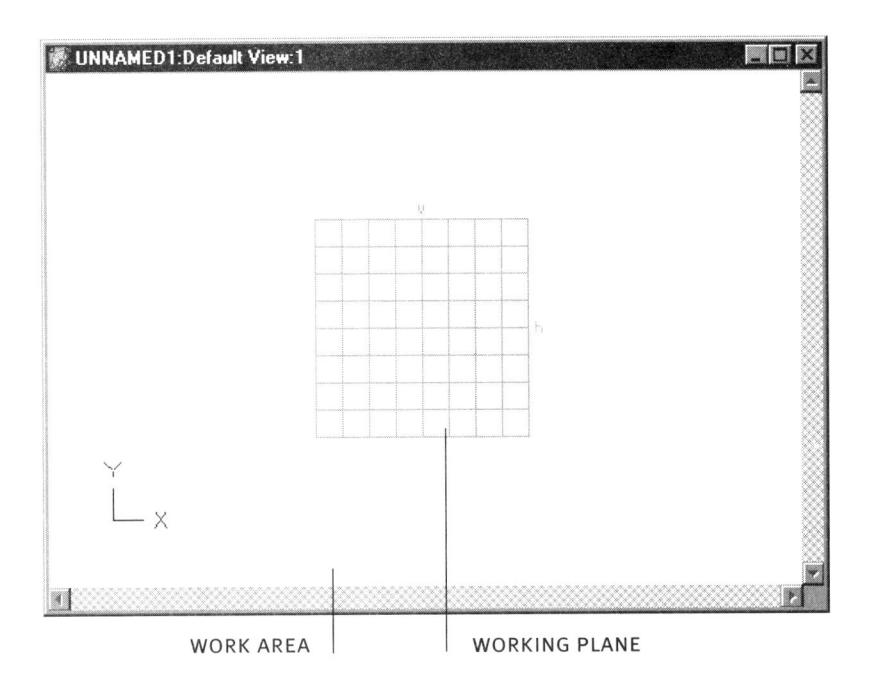

WORK AREA | WORKING PLANE

2] Choose Render › Set Background.

The Set Background dialog box opens.

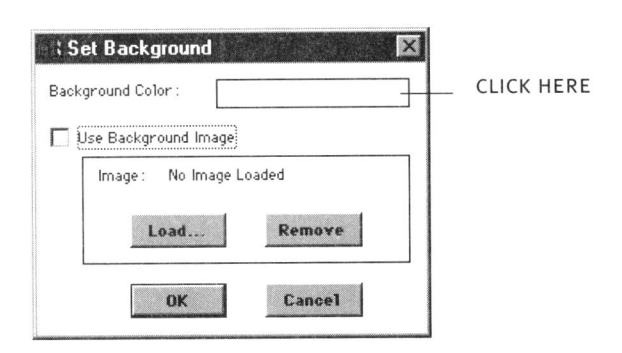

CLICK HERE

3] Click the Background Color rectangle to open the color palette. Click the black square and then close the color palette. Click OK to close the Set Background dialog box.

The background is now black.

4] Double-click the Text tool to open the Text Tool Preferences dialog box.

The Text Tool Preferences dialog box allows you to set the font and size.

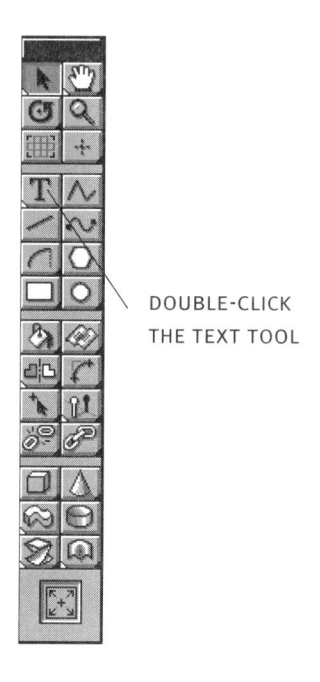

DOUBLE-CLICK
THE TEXT TOOL

5] Use the default font and set the size by typing .75. Click OK to close the dialog box.

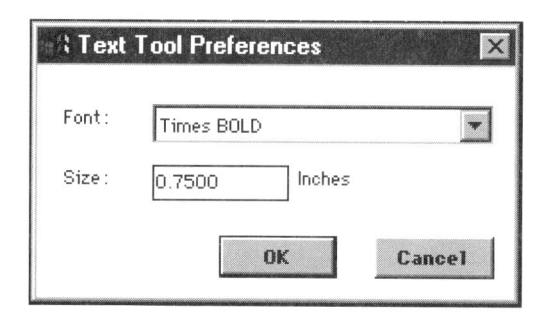

6] Click the work area to set the origin of the text. Then type *Tools* and press Enter on the numeric keypad.

You will not see any text in the work area until you press Enter, but as you type you can see and modify your entry in the tool space at the bottom left of the screen. When you press Enter, an outline of the word *Tools* appears in the work area.

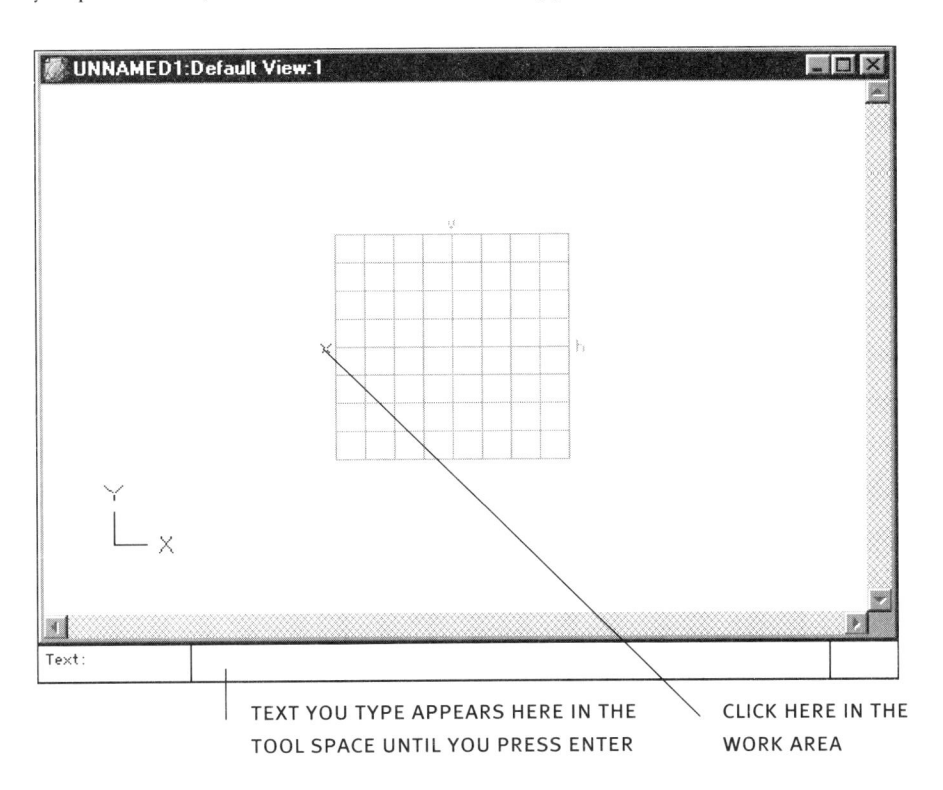

TEXT YOU TYPE APPEARS HERE IN THE TOOL SPACE UNTIL YOU PRESS ENTER

CLICK HERE IN THE WORK AREA

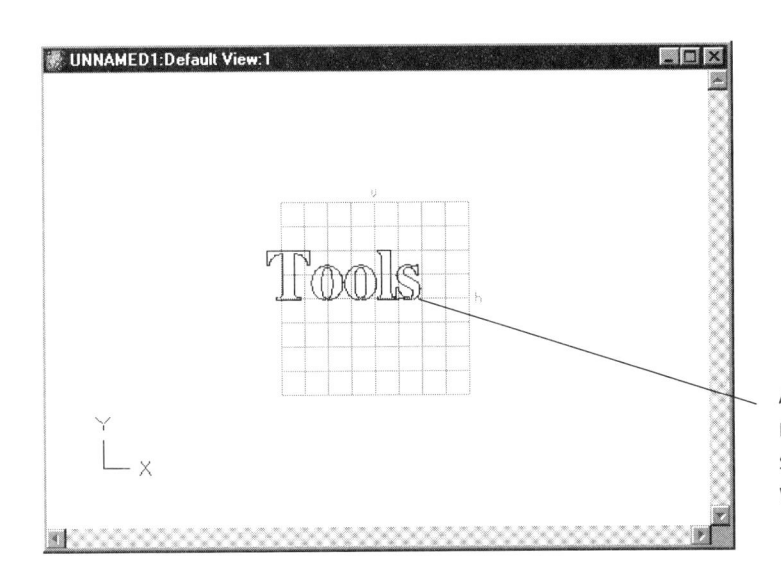

AFTER YOU PRESS ENTER, YOU WILL SEE TEXT IN THE WORK AREA

7] To center the word in the window, drag the word by the letter *T* to the middle of the work area.

For all text, if the first letter is red, the entire word is selected, and you can drag the word by the first letter. You can also move selected objects incrementally by using the arrow keys.

Now you will extrude the text—stretch it out along the Z-axis—to make it 3D. You'll use a special kind of extrusion that creates a beveled (chiseled) edge on the 3D object.

8] Select the Bevel Extrude tool in the tool palette by clicking the Extrude tool and continuing to hold down the mouse button and then selecting the Bevel Extrude tool that pops up to the right.

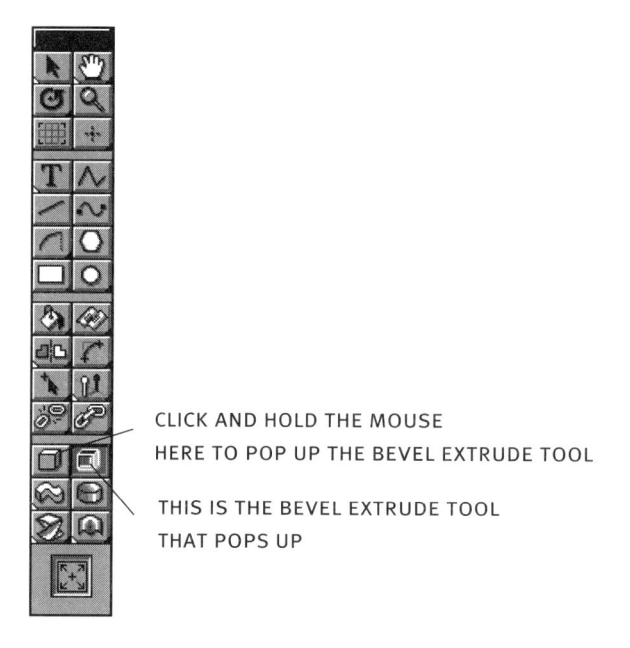

CLICK AND HOLD THE MOUSE
HERE TO POP UP THE BEVEL EXTRUDE TOOL

THIS IS THE BEVEL EXTRUDE TOOL
THAT POPS UP

The Bevel Extrude tool creates a beveled edge on an extruded object. This tool is especially useful for creating 3D text characters with rounded edges.

9] Press the Tab key to select the Extrude Depth field in the tool space at the bottom of the work area. Accept the default depth, 1, and press Tab again. Accept the default bevel width by pressing Enter. Click the work area to deselect the text.

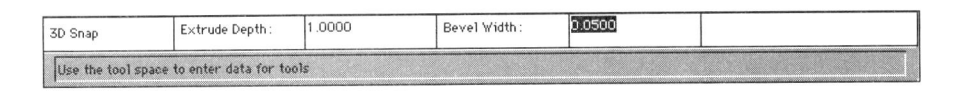

The text is now extruded and looks three-dimensional.

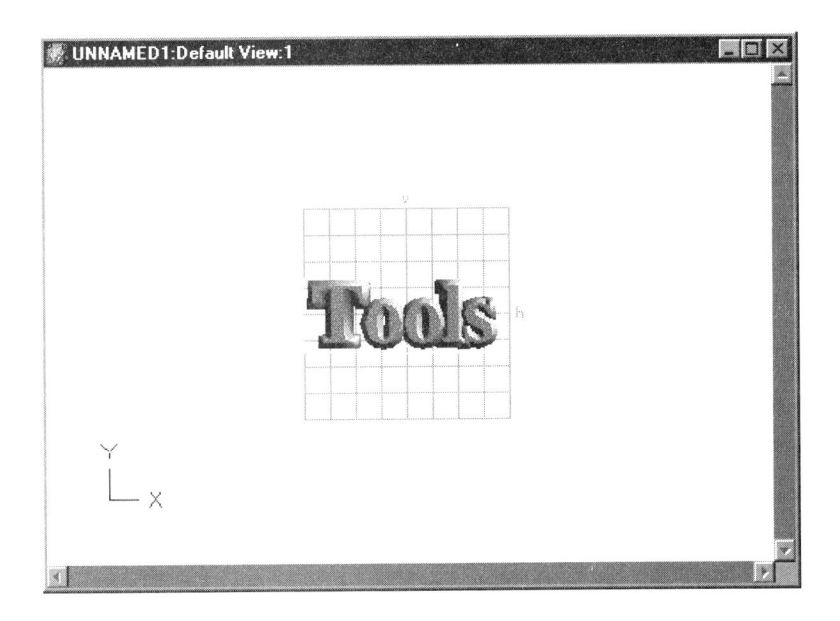

10] Choose Object > Show Working Plane to hide the working plane.
If you don't hide the working plane, it will appear in the exported file.

11] Choose File > Export > Bitmap (Windows) or File > Export > Paint PICT (Macintosh).
You're going to export the text as a picture file so it can be imported into Director.

12] Name the file Text.pct and save it in your MyWork folder.
You now have 3D text to use in your multimedia application.

13] Choose File > Exit (Windows Alt+F4) or File > Quit (Macintosh Command+Q) to close Extreme 3D.
Because you've already exported the file, you don't need to save any changes.

MODIFYING SOUNDS WITH SOUNDEDIT 16 OR SOUND FORGE

Sound can transform your work from interesting to engaging. Director features two sound channels in the score that allow you to easily combine voice-over with soundtrack or sound effects. Director also includes commands for controlling CD audio, sound files, and cast member sounds, including fade-in and fade-out.

The sound editing programs that come with the Director Multimedia Studio help you create and edit the sounds you'll use in Director movies. SoundEdit 16, version 2 (for the Macintosh), is a 16-bit, 44 kHz sound editor capable of creating multitrack CD-quality soundtracks without additional hardware. Sound Forge XP is a general-purpose sound editor for Windows. Both products let you adjust input levels, apply effects, and more. In this task, you will use the fade-out effect for an audio file that will be incorporated into the speaker support application you will create in the next lesson.

Windows only: If you are using the demo versions of the Director Multimedia Studio provided with this book, you will not be able to complete this task.

1] Open the sound editing program (on the Macintosh, SoundEdit 16; in Windows, SoundForge).

The main window appears.

2] Choose File > Open and open Leader.aif in the Media folder.

Leader.aif is an AIFF file, a common cross-platform format.

3] Double-click the waveform to select it. Then press the spacebar to play the selection.

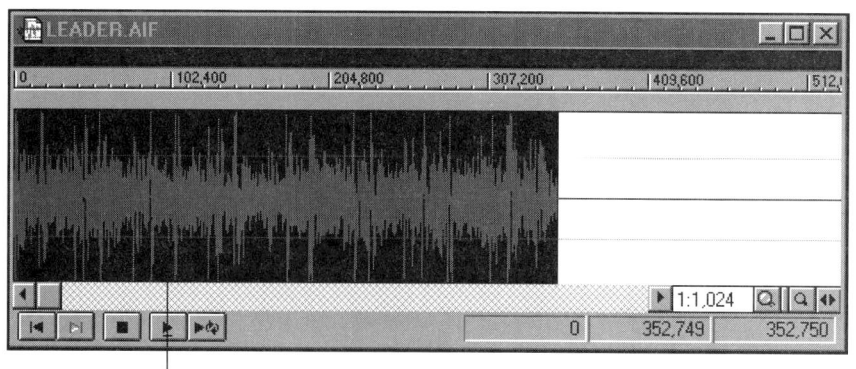

DOUBLE-CLICK THE WAVE FORM

You should hear the sound play.

4] If you're using a Macintosh, choose Effects › Fade Out; then in the dialog box, click Fade. If you're using Windows, choose Process › Fade › Out.

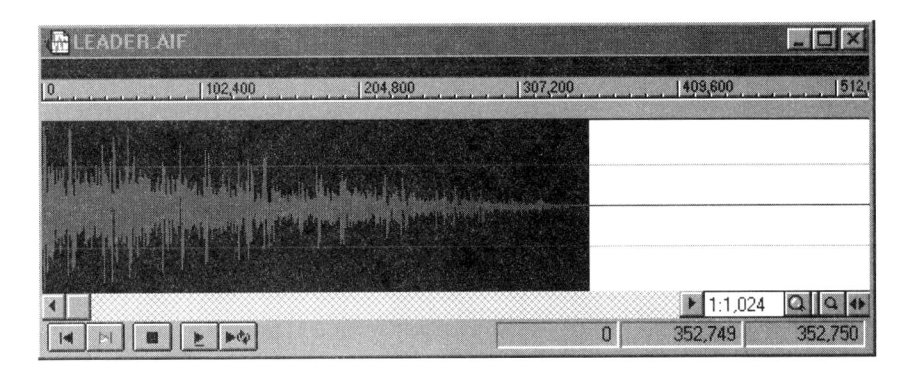

Notice the change in the appearance of the waveform toward the end. This is the fade-out you just added.

5] Press the spacebar to hear the difference in the sound file.

Adding the effect caused the sound to fade away slowly.

6] Choose File › Save and save the file as Leader.aif in your MyWork folder.

7] Close SoundEdit 16 or Sound Forge.

You are now ready to add these elements to a multimedia production.

WHAT YOU HAVE LEARNED
In this lesson you have:

Used xRes to add a Gaussian blur to an object [*page* **138**]

Used the Bevel Extrude tool in Extreme 3D to extrude text [*page* **147**]

Faded out a sound file with SoundEdit 16 or Sound Forge [*page* **152**]

sprite properties and palettes

Speaker support programs are used for many reasons: sales people use them during sales calls as backup for their discussions, and business people use them for presentations instead of overhead slides. These programs are sometimes left behind with customers after the presentation so the customers can review the material again on their own. In this lesson you will build the front-end of a speaker support program with navigation controls.

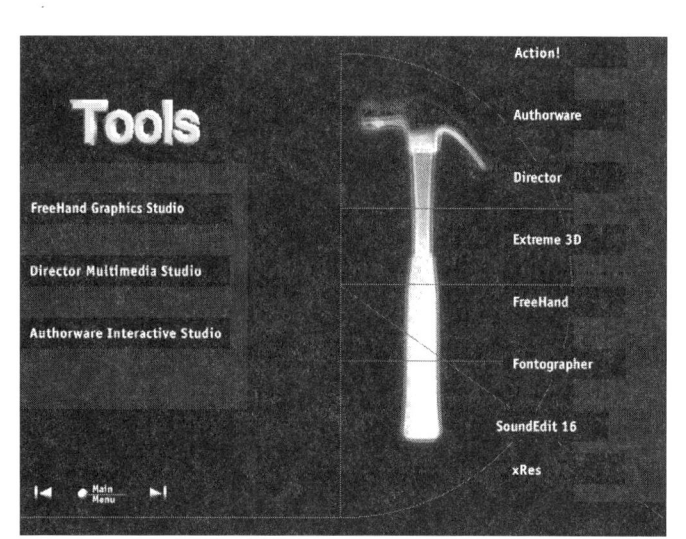

The Showcase CD includes one screen from which you can access information about each of Macromedia's studio products. In this lesson you will incorporate the multimedia elements you created in the previous lesson to create that screen. (The Showcase CD 5.0 was produced for Macromedia by Xronos, Inc.)

LESSON 11

If you would like to view the final result of this lesson, open the Complete folder in the Lesson11 folder and play Speaker.dir.

WHAT YOU WILL LEARN
In this lesson you will:

Practice setting a movie palette

Practice setting the background color of a movie

Organize cast members in a logical sequence

Set locations of sprites

Make sprites smaller

Use the tool palette to color sprites

Locate colors in a palette using an index number

Modify the dimensions of a sprite

Use grid settings to align objects

Practice adding a sound

APPROXIMATE TIME
It usually takes about 2 hours to complete this lesson.

LESSON FILES
Media Files
Lesson11\Media
Starting Files
None
Completed Project
Lesson11\Complete\Speaker.dir

IMPORTING MEDIA ELEMENTS

After your media elements are developed, the first step in creating a speaker support program is to import the media into Director and set some movie properties. In the previous lesson you used the products in the Director Multimedia Studio to create or modify some media elements for use in this speaker support program. Now you'll import those media elements along with other graphics. If you did not complete the previous lesson, you will still be able to complete this lesson.

1] Open a new file (Windows Ctrl+N, Macintosh Command+N).

An empty stage appears.

2] Choose File > Import to open the Import dialog box (Windows Ctrl+R, Macintosh Command+R).

You're going to import all the media elements now.

3] Locate the Media folder in the Lesson11 folder and click Add All.

All the file names appear in the file list.

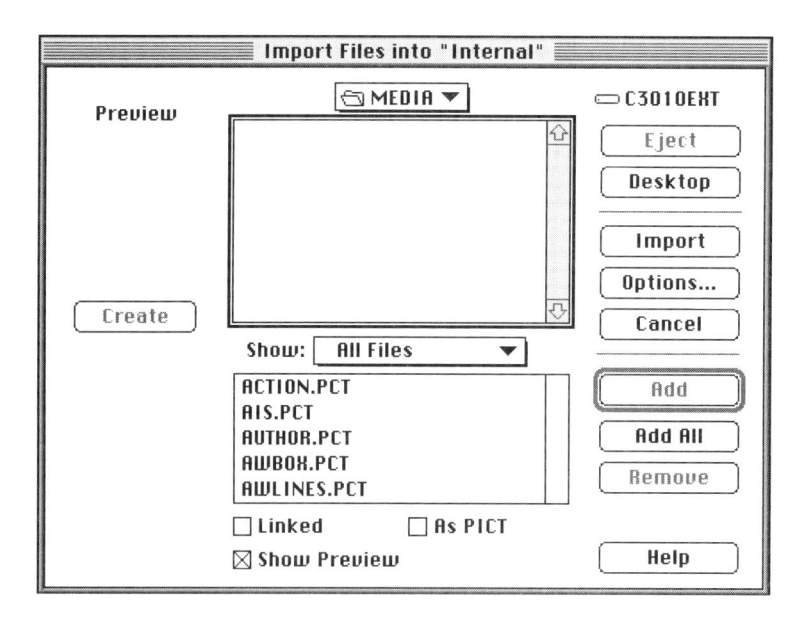

4] Click Import.

The Image Options dialog box appears.

5] In the Image Options dialog box, choose Stage (8 bits).
The graphics were created in a higher bit depth than the current stage is set to. To prevent any ugly color flashes, you need to set the images to 8 bits, the bit depth of the stage.

6] Macintosh only: From the Palette menu choose Remap to System-Win.
The images were created with the Windows system palette, which uses different colors than the Macintosh system palette. When you remap the images to the Windows system palette, Director can display these images with the correct colors.

7] Check Same Settings for Remaining Images and click OK to close the dialog box.
All the images should be set to these same settings. Choose Same Settings for Remaining Images so this dialog box isn't displayed for every image that you're now importing.

8] If you completed Lesson 10, import the files you created and saved in the MyWork folder.
The files are Hammer.pct, Leader.aif, and Text.pct. As you import these files, you can replace Hammer.pct, Leader.aif, and Text.pct now in the Cast window. These are files you imported in steps 3 and 4, and you are replacing them with your versions of those files.

SETTING A MOVIE PALETTE

Next you'll use the Movie Properties dialog box to set a color palette, background color, and stage size for the movie. In many cases, a specific color palette may have been used to create graphics on a particular platform. When you move the graphics to another platform, that platform may have its own default palette, which will most likely not match the palette that was used to create the graphics. When this happens, the graphics may be displayed on the screen in unattractive, clashing colors. To resolve this issue, you can switch the default movie palette to the same palette that was used to create the graphics.

1] Choose Modify > Movie > Properties.
The Movie Properties dialog box opens.

2] Macintosh only: In the Default Palette pop-up menu, choose System-Win and then click OK.
This sets the movie's default palette to the Windows palette.

In this project, the graphics were created using the default Windows palette. To ensure that the graphics look good on the Macintosh, you also need to set the movie palette to the Windows system palette. Now the palette for the movie matches the palette used to create the graphics. This is different from setting the palette for specific graphics, as you just did when you imported the graphics. In this case, you are setting the palette for the entire movie, so the movie uses one palette throughout. Windows users do not need to change the movie's default palette because it's already set to the Windows system palette.

3] Set the movie background color to black.

To do this, click the Stage Color chip and select black from the palette.

4] Set the stage to 640 x 480 and close the dialog box.

To do this, select the size from the Stage Size pop-up menu.

ORGANIZING THE CAST

Next you'll organize the cast so all related cast members are in a logical order. This will help you easily locate cast members. Devising a scheme for the cast is not a necessary step for Director development, but it will help you keep organized, especially if you are working with many cast members.

1] Drag the cast members into any logical order that you find useful. For example, place the buttons that go on the main screen next to each other, place the graphics that go on the main screen next to each other, and so on. Then do the same thing for each destination screen.

Placing cast members in a logical order will help save you valuable search time later. The following list is a suggested order for the cast members. To see a cast member name, click the cast member. The name will be displayed at the top of the Cast window.

Here's one order to try:

1 AIS	13 Lines	25 Dirlines
2 DMS	14 Leftbtn	26 Text
3 FGS	15 Mainbtn	27 Leader
4 Font	16 Ritbtn	
5 Author	17 AWtext	
6 Fhand	18 FHtext	
7 E3D	19 Dirtext	
8 Direct	20 Awbox	
9 Action	21 Fhbox	
10 SE16	22 Dirbox	
11 xRes	23 Awlines	
12 Hammer	24 Fhlines	

This is how the cast members should appear in the Cast window.

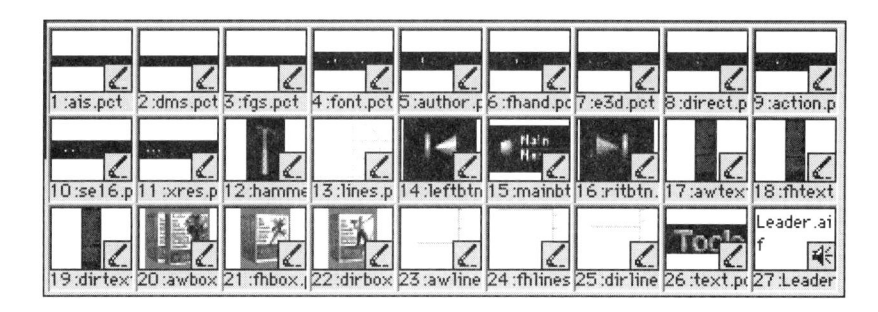

2] Save your work as Speaker.dir in your MyWork folder.

SETTING THE LOCATION OF A SPRITE

Next you'll starting adding elements to the stage. In this task, you will set the location of sprites on the stage by defining exact locations using the Sprite Properties dialog box.

1] Drag cast member Hammer from the cast window to channel 1, frame 1.

This is the image to which you applied a glow in the previous lesson.

2] Choose Modify › Sprite › Properties (Windows Ctrl+Shift+I, Macintosh Command+Shift+I) to open the Sprite Properties dialog box. Set Location Left to *275* and Top to *30* and close the dialog box.

The Location fields set the location of the sprite relative to the upper-left corner of the stage.

Remember that the stage size is not necessarily the same size as the screen. Recall that you set the stage size in the Modify › Movie › Properties dialog box. The Location boxes set the location of the sprite relative to the upper-left corner of the *stage*, not the upper-left corner of the *screen*.

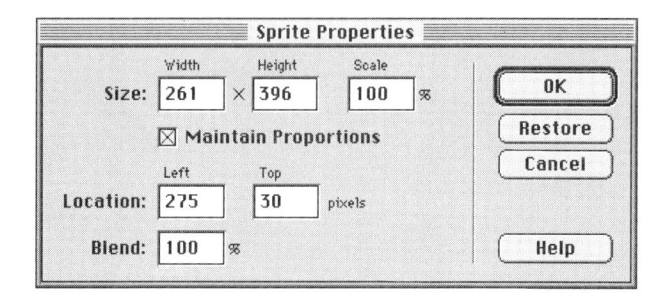

160

LESSON 11

REDUCING THE FILE SIZE OF A BITMAP

You will frequently be concerned with keeping file size to a minimum to help reduce download time for Shockwave files or to ensure that you final product will fit on the disk on which it will be shipped. Here's one technique for reducing the size of a graphic cast member.

1] Select the Lines cast member in the cast and click the Cast Member Properties button.

Notice the size of the graphic in the lower-left corner of the dialog box.

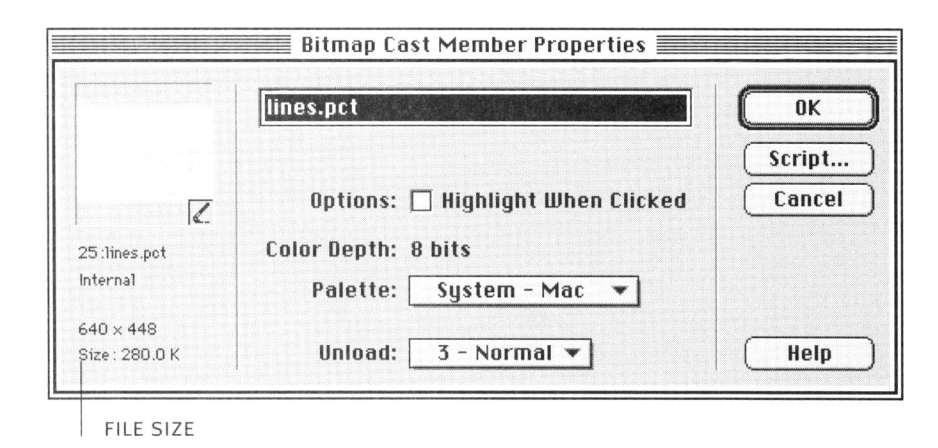

FILE SIZE

2] Close the dialog box.

3] Select the Lines cast member and choose Modify > Transform Bitmap.

The Transform Bitmap dialog box opens.

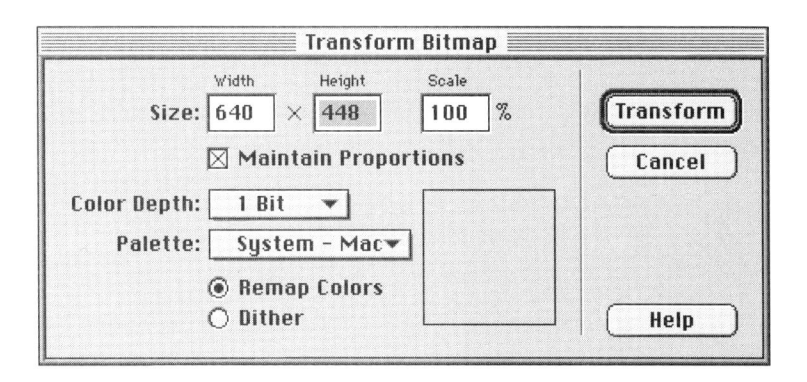

161

SPRITE PROPERTIES AND PALETTES

4] In the Color Depth pop-up menu, choose 1 Bit. Then choose Remap Colors and click Transform. In the dialog box that opens, click OK to confirm your choice.

This reduces the size of your graphic. The original graphic was 8 bits. An 8-bit graphic stores more color information and therefore takes more disk space than a 1-bit graphic; 1-bit graphics are black and white.

5] Select the Lines cast member in the Cast window. Then click the Cast Member Properties button to check the size of the graphic.

Notice the size of the graphic in the lower-left corner of the dialog box. The graphic is much smaller than before.

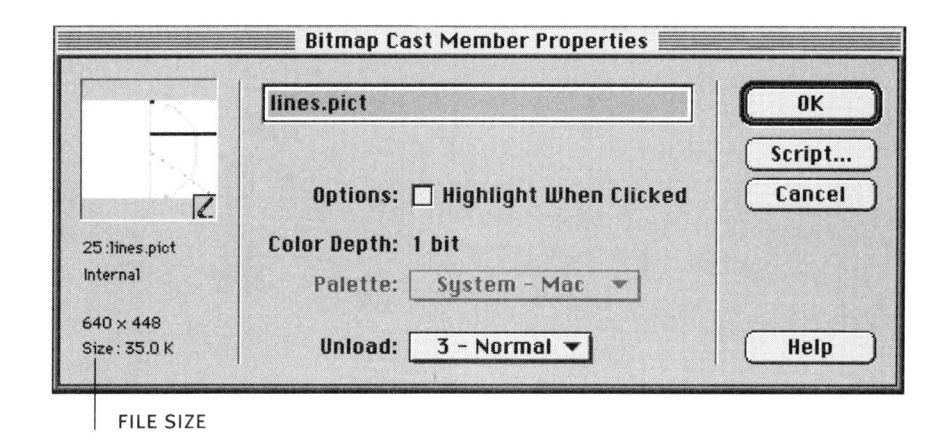

FILE SIZE

shockwave tip *Depending on the user's modem speed, using as little storage space as possible can be very important. Transforming graphics from 8 bits to 1 bit reduces the amount of storage space the bitmap needs and also enables faster downloading.*

6] Drag the Lines cast member to channel 2, frame 1, and center it on the stage. Set the ink to Bkgnd Transparent.

Because both the lines and the stage are black, you'll just see a few lines going across the hammer. You'll fix this in the next task.

tip *A quick way to ensure that a full-screen graphic is centered is to choose Modify › Sprite › Properties and set Location Left to 0 and Top to 0.*

7] Set the ink to Bkgnd Transparent.

This ink makes the pixels in the background color of the sprite appear transparent and permits the background to be seen.

FINDING AN INDEX COLOR NUMBER

Index color numbers are associated with each color in a color palette. These numbers help you identify colors. Index color 0 is always at the top left of the palette. Index color 255 is always at the bottom right of the palette (assuming that the palette contains 256 colors). Colors are numbered from top to bottom, left to right. Note that you cannot assign a color to an object from this dialog box.

If you know the exact location of a color in the color palette (by determining its index color number), you can apply that same color to another object. Also, if another person is working on a graphic that requires a specific color in a palette, you can specify the index color number to use. Of course, you could simply look closely at the color palette and describe the location of the color: for example, "it's 2 over and 9 down." However, index color numbers are much easier to use.

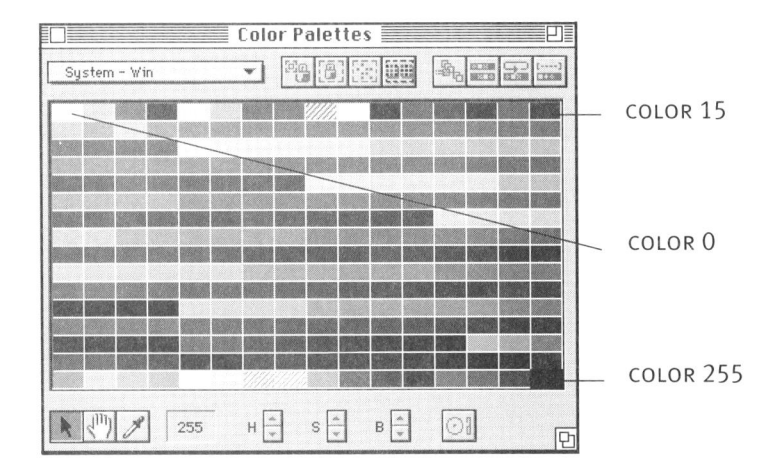

Index color numbers are used to identify the location of a color in a palette. For all palettes, Color 0 is in the upper left corner. Colors are numbered left to right in the palette.

1] **Select channel 2, frame 1, in the score and choose Window > Tool Palette (Windows Ctrl+7, Macintosh Command+7).**
The tool palette opens.

2] Click the foreground color chip and choose a dark red from the palette.

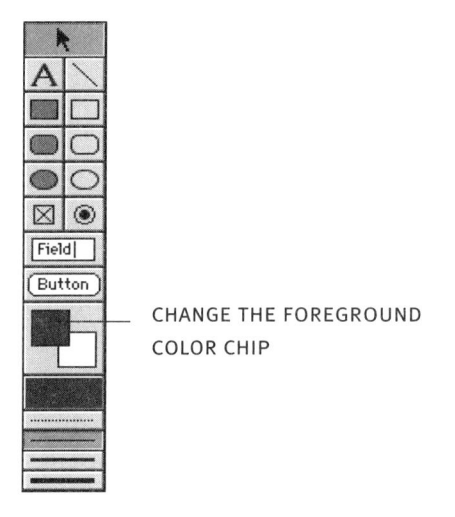

CHANGE THE FOREGROUND COLOR CHIP

Color chip (index color) 254 of the Windows palette is a good dark red.

To see what index color 254 looks like, choose Window › Color Palettes and open the color palette you want. In this case, the System-Win palette is the one you want; it may already be open (Windows and Macintosh computers have different system palettes; for example, index color 5 in the Windows palette is green, and in the Macintosh palette, it's yellow).

Click a color in the palette to display the index color number in the bottom part of the dialog box. Index color 255 is at the bottom right of the palette. Colors are numbered from top to bottom, left to right, so index color 254 is one left from the bottom right of the palette.

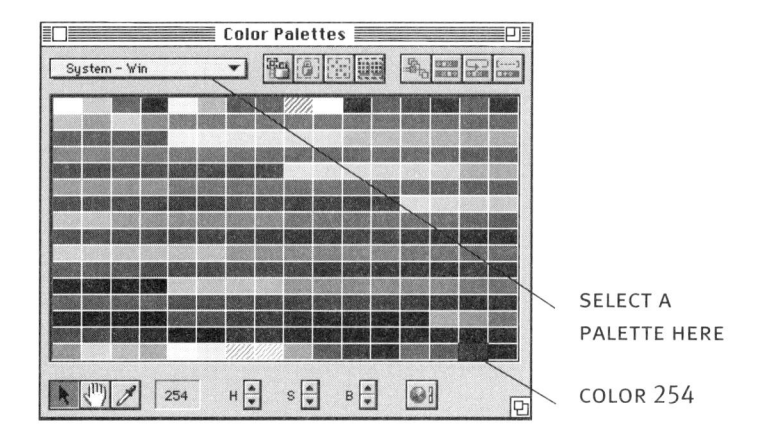

SELECT A PALETTE HERE

COLOR 254

Now that you know the location of the color in the palette, you can select the color from the palette that is displayed when you click the foreground color chip.

Now the lines across the hammer should be dark red.

shockwave tip *The ability to color 1-bit sprites like this is very useful. It reduces the size of the Director movie by allowing a black 1-bit cast member to become any color in the current palette. It is a great technique for shrinking movies for playback with Shockwave.*

MODIFYING SPRITE PROPERTIES

You set the location of sprites and modify their dimensions in the Sprite Properties dialog box. You'll do that next.

1] Click channel 4, frame 1. Then use the Filled Rectangle tool in the tool palette to create a rectangle of about 2 x 3 inches on the stage.

You'll use the rectangle as a design element on the stage. The rectangle is added to the Cast window when you create it.

You are going to set the exact size of the rectangle in the next step, so you don't need to be very concerned about its size right now.

tip *Note that you are skipping over channel 3 in the score. Leaving empty spaces makes the score easier to read.*

2] Choose Modify > Sprite > Properties. Uncheck Maintain Proportions. For the width and height of the rectangle, specify *93 x 448*, and set Location Left to *549* and Top to 0. Close the dialog box when you're done.

Be sure Maintain Proportions is unchecked; otherwise, the rectangle will be scaled proportionately.

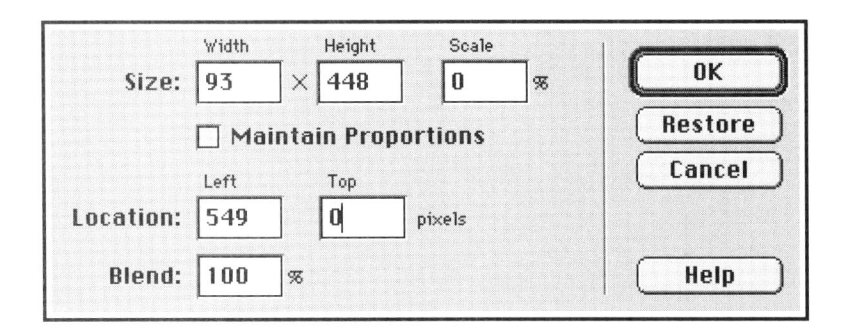

165

SPRITE PROPERTIES AND PALETTES

Now the rectangle is resized and in a new location.

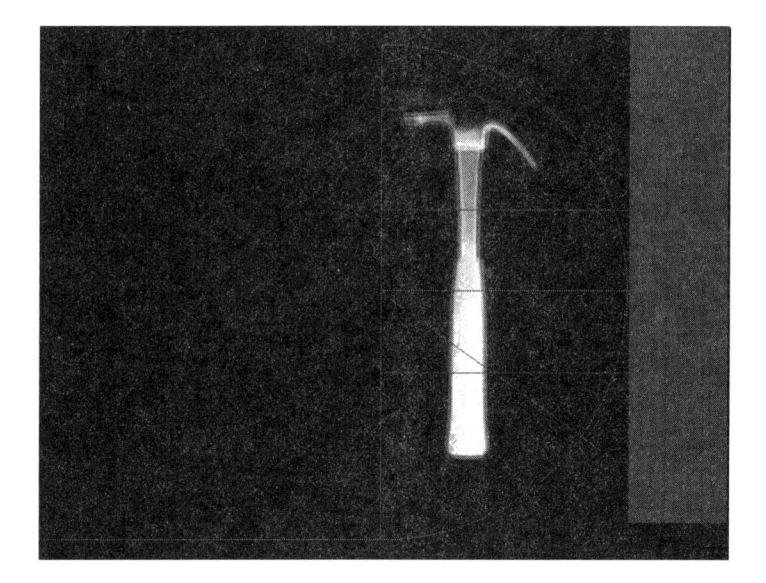

As you can see, the Sprite Properties dialog box is very useful. You will be using it frequently in your Director development.

3] Use the tool palette to color the rectangle a very dark red.

Click the foreground color chip to open the color palette. Index color 179 would be a good choice.

4] In the Cast window, select the rectangle. Then click the Cast Member Properties button.

Now you're going to give this new cast member a name.

5] Name the cast member *Rectangle*. Then click OK to close the dialog box.

Naming cast members is a good habit to get into so you or someone else can easily locate them later.

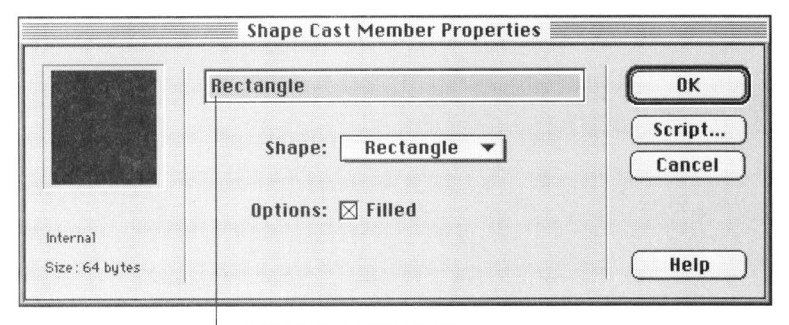

TYPE THE NAME HERE

6] Drag the cast member you just named Rectangle from the Cast window into channel 5, frame 1.

The rectangle will be the same color and size as before because it retains the size and color it previously was assigned. Position the rectangle on the left side of the stage. Now you will change some properties of this sprite to make it appear different from its other use here.

tip *All objects created with the tool palette tools can be modified without affecting the parent cast member. Note that Director can much more quickly display resized objects that are created using the tools in the tool palette than it can resize imported graphics or ones created with the paint tools. Reusing the same cast member saves storage space. Once the cast member is on the stage, you can resize the sprite or change any of its attributes, and it will look like a different cast member entirely. Note that the parent cast member will not be affected.*

7] Select the sprite in channel 5, frame 1, and set the ink to Copy.

You have used this ink before. Copy ink is useful for backgrounds or for sprites that do not appear in front of other artwork.

8] Choose Modify > Sprite > Properties and uncheck Maintain Proportions. Set the width and height to *226 x 237* and set the location to *0, 122*.

Now the sprite has a new location and new dimensions.

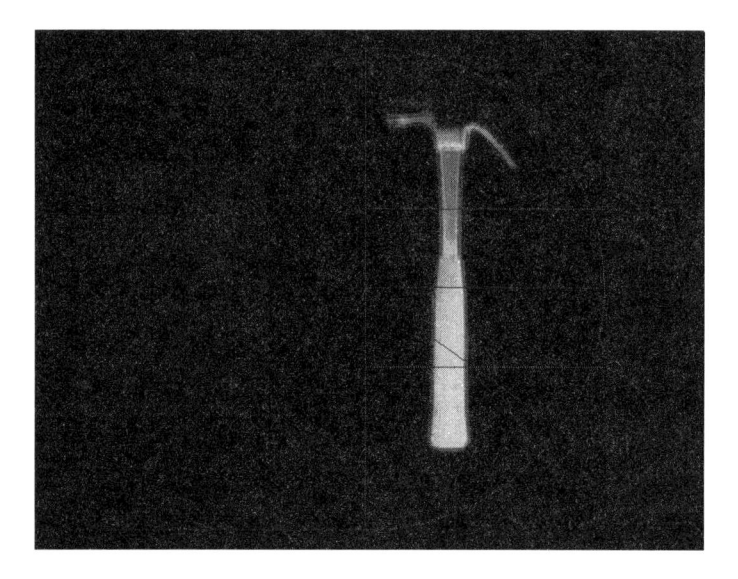

EDITING A CAST MEMBER

Now you'll use the Paint window to edit a cast member, cutting away extra parts.

1] Double-click the cast member named Text to open the Paint window.

Recall that this is the extruded text you created in the previous lesson. The text is the word *Tools*. You need to cut away the outer parts of the graphic so only the small rectangular area around the text remains.

2] Click the Marquee tool.

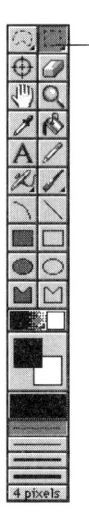

MARQUEE

3] **Draw a rectangle around the lower part of the graphic to select the large black area. Then choose Edit › Cut. Repeat this process for the upper part and the left and right parts of the graphic, until only the word *Tools* remains.**

Cutting away extraneous parts of the graphic reduces its size.

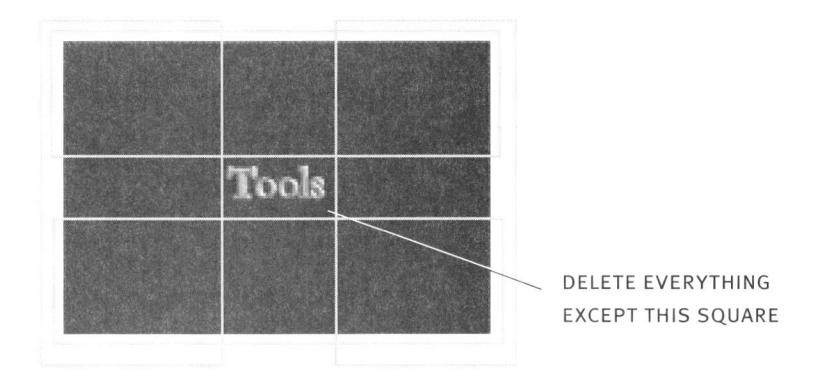

DELETE EVERYTHING EXCEPT THIS SQUARE

4] **Close the Paint window when you're done.**

Now the graphic is ready to be placed on the stage.

5] **Drag the Text cast member (the word *Tools*) from the Cast window to channel 6, frame 1, of the score.**

The text is automatically centered on the stage.

6] **Drag the text to the upper-left corner of the stage and center it above the dark red rectangle. In the Score, set the ink to Copy.**

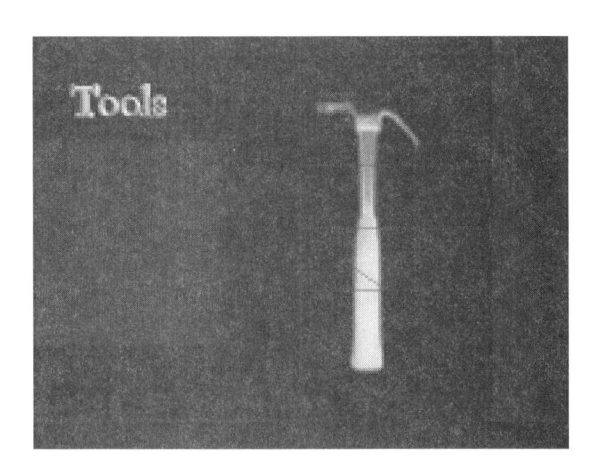

7] **Save your work.**

SPRITE PROPERTIES AND PALETTES

SNAPPING TO THE GRID

In this task you will add several elements to the stage at one time. Then you'll use the grid to align these elements quickly and easily.

1] Drag these cast members to frame 1 in the score, starting in channel 20:

Channel	Cast member
20	Action
21	Author
22	Direct
23	E3D
24	FHand
25	Font
26	SE16
27	xRes

These cast member names will be listed on the right side of the stage.

Notice that you're leaving extra space in the score. There are two reasons for this. First, you will be filling in many of the empty channels over the next few lessons. Second, leaving space in the score makes the score easier to read.

2] Select all the sprites in frame 1, channels 20 through 27, and set the ink to Copy.
Copy ink is useful for sprites that do not appear in front of other artwork, and sprites with Copy ink animate faster than sprites with any other ink, so this is a good choice.

The sprites should all be readable now, but they aren't placed where you want them. You will place them in the next several steps.

3] Select channel 20, frame 1, and set its location to *481, 0*.
Remember: To set the exact position of a sprite, you choose Modify > Sprite > Properties.

You need to place the remaining sprites vertically at 60-pixel intervals, in the order they are listed in step 1. A quick way to place the sprites precisely is to use the grid.

4] Choose View > Grid > Settings, type *60* in the Width and Height boxes, and close the dialog box.
This creates a grid with 60-pixel intervals.

5] Choose View > Snap To to turn on grid snapping. Then choose View > Grid > Show.
Now you can see the grid. Grid snapping ensures that anything you drag near a grid line will be automatically aligned with it.

6] Using the following illustration as your guide, drag the seven remaining graphics to the right side of the stage.
Because grid snapping is turned on, the graphics jump to the grid lines, which makes aligning them much easier.

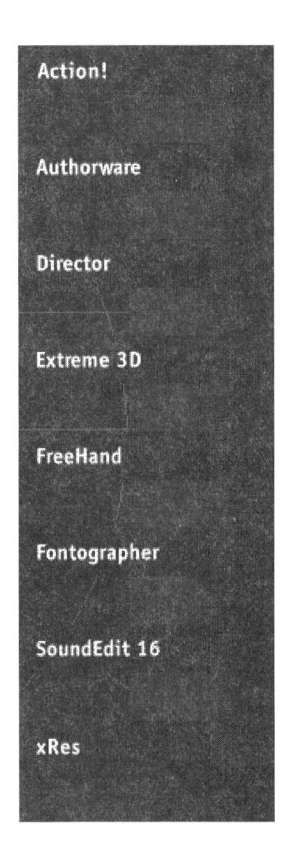

7] Turn the grid and grid snapping off.
To do this, choose View > Grid > Show and View > Snap To to uncheck those options.

ADDING NAVIGATIONAL ELEMENTS

In this task you will add buttons for navigation and complete the first frame of the speaker support project.

1] Drag cast members Leftbtn, Ritbtn, and Mainbtn into frame 1 in channels 13, 14, and 15.

These buttons will take the user forward, backward, or to the main menu. This screen will be the main menu for the speaker support program. You will build destination frames in the next two lessons.

2] On the stage, drag the buttons to the bottom left of the stage.

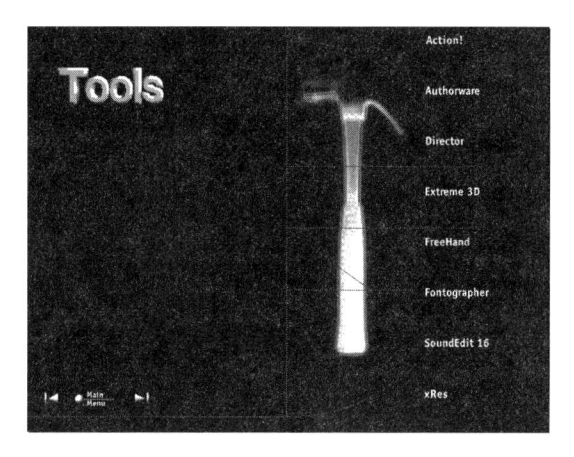

3] Use the Align tool to align the buttons evenly.

You can click the Align tool on the toolbar or choose Modify › Align.

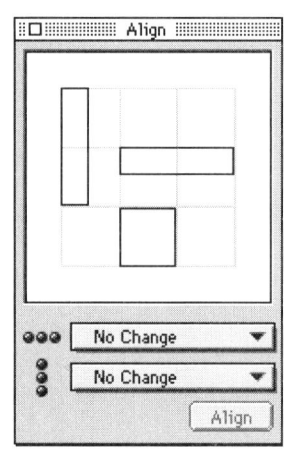

4] Set the ink to Copy for all of these sprites.
With Copy ink set, the sprites should look better on the black background.

5] Drag cast members FGS, DMS, and AIS into frame 1 in channels 28, 29, and 30.
These are "hot areas" that will branch users to the FGS, DMS, and AIS sections of the speaker support program. (You will build these destination frames in the next two lessons.)

6] Choose Modify > Sprite > Properties and set the locations of the sprites as follows:
FGS: (0, 151)
DMS: (0, 211)
AIS: (0, 271)

7] Set the ink to Copy for these three sprites.
The layout of the main menu screen is now complete, including graphics and navigation controls.

ADDING SOUND

Now you'll add a sound to play while the main menu frame is displayed.

1] Drag cast member Leader.aif to sound channel 1, frame 1, in the score.

This is the sound you modified in the previous lesson. Whenever this frame is displayed, the music will play.

tip *Instead of dragging a sound from the Cast window, you can double-click the sound channel to display a dialog box that lists available sounds. Choosing Modify › Frame › Sound opens the same dialog box.*

2] In-between the sound channel from frame 1 to frame 2.

tip *If you have sound in only one frame, occasionally it won't play smoothly. To avoid this problem, always in-between sounds so they're at least two frames long.*

3] Play the movie.

Now the first screen of the speaker presentation is complete, and you can hear the sound start to play in the background. Because the movie has only two frames, the playback head moves only from frame 1 to frame 2, so you don't see much when you play the movie. That's because, so far, you have been concentrating on just creating the layout of the opening menu. You'll be adding more frames to this movie in the next two lessons.

WHAT YOU HAVE LEARNED

In this lesson you have:

Set a movie palette [*page* **157**]

Set the background color of a movie [*page* **158**]

Organized cast members in a logical sequence [*page* **159**]

Used the Sprite Properties dialog box to set locations of sprites [*page* **160**]

Transformed sprites from 8 bits to 1 bit [*page* **161**]

Used the tool palette to color sprites [*page* **163**]

Determined a color's index color number [*page* **163**]

Modified the dimensions of a sprite [*page* **165**]

Used grid settings and snapping to align objects [*page* **170**]

Added a sound [*page* **174**]

text, blending, and navigation

In the previous lesson you created the main menu frame for a speaker support program by adding graphics and navigation controls. In this lesson, you will create a destination frame for one of the navigation controls to jump to. By incorporating color blending techniques, you will highlight and dim hot areas to let users know what areas of the screen they can click. You will also instruct the playback head to wait for user input and to branch to various sections in a movie.

In this lesson you will build a destination screen of the product information section for the Showcase CD. You will incorporate navigation capability, add highlights, and dim buttons to provide user feedback.

LESSON 12

If you would like to view the final result of this lesson, open the Complete folder in the Lesson12 folder and play Speaker2.dir.

WHAT YOU WILL LEARN
In this lesson you will:

Practice adding markers and labelling them

Practice pausing the program to wait for user input

Create and modify text

Set spacing and kerning

Set text color

Add a highlight to a hot area

Dim buttons

Change the background transparent color

Practice navigating to markers

APPROXIMATE TIME
It usually takes about 2 hours to complete this lesson.

LESSON FILES
Media Files
None
Starting Files
Lesson12\Start.dir
Completed Project
Lesson12\Complete\Speaker2.dir

ADDING MARKERS

You'll start by adding markers for the frames. Just as in earlier lessons, you will use markers to indicate where certain sections of the movie are located so Director can branch to those sections using Lingo commands.

1] Open Start.dir in the Lesson12 folder and save it as Speaker2.dir in your MyWork folder.

This is the prebuilt file that contains the main menu. If you completed the last lesson, you can use the movie you created there instead. Save it as Speaker2.dir in your MyWork folder.

2] Drag/copy channels 4 and 5, frame 1, into frame 5. Then do the same for channels 13 through 30.

To drag/copy, select the frames you want to copy with the arrow pointer. Press the spacebar to change the arrow to a hand pointer and at the same time press Alt (Windows) or Option (Macintosh). While holding these keys down, drag to the new frame and release the mouse.

You now have a copy of the opening menu to use as a basis for a destination frame. That was easy.

Now that you have a few different sections in the movie, you will add some markers for those sections.

3] Drag a marker to frame 1 and label it *Main*.
This marker indicates the location of the main menu frame.

4] Drag a marker to frame 5 and label it *FreeHand*.
This marker indicates the location of the FreeHand destination frame.

5] Save your work.

6] Rewind and play the movie.
The playback head moves from left to right through the movie, displaying every frame until it reaches the end of the movie, which is frame 5. However, you want the playback head to stay on the main menu frame so the user can make a selection from that frame. You'll accomplish this next.

PAUSING THE PLAYBACK HEAD TO WAIT FOR USER INPUT

This main menu frame should be displayed and paused so the user can choose a topic. You need to add a script that holds the playback head on this frame so the playback head doesn't continue through the score until the user makes a selection. If you have completed all the lessons so far, you have already learned two methods for doing that using Lingo: using *pause* to pause the playback head at a certain frame, and using *go to the frame* to keep replaying the current frame. You have also added markers and used *go to frame "marker"* to branch to a marker. This time, you'll use *go to the frame* again.

tip *In many cases, pausing is recommended instead of looping on the same frame (with* go to the frame*) or looping between two frames. This is because a pause operation uses much less processor time than repeatedly moving the playback head to the beginning of the frame. Note that the* pause *command stops the playback head entirely, so you should not use it when you want to animate or when you are using a film loop.* Go to the frame *replays the current frame.*

1] Double-click the script channel in frame 1.
The Script window opens with *on exitFrame* and *end* already in it.

2] Type *go to the frame* below *on exitFrame*. Then close the window.
As usual, the playback head will try to move left to right across the score when you play the movie. As it exits frame 1, it sends the *exitFrame* event message to Director. Then Director encounters the *go to the frame* command and sends the playback head back to frame 1. Check it out.

```
on exitFrame
    go to the frame
end
```

3] Rewind and play the movie.

Look at the playback head. It's stopped on frame 1 because of the script you added.

4] Stop the movie.

ADDING SPRITES TO THE STAGE

Now you'll start modifying and adding sprites to the new FreeHand frame.

1] Drag the Rectangle cast member in the Cast window to channel 1, frame 5, in the score.

You created and named this rectangle in the previous lesson.

2] Use the Sprite Properties dialog box to resize the rectangle to *263 x 447* and set its location to *(286, 0)* (Windows Ctrl+Shift+I, Macintosh Command+Shift+I).

To do this, choose Modify › Sprite › Properties. Type *263* in the Width box, *447* in the Height box, *286* in the Left Location box, and *0* in the Top Location box.

3] Select the rectangle on the stage and use the tool palette to change the color to the darkest gray on the top row of the color palette.

Use the sixth color chip in from the top right of the color palette (index color number 10).

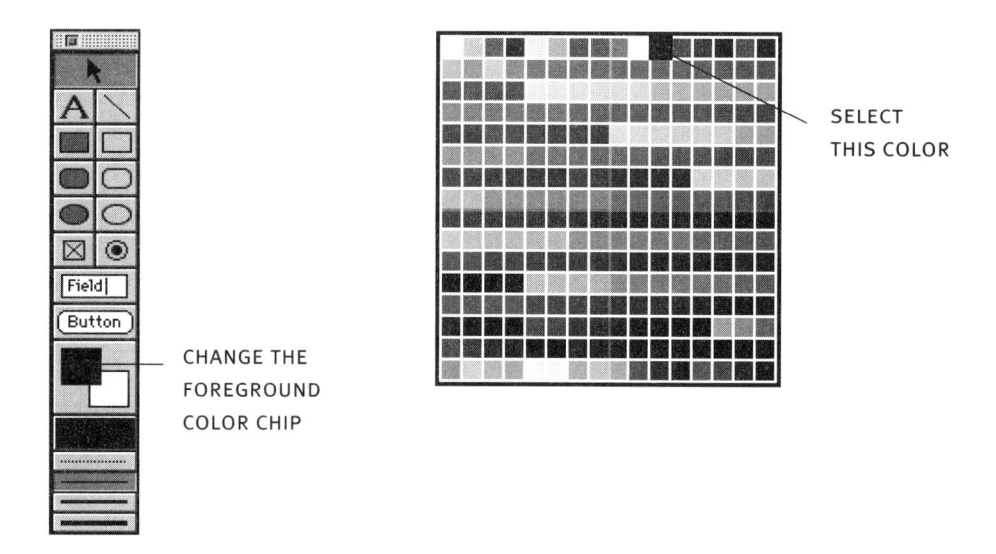

CHANGE THE FOREGROUND COLOR CHIP

SELECT THIS COLOR

4] Drag cast member FHtext to channel 6, frame 5, and position it in the gray rectangle you just created.

180

LESSON 12

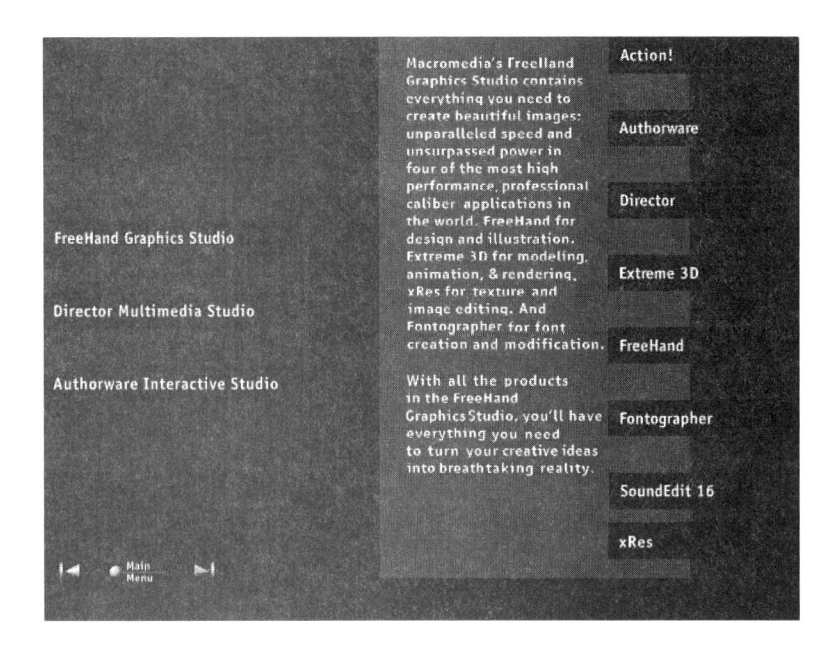

5] Set the ink of this sprite to Lightest in the score.

With this ink set, Director compares pixel colors in the foreground and background, and uses whichever pixel color in the foreground or background is lightest. Now you should be able to read the text more clearly.

Next you will create header text for this frame.

6] Select channel 7, frame 5. Choose the Text tool from the tool palette and click the stage with the Text tool to create a text block on the stage.

This sprite should be in channel 7, frame 5.

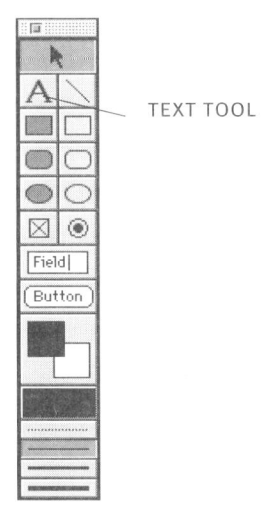

TEXT TOOL

7] Type *FGS* in the text block, highlight the text, and choose Modify › Font to open the Font dialog box (Windows Ctrl+Shift+T, Macintosh Command+Shift+T).

You're about to modify the font type, size, and color.

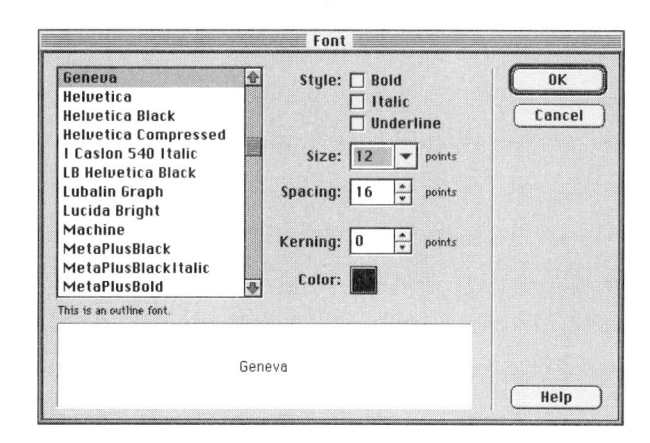

8] Select Courier or Courier New from the font list, choose 72 points from the Size menu, click the Color chip, and choose off-white from the color palette. Close the dialog box when you're done.

Now the text will look larger in the text window.

9] Drag the text to the upper left of the stage, above the red rectangle.

10] In the score, set the ink of this sprite to Bkgnd Transparent.

To be more precise, you can set the location of this text to (*12, 39*) in the Sprite Properties dialog box. With Bkgnd Transparent ink set, you can see through to the background.

11] Select channel 8, frame 5, and drag cast member FHlines to the stage. The top-left line should point to *FreeHand Graphics Studio*, the top-right line should point to *Extreme 3D*, and the bottom-right line should point to *xRes*. Use the following illustration as your guide.

LESSON 12

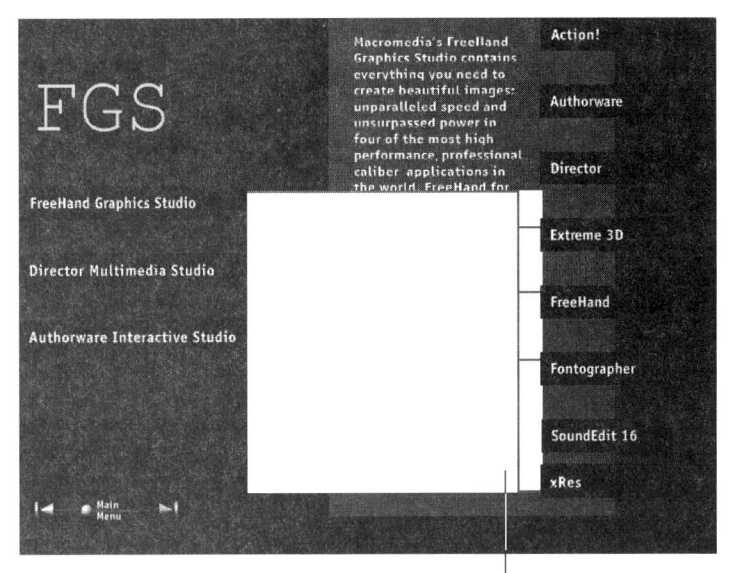

ALIGN THE FHLINES CAST
MEMBER AS SHOWN HERE

12] Set the ink of this sprite to Bkgnd transparent in the score.

Now you can see the background colors behind the lines.

CHANGING THE BACKGROUND TRANSPARENT COLOR

In this task you will use a technique to deal with images that contain lots of black and white. What's the issue with black and white images? When you use the Bkgrnd Transparent ink, usually the color that is made transparent is black or white. Most of the images you've imported have been a solid color with either black or white around the edges. After dragging them to the stage, you have set the ink to Bkgrnd Transparent so the black or white around the edges becomes transparent and the image looks better on the stage. What if the image itself has lots of black or white in it? If you set the ink to Bkgrnd Transparent, most of the image will become transparent, which is not what you want. You usually want only the *edges* of the graphic to become transparent, not the colors within the image. One technique for accomplishing this is to use a color other than black or white around the edges of the graphic so you can make that color transparent instead of the black or white.

1] Drag cast member FHbox to channel 10, frame 5. On the stage, position it below the names on the left.

Wow—look at that pink! It's no mistake. The image has black and white in it, but black and white are the colors that are commonly made transparent with the Bkgrnd Transparent ink in the score. However, if the white in this image were made transparent, parts of the graphic would also disappear. Here pink is used around the graphic to retain the white in the image itself. Now you need to make the pink transparent.

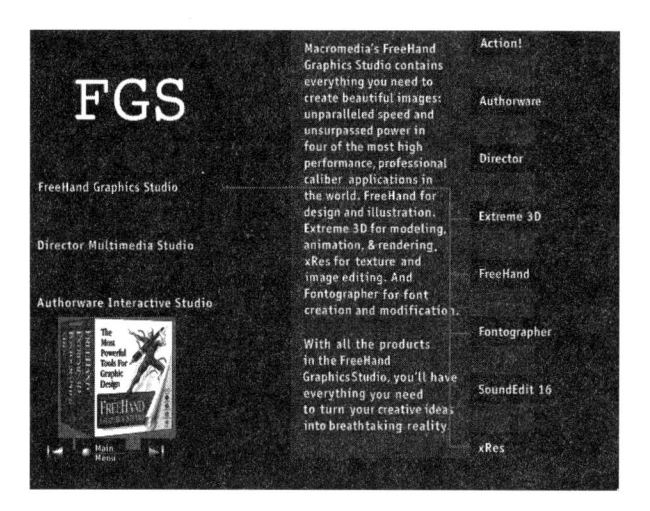

To make the pink transparent, you need to determine which color it is in the color palette, change the background color for that sprite to pink, and set the ink to Bkgnd Transparent.

2] Double-click the graphic to open the Paint window. Using the Eyedropper tool, click the pink to determine the index color of the pink. Close the Paint window.

Remember: To determine the index color, choose Window › Color Palettes. The pink is highlighted in the color palette, and the index number is displayed at the bottom of the dialog box. The pink is index color 33.

EYEDROPPER

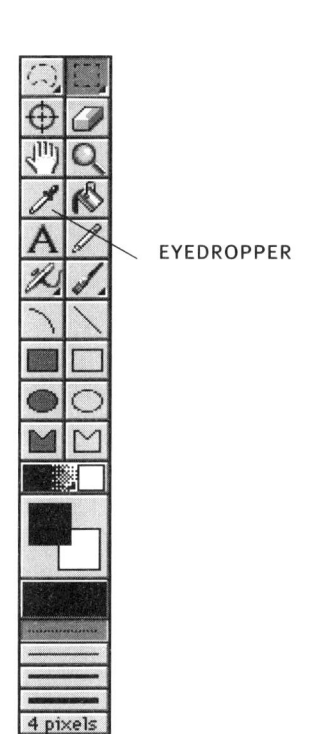

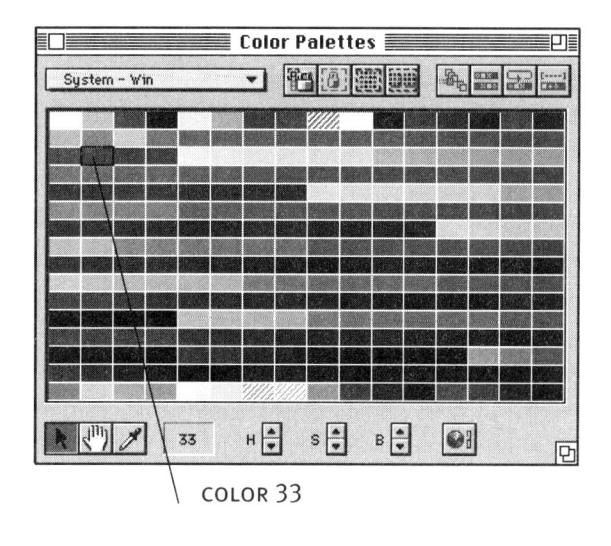

COLOR 33

3] In the score, select the box sprite (channel 10, frame 5). In the tool palette, change the background color chip to the same pink.

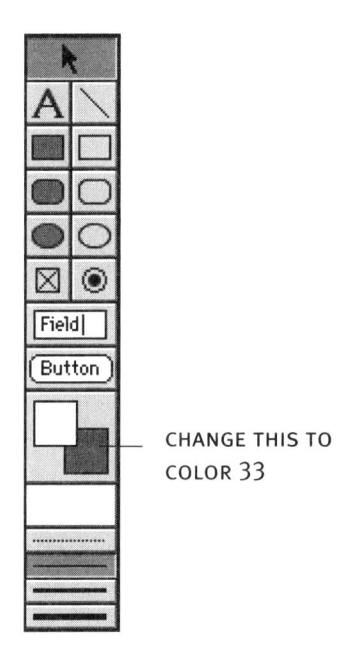

CHANGE THIS TO COLOR 33

185

TEXT, BLENDING, AND NAVIGATION

4] In the score, select the box sprite (channel 10, frame 5) and set the ink to Bkgnd Transparent.

On the stage the graphic should now have a transparent background, so you can see through to the black. If the background is not transparent, you have selected the wrong pink from the tool palette's background color chip. Be sure you select color 33.

USING HIGHLIGHTS AROUND A HOT AREA

In this task you will add a highlight around the words *FreeHand Graphics Studio*. Adding a highlight to one item in a menu is a common way to indicate that the item is the currently selected option.

1] Select channel 11, frame 5.

You're going to create a rectangle sprite here and use it as a highlight.

2] In the tool palette, click the 2-pixel line and the Unfilled Rectangle tool.

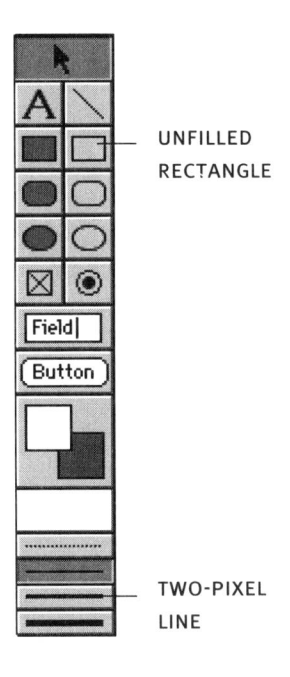

UNFILLED RECTANGLE

TWO-PIXEL LINE

3] On the stage, create a rectangle around the words *FreeHand Graphics Studio*. Color it index color 128 so it matches the lines that point to the product names on the right side of the stage.

To determine the index color, choose Window › Color Palettes. Index color numbers are at the bottom of the dialog box. Click the palette until you locate index color 128. Then select the rectangle on the stage, and in the tool palette choose the foreground color chip and select the appropriate color in the color palette. This sets the rectangle to index color 128.

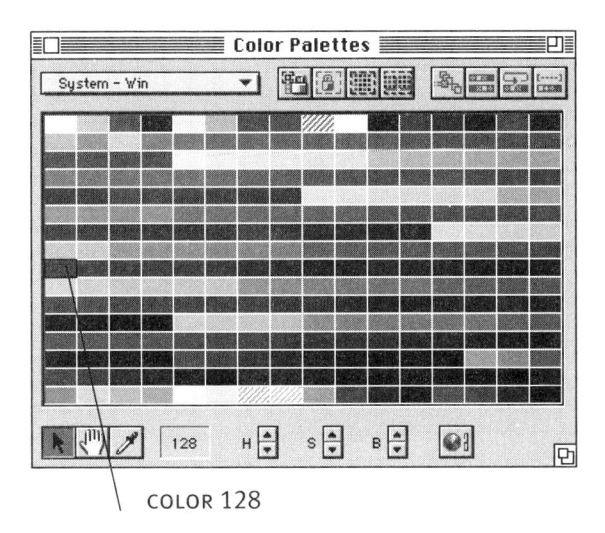

COLOR 128

BLENDING COLORS

Next you will dim the other two text blocks by blending them with the background. Dimming menu items is a common way of showing that they are unavailable for use. Color blending is a processor-intensive operation and should be used sparingly. Director builds each frame as the playback head moves through the movie. This means that each time you run the movie, Director needs to determine the requirements for each frame. If you use blending, Director must also determine the amount of blend, the color depth, and other color information. Because Director is busy with all these calculations, less processing power is available for other work, which slows down the animation or anything else that is going on in the frame. The destination screen you are building, however, consists of a lot of static text and graphics and very little animation, so blending will not have a huge effect on Director's ability to quickly display the frame.

tip   *A good technique for handling this problem is to apply the blend and then export the frames from Director to .PICT images or to QuickTime. Then you can reimport the images and replace the sprites you originally blended with the pictures of the blend. Director can display pictures much faster.*

1] Select the sprites in channels 29 and 30, frame 5, choose Modify > Sprite > Properties, and set the blend to 50%. Click OK to close the dialog box.

The sprites on the stage now look dimmed because their colors have been blended with the colors underneath them.

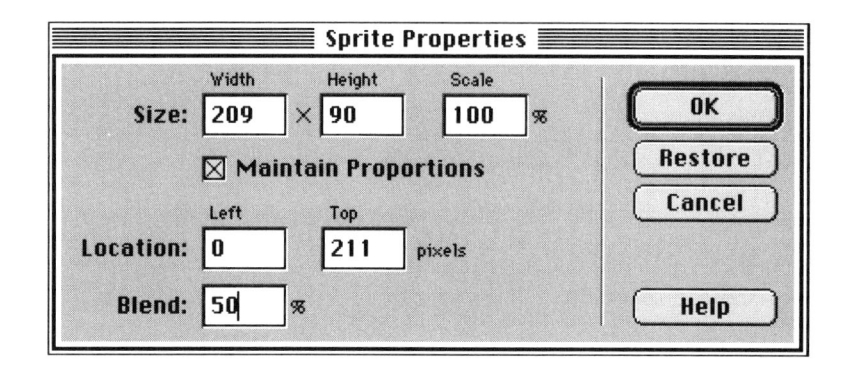

2] Save your work.

Now you'll add some scripts for navigation.

NAVIGATING TO A MARKER

When the movie plays, you want to be able to get to the FreeHand frame from the main menu by clicking the FreeHand Graphics Studio button on the left side of the stage. To make that happen, you will create a script.

In Lesson 9, you created *sprite scripts* by associating a script with a sprite. First you selected a sprite in the score, and then you chose New Script from the Script menu in the score. You created sprite scripts for buttons called Send the Document and Receive the Document. These buttons are displayed in only one frame, so using a sprite script is appropriate. If the buttons were in multiple frames, however, you would have to locate all of the frames with those buttons, select the sprites, and create the same script for each of the sprites. That's time consuming!

There is an easier way to do this for a button that appears in multiple frames: You can create a *cast member script*. You do this by associating the script with the cast member itself, instead of a sprite (remember that a sprite is an instance of a cast member). Then, when you place the cast member on the stage, it will have the script already associated with it. In this project, the FreeHand Graphics Studio button will be displayed in several frames, so you will create a cast member script for this button.

1] Select cast member FGS in the Cast window. Then click the Cast Member Script button to open the Script window. The FGS cast member contains the text *FreeHand Graphics Studio*.

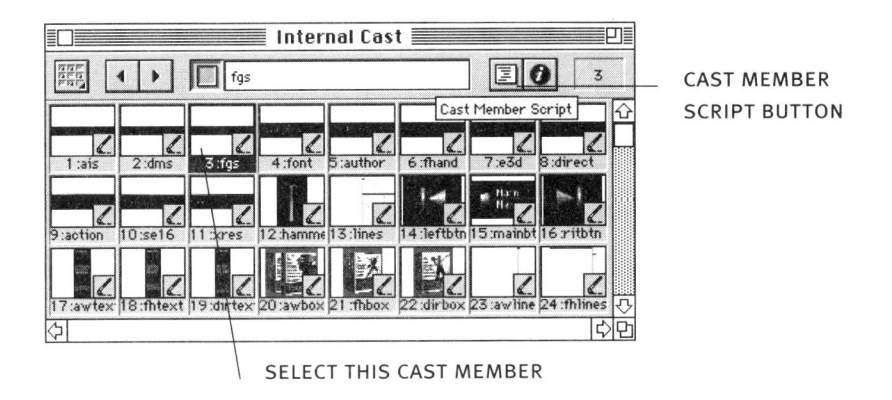

CAST MEMBER SCRIPT BUTTON

SELECT THIS CAST MEMBER

2] Type *go to frame "FreeHand"* below *on mouseUp* and then close the Script window.

```
on mouseUp
    go to frame "FreeHand"
end
```

The Script window already contains *on mouseUp* and *end*.

Be sure to use the same spelling as the marker label you created in frame 5. Remember that capitalization does not have any affect on the script.

Now when the FGS sprite is clicked, a *mouseUp* event message is sent to Director, which sends the playback head to the FreeHand marker.

tip   *You can use go to frame "marker", go frame "marker", or go "marker". Any of these will go to the named marker.*

3] Rewind and play the movie.

The playback head is held on the main frame because of the *go to the frame* script you added earlier.

4] Click the FreeHand Graphics Studio button and watch the playback head.

The playback head branches to the FreeHand marker because of the *go to frame "FreeHand"* script you added. Then the playback head stops there because there are no other frames in the movie. What's going to happen when you add more frames to this movie? The playback head will continue to play through any frames after this marker. To keep the playback head on this frame, you can loop on the frame. You will do that next.

5] Double-click the script channel, frame 5, and type *go to frame "FreeHand"* **below** *on exitFrame.*

```
on exitFrame
    go to frame "FreeHand'
end
```

The Script window already displays *on exitFrame* and *end*.

Now when the playback head branches to this frame, it will stay in this frame because it will keep looping to frame "FreeHand".

You may have been wondering what the difference is between scripts created by double-clicking the script channel and the other two scripts types you have used: sprite scripts and cast member scripts. When you double-click the script channel, you create a frame script. You use frame scripts when you want something to happen during frame events, such as *exitFame* and *enterFrame*. So far you have used frame scripts to handle the *exitFrame* event.

6] Stop the movie and save your work.

Good work! You've just built a destination frame and added navigation to the speaker support program.

WHAT YOU HAVE LEARNED
In this lesson you have:
Added markers and labeled them [*page* **178**]
Paused the playback head with *go to the frame* [*page* **179**]
Created and modified text with the Text tool [*page* **181**]
Changed the background transparent color [*page* **183**]
Added a highlight to a hot area [*page* **186**]
Dimmed buttons with a blending technique [*page* **187**]
Used *go to frame "marker"* to navigate to markers [*page* **188**]

color cycling

LESSON 13

In the previous lesson you continued working on the speaker support program by adding a destination frame for the navigation controls to jump to. By incorporating color blending techniques, you added highlights and dimmed hot areas. Next you will use an animation technique called color cycling. In this lesson, you will also learn to refer to navigation markers in a new way, as relative markers, rather than by name. As you go along, you'll see why this is such a powerful feature.

Color cycling is a technique used to create animation without having to create different images. It adds great visual impact and attracts attention quickly. You'll incorporate color cycling into the Showcase CD project you've been developing.

If you would like to view the final result of this lesson, open the Complete folder in the Lesson13 folder and play Speaker3.dir.

> **note** *To complete the color cycling lesson, the monitor must be set to 8-bit color.*

Cycling a range of colors through a graphic creates a visual effect of movement, even though the sprite itself is not actually moving. You may have seen an old clock-light in a restaurant that has a clear graphic of a waterfall on it. The waterfall has a strip of color behind it that ranges from white to light blue to dark blue. This color strip cycles behind the waterfall and makes the water appear to be falling. That illusion is created with color cycling.

Color cycling is a low-overhead way to create animation because you reuse the same cast member; the colors shift, and you don't need multiple cast members. Note that color cycling works only with 8-bit graphics (256 colors).

WHAT YOU WILL LEARN
In this lesson you will:
Branch to markers relative to the playback head
Define a color gradient
Use an animation technique to cycle colors

APPROXIMATE TIME
It usually takes about 2 hours to complete this lesson.

LESSON FILES
Media Files:
None
Starting Files:
Lesson13\Start.dir
Completed Project:
Lesson13\Complete\Speaker3.dir

USING RELATIVE MARKERS IN SCRIPTS

For color cycling to work continuously, the playback head needs to keep returning to the start of the cycling section. You can accomplish this by using marker labels as you have in previous lessons, or you can use relative markers. As you know, when you play a movie, the playback head moves left to right across the score, and there can be markers anywhere in the score. In handlers, you can refer to a marker by its label (as in *go to frame "FreeHand"*, the command you used in the previous lesson) or by its position relative to the playback head. As the playback head moves, marker(0) is the marker in the current frame or the marker the playback head has most recently passed. The first marker to the right of marker(0) is marker(1) and so on. The first marker to the left of marker(0) is marker(-1) and so on. These markers are numbered *relative* to the position of the playback head, and they always refer to a marker based on the current position of the playback head, not to a marker in a specific frame.

Study the following two illustrations of the score. They're the same except that the position of the playback head is different. Notice how the relative marker locations change based on the location of the playback head.

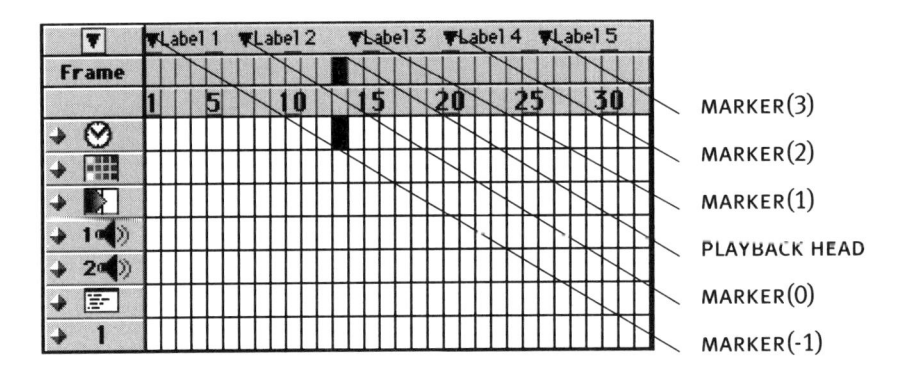

Marker (0) is the marker in the current frame or the marker the playback head has most recently passed. In this illustration, the playback head is in frame 13, which has no marker. The marker the playback head has most recently passed is in frame 7. So marker(0) is the marker called Label2.

194

LESSON 13

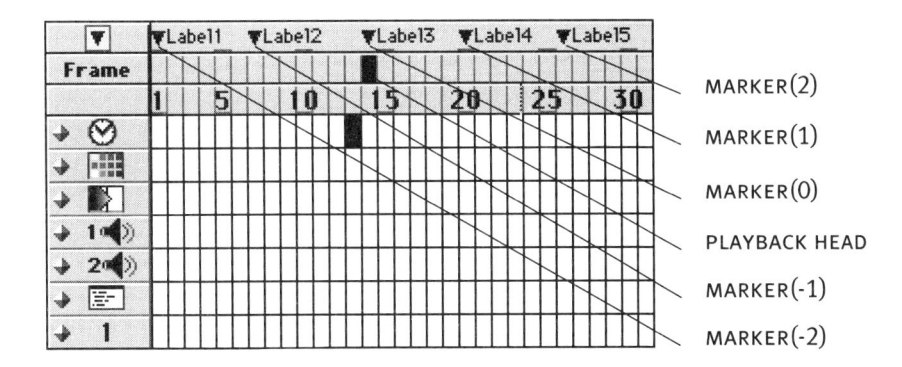

The markers in this illustration are exactly the same as the ones in the previous illustration. The difference here is that the playback head is now in frame 14. This frame has a marker on it, so marker(0) is the marker on this frame, called Label3.

In this task, you'll add a relative marker in a script.

1] Open Start.dir in the Lesson13 folder and save it as Speaker3.dir in the MyWork folder.

This is the prebuilt file. If you completed the last lesson, you can use the movie you worked on there. Save it as Speaker3.dir in your MyWork Folder.

2] Select all the cells in frame 5 and copy them to frame 6.

You could copy and paste, but try this method: To copy an entire frame and paste it next to itself, first select the frame you want to copy and then choose Insert › Frame. The entire frame is copied and pasted next to itself. Notice that this moves the FreeHand marker to frame 6. You'll need to move it back to frame 5.

tip   *Like blending, color cycling taxes system resources because Director needs to do a great deal of work to cycle colors. Making a color cycling section more than one frame long spreads out the work Director needs to do and so reduces the risk that other effects will be delayed while Director works on creating the color cycling effect.*

3] Drag the FreeHand marker back to frame 5, the beginning of the FreeHand section.

When you copy and paste frames with markers, the markers move, so always be sure the markers are where you want them to be.

4] Select the script channel, frame 5, and delete it.

The script was *go to frame "FreeHand"*. You placed this here in the previous lesson to keep the playback head on this frame so the users could stay on this frame as long as they desired. You still need to keep the playback head on this frame, but you're going to refer to a relative marker instead.

The *go to frame "FreeHand"* script would still work, of course, but a reference to a marker label is less flexible than a reference to a relative marker. Suppose you had to change the marker label from *FreeHand* to *FreeFoot*. You would need to open this script and change the reference to *FreeHand* in the script. If several scripts referred to the FreeHand marker label, you would need to locate all those scripts and change them as well. This could get very complicated! If you use a relative marker in a script, you will not need to worry about changing references in the script. Using relative markers helps save time by allowing you to write just one script and have it work effectively in many sections.

5] Select the script channel, frame 6, and choose New Script from the Script pop-up menu. Type *go marker(0)* below *on exitFrame* and close the window.

```
on exitFrame
    go marker (0)
end
```

Now when you click the FreeHand Graphics Studio button on the main screen, the playback head will branch to frame 5 (just like before) and then move to frame 6. As the playback head begins to exit frame 6, it will encounter the command *go marker(0)*. At this time, marker(0) (the marker the playback head has passed most recently) is the FreeHand marker in frame 5. As the playback head begins to exit frame 6 and Director instructs it to go to marker(0), it looks for a marker in the current frame (in frame 6); there isn't one, so it looks for the marker it just passed (the one in frame 5). So the playback head goes back to frame 5. When it moves to frame 6, Director instructs it to go to marker(0) again. Thus, the playback head will loop between frames 5 and 6.

Remember that marker(0) is *relative* to the position of the playback head. Relative markers always refer to a marker based on the current position of the playback head, not to a marker in a specific frame.

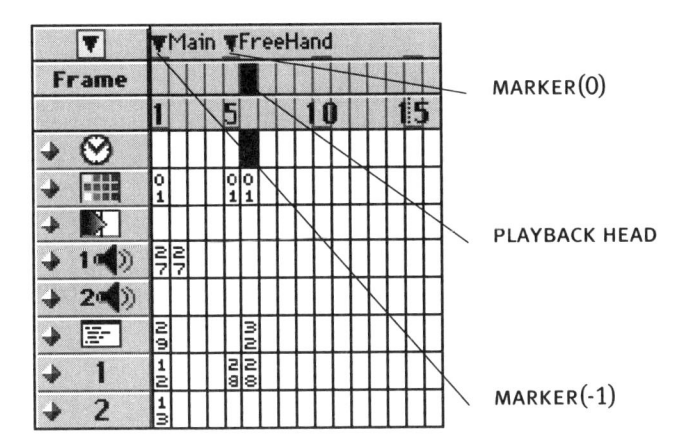

6] Rewind and play the movie. Click the FreeHand Graphics Studio button.
Everything still works as it did before, but now the script refers to a relative marker instead of a marker label. Look at the playback head and notice that it is looping between frames 5 and 6. You'll be happy you made this change because in the next lesson you will add more sections that can use this same script. You won't need to rewrite it—just copy and paste, and it will work!

7] Stop the movie and save your work.

SETTING A GRADIENT
Now you'll define a color gradient to apply to a line sprite, so the line has a blend of colors applied to it. Once you have a blend of colors applied to the line, you can cycle through that range of colors to create animation.

1] Choose Window > Color Palettes and find the locations of colors 230 and 238.
You will be using these colors in the next few steps, so be sure to note their exact locations in the color palette. To find the number for a color, click a color. The color number will be displayed in the lower left of the dialog box.

COLOR CYCLING

COLOR 230   COLOR 238

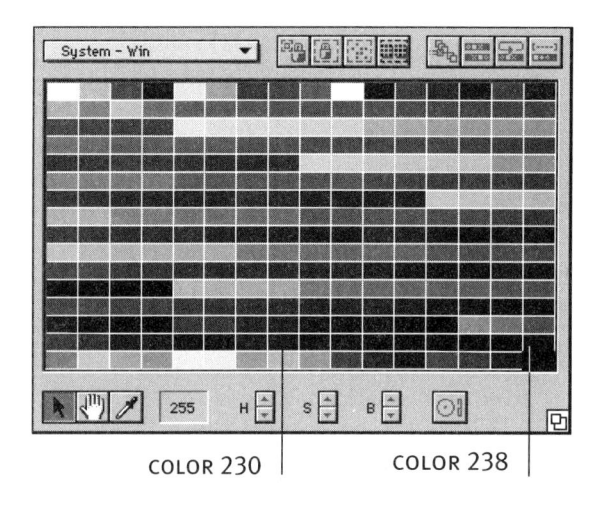

2] In the score, click channel 8, frame 5 (the Lines sprite).

On the stage, the Lines sprite should be selected.

3] Double-click the Lines sprite on the stage to open the Paint window.

The Paint window should be open with the Lines sprite in it.

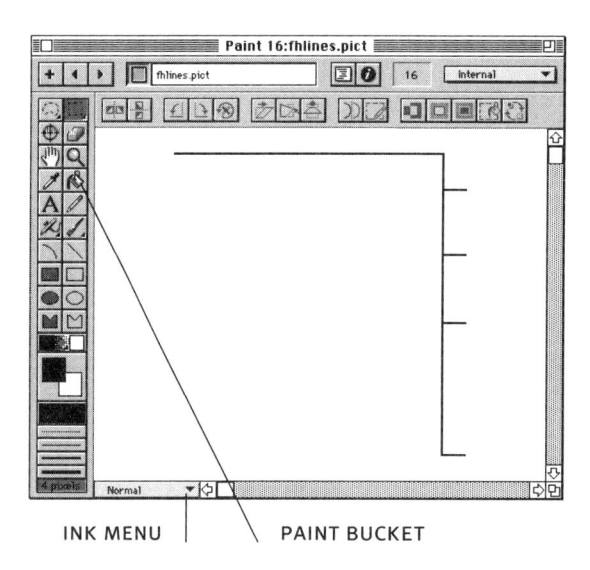

INK MENU   PAINT BUCKET

4] Select the Paint Bucket tool and set the Ink menu selection to Gradient.

The Paint Bucket tool is now set to paint a gradient color instead of a solid one. When you paint with Normal set, one solid color is applied to an object. When you paint with a gradient, a blend of colors will be applied, often shading from light to dark. For example, a gradient color could go from a light blue to a dark purple. Next you will set the way the gradient flows in the graphic.

5] Double-click the Paint Bucket tool to open the Gradient Settings dialog box.
In this dialog box you can choose the exact parameters (such as color, method, and direction) that will be used to create the gradient.

6] Select the first color chip below *Destination* to open its color palette. Select a bright blue (index color 230) as the starting color. Select the color chip on the right to open its color palette and set the destination color to dark blue (index color 238).

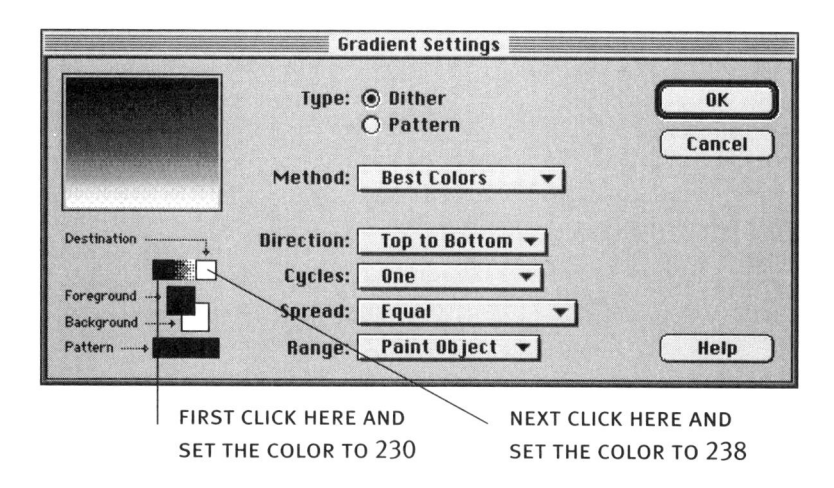

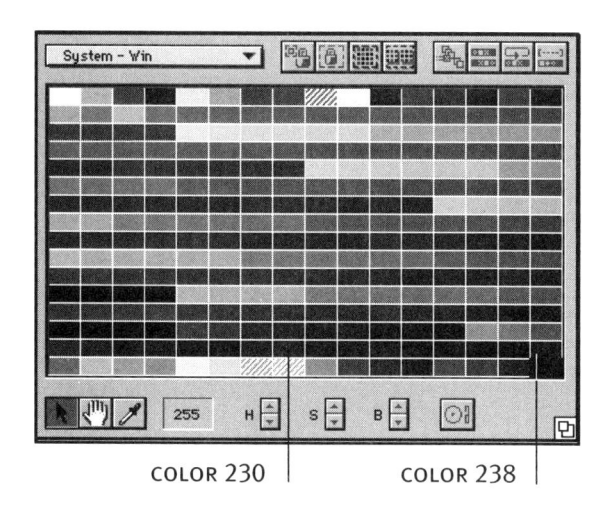

FIRST CLICK HERE AND SET THE COLOR TO 230

NEXT CLICK HERE AND SET THE COLOR TO 238

COLOR 230

COLOR 238

COLOR CYCLING

7] From the Method menu, choose Adjacent Colors.

You are setting a color gradient from one shade to another. Choosing Adjacent Colors means that the gradient shades will be created by using the colors between the two colors you just selected.

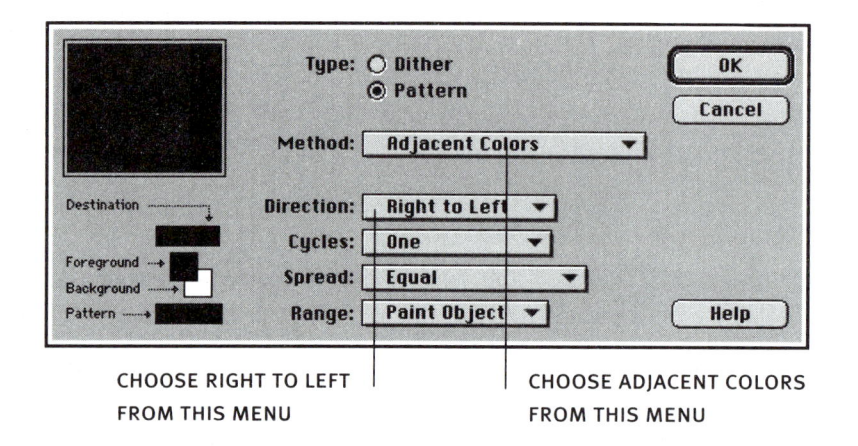

CHOOSE RIGHT TO LEFT FROM THIS MENU

CHOOSE ADJACENT COLORS FROM THIS MENU

8] From the Direction menu, choose Right to Left. Leave the other settings as they are. Then click OK to close the dialog box.

The Direction menu selection determines the way the gradient fills an area in the Paint window. Right to Left puts the starting color on the right and the destination color on the left.

9] Select the Magnifying Glass tool and click the line graphic to zoom in for a better view.

You should see a larger view of the lines.

10] With the Paint Bucket tool, click the line graphic.

The gradient with the colors you just defined fills the lines.

11] Save your work.

ANIMATING WITH COLOR CYCLING

Now that you have a specific gradient color applied to the Lines sprite, you'll set up the color cycling.

1] Close the Paint window and double-click the palette channel, frame 6.

The Palette dialog box opens.

DOUBLE-CLICK HERE

2] Next to Action, click Color Cycling and drag the Rate slider to 25. In the color palette, drag to select the range of blues you just used in the gradient and close the dialog box.

The Rate slider controls the speed at which the colors cycle. The colors you selected are the ones that will cycle. In this case, you select the range of blues you used to create the gradient. You must be precise when you select these colors or the color cycling effect will not work.

tip *If any other sprites being displayed in the frames that are cycling use any of the blues in the range you selected, they will start cycling, too, so unless you want that effect, make sure only the item you want to use color cycling on uses those colors.*

COLOR 230   COLOR 238

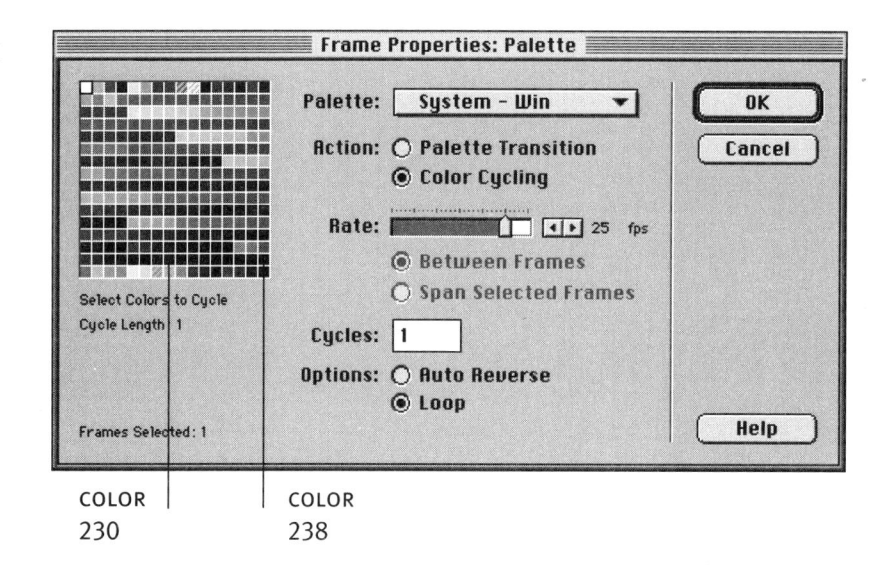

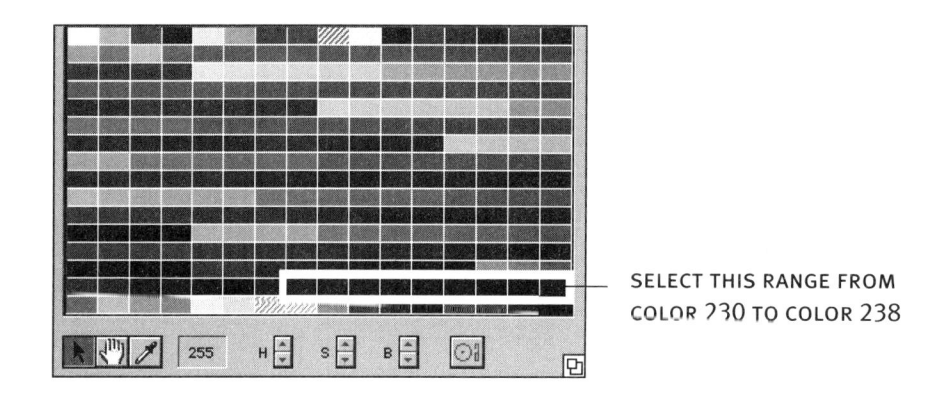

SELECT THIS RANGE FROM COLOR 230 TO COLOR 238

3] Rewind and play the movie and click the FreeHand Graphics Studio button.

It looks as though color shoots out along the lines! This animation technique makes the screen come alive by cycling colors across one sprite.

4] Save your work.

As you can see, color cycling is an great way to simulate motion without creating different artwork. The process is achieved by cycling through the current palette in the selected range. As the cycling progresses, each of the colors in the range is moved over one by one, which causes the eye to see continuous movement. Keep this technique in mind when you need animation effects like water movement.

WHAT YOU HAVE LEARNED
In this lesson you have:

Used a relative marker to loop on a frame **[*page* 194]**

Defined exact gradient settings in the Paint window **[*page* 197]**

Used the palette channel to define color cycling **[*page* 201]**

reusing your work

LESSON 14

Presentations such as this one frequently contain many sections with the same overall skeleton but with specific text and graphics for each section. This is the case with the presentation you are building now. In previous lessons you built the main menu frame and a destination frame for a speaker support program. This lesson is intended to solidify the concepts presented to you in the previous lessons and to show you how to reuse your work to build similar parts of a movie quickly.

The remaining screens in the product information section of the Showcase CD are very similar to the ones you've already built. In this lesson you learn some techniques for quickly and effectively building the remaining sections by reusing elements you've already created.

If you would like to view the final result of this lesson, open the Complete folder in the Lesson14 folder and play Speaker4.dir.

WHAT YOU WILL LEARN
In this lesson you will:

Practice exchanging cast members

Practice using relative markers for navigation

APPROXIMATE TIME
It usually takes about 1.5 hours to complete this lesson.

LESSON FILES
Media Files
None
Starting Files
Lesson14\Start.dir
Completed Project
Lesson14\Complete\Speaker4.dir

BUILDING A FRAME BY EXCHANGING CAST MEMBERS

You need to add a few more frames to this program before you can call it complete. Proper planning and construction of any presentation will allow you to build quickly by reusing work as you do in this lesson. You'll begin by copying and pasting frames you've already created.

1] Open Start.dir in the Lesson14 folder and save it as Speaker4.dir in the MyWork folder.

This is the prebuilt file. If you completed the last lesson, you can use the movie you worked on there. Save it as Speaker4.dir in the MyWork folder.

2] Copy all channels in frame 5 and paste them into frame 10. Drag a marker to frame 10 and label it *Director*.

To select the entire frame, you can click and drag over the number 5 in the frame area at the top of the score. To copy the selected frame, choose Edit › Copy. To paste the contents, click frame 10 and then choose Edit › Paste.

You're going to use the existing screen layout and simply swap as many cast members as possible with the Exchange Cast Members button you used in earlier lessons. Exchanging cast members puts the new cast member in the same place on the stage as the original cast member.

3] Select channel 8, frame 10, in the score: the FHlines sprite to which you applied color cycling in the previous lesson. Select cast member Dirlines in the Cast window. Swap the cast members by clicking Exchange Cast Members on the toolbar (Windows Ctrl+E, Macintosh Command+E).

The Dirlines cast member is displayed in place of the FHlines cast member. This graphic is similar to FHlines, except the left and right lines point to different areas of the stage.

4] On the stage, reposition the new graphic so the left line points to the words *Director Multimedia Studio*.

THE LEFT LINE POINTS HERE

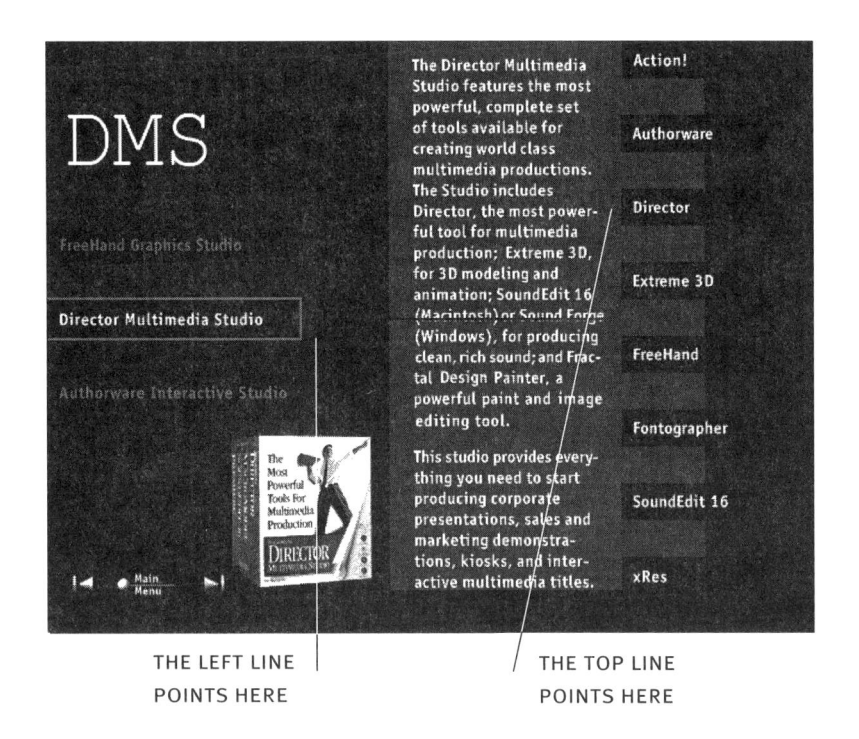

THE TOP LINE POINTS HERE

5] Select channel 6, frame 10, in the score (the FreeHand text) and select cast member Dirtext in the Cast window. Swap the cast members.

Now you should see the new text that describes the Director Multimedia Studio.

Next you will create a new cast member with *DMS* in it and exchange it with the *FGS* text.

6] In the Cast window select the *FGS* text you created and choose Edit > Duplicate to create a duplicate cast member in the Cast window. Double-click this new cast member to open the Text window, select the text and replace it with *DMS*, and close the window. Select the new DMS cast member in the Cast window, select channel 7, frame 10, in the score, and exchange the cast members.

By duplicating the cast member instead of creating a new text block, you ensure that the text options and placement match the previous text exactly.

7] Select channel 10, frame 10, in the score, select Dirbox in the Cast window, and then click Exchange Cast Members on the toolbar.

This replaces the FreeHand box graphic in channel 10, frame 10, with the Director box graphic.

8] Select channel 11, frame 10 (the rectangle around the text). On the stage, move the rectangle so it covers the words *Director Multimedia Studio*.

DRAG THE HIGHLIGHT HERE

All the remaining screen elements are the same, so you don't need to exchange any more cast members.

9] Save your work.

ADDING COLOR CYCLING AND HIGHLIGHTS

You still need to create the color cycling animation for this section and dim and highlight the appropriate hot areas. You'll do that next.

1] Select frame 10 and duplicate it by choosing Insert > Frame (Windows Ctrl+], Macintosh Command+]). Don't forget to drag the Director marker back to frame 10, the beginning of the section.

Remember that color cycling taxes system resources, so you need to add another frame to this color cycling section.

Now you need to copy the script you used in the previous lesson.

2] Copy the script channel, frame 6 (from the FreeHand section), and paste it into the script channel, frame 11.

Remember that this is the *go marker(0)* script that enables the color cycling to play back repeatedly. If you had left *go to frame "FreeHand"* in the script (as it was in an earlier lesson) instead of using a relative marker, you would not have been able to copy and reuse this script as you've just done.

3] Select the sprites in channel 28, frames 10 and 11. Then choose Modify › Sprite › Properties. Set the Blend to 50%.

This dims the FreeHand Graphic Studio button.

4] Select the sprites in channel 29, frames 10 and 11. Then choose Modify › Sprite › Properties. Set the Blend to 100%.

This highlights the Director Multimedia Studio button.

5] Select channel 8, frame 10. Then double-click Dirlines on the stage to open the Paint window.

All the settings should be the same as they were when you previously set them. If they are not, go back to the previous lesson and follow the instructions to set the gradient.

6] Use the Magnifying Glass to zoom in, use the Paint Bucket to paint the lines, and then close the Paint window.

This sets the same gradient colors for the new lines as you used for the lines in the main menu section.

7] Copy the palette channel, frame 6, to the palette channel, frame 11.

Remember that in the previous lesson you set up some color cycling options in the palette channel. You can reuse your work by copying the cell.

That's it! Now you have completed the second destination frame.

8] Save your work.

NAVIGATING WITH MARKERS

Next you need to add navigation to the Director Multimedia Studio text block in the main frame.

1] Select cast member DMS in the Cast window and click the Cast Member Script button to open the Script window. This cast member is the text *Director Multimedia Studio*.

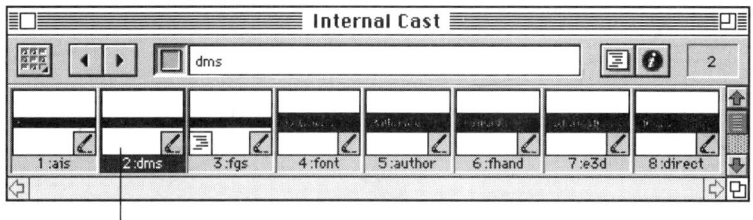

SELECT THIS CAST MEMBER

You'll add a script to this cast member that is similar to the one you added to the FGS cast member in the previous lesson.

2] Type *go to frame "Director"* below *on mouseUp*.

```
on mouseUp
    go to frame "Director"
end
```

Be sure to use the same spelling as the marker label you created in frame 10.

You are referring to a marker label instead of a relative marker because this cast member will always branch to the Director frame, no matter where the playback head is located.

3] Rewind and play the movie. Then click the Director Multimedia Studio button.

You can now navigate to the Director frame.

4] Stop the movie and save your work.

You can now jump to two screens from the main frame, but you can't use the navigation buttons at the bottom of the stage. How do you think relative markers might be used with the navigation buttons?

You can add the script *go marker(1)* to the right arrow and *go marker(-1)* to the left arrow so these arrows move the user to the next or previous markers. In this case, using relative markers is the best way to navigate because the next and previous frames in the presentation are based on the location of the playback head.

5] Select Leftbtn from the cast. Then click the Cast Member Script button in the Cast window.

You'll add a script to this cast member.

6] Type *go marker(-1)* below *on mouseUp*. Then close the Script window.

211

REUSING YOUR WORK

This script will cause Director to display the frame with a marker to the left of the marker at which the playback head is currently located.

```
on mouseUp
    go marker(-1)
end
```

7] Select Ritbtn from the cast. Then click the Cast Member Script button in the Cast window. Type *go marker(1)* below *on mouseUp*. Close the Script window when you're done.

This script will cause Director to display the next frame with a marker that is to the right of the marker at which the playback head is currently located.

```
on mouseUp
    go marker(1)
end
```

8] Save your work. Then rewind and play the movie and use the left and right arrows to navigate.

The left and right navigation buttons move you forward and backward through the speaker support program because of the relative markers you used in the scripts.

If you click the left arrow in the main frame, nothing happens because when you're in frame 1, there is no marker(-1): that is, there are no markers to the left of frame 1.

Similarly, when you're in frame 10 and you click the right arrow, nothing happens because there is no marker(1): that is, there are no markers to the right of frame 10.

Now you need to activate the Main Menu button.

9] Select Mainbtn from the cast, click the Cast Member Script button in the Cast window, type *go to frame "Main"* below *on mouseUp*, and close the window.

```
on mouseUp
    go to frame "Main"
end
```

Now when the viewer clicks this button, the playback head will branch to the Main frame.

10] Save your work and rewind and play the movie. Test all the buttons.
Everything works!

ON YOUR OWN

You can quickly create the last destination frame by using the same techniques you used to create the Director frame. First copy all channels in frame 10 to frame 15. Then drag a marker to frame 15 and label it *Authorware*. Go through each channel in the Authorware frame to see if it's okay as is, needs to be moved, or needs to be replaced with new artwork. Don't forget to add the *go to frame "Authorware"* script to the AIS cast member. You'll also need to dim the DMS hot area, highlight the AIS hot area, and check the gradient for the lines. You can further enhance this program by deleting the arrows and the Main Menu button in the main menu frame because they're not needed on that screen.

WHAT YOU HAVE LEARNED
In this lesson you have:

Exchanged cast members to quickly create similar frames [*page* **206**]

Added color cycling and highlights to lines and buttons [*page* **208**]

Used markers and relative markers for navigation [*page* **210**]

shockwave for director

LESSON 15

Shockwave is the software that lets multimedia developers prepare Director multimedia for the World Wide Web and lets Web users read the Director files once they're posted on the Web. There are versions of Shockwave for almost all Macromedia products; in this lesson, you'll learn about Shockwave for Director.

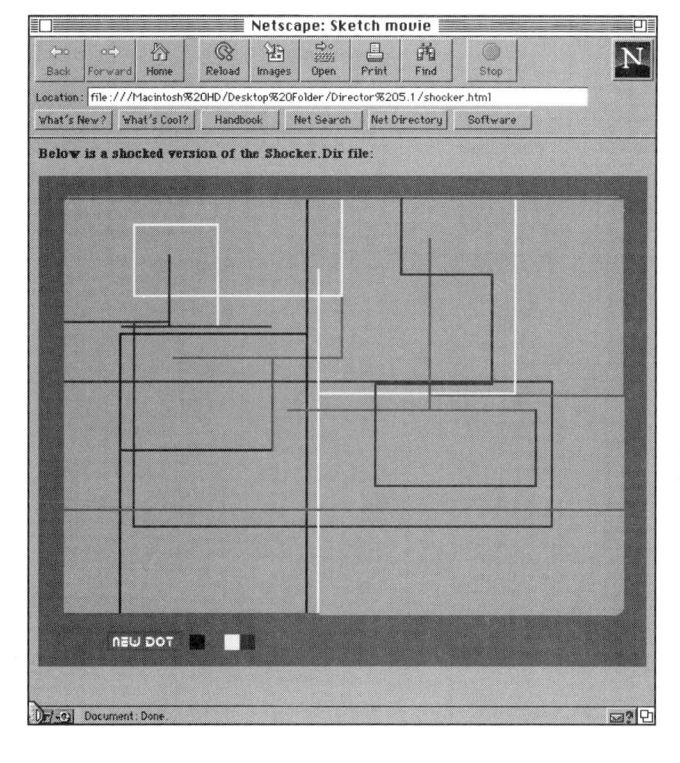

Shockwave is the latest in Web technology for delivering interactive multimedia and large sound files over the Internet. In this lesson you will shock a Director movie and then embed it in an HTML document for playback over the Web. Artwork and programming for this lesson were developed by Mark Castle, Castle Productions. The sound file was provided by Jeff Essex, Audiosyncrasy.

Shockwave for Director delivers high-impact Director movies—with interactivity, graphics, sound, and animation—to the World Wide Web. This lesson guides you through the steps of "shocking" a Director movie.

You create a Director movie for use with Shockwave and the World Wide Web the same way you create any other Director movie. Movies for the Web can include almost any effect any other Director movie can include: interactivity, animation, and the rest. However, there are some features that Shockwave movies can't include at this time, such as QuickTime movies and add-in features, such as those created with Xtras that aren't part of Director's standard features. Also, when creating movies for the Web, you should keep file sizes as small as possible to minimize the amount of time users must wait for the file to download online. (The Shockwave tips throughout this book point out ways to do this.) After the movie is complete, you simply "shock" it to prepare it for the Web.

WHAT YOU WILL LEARN
In this lesson you will:

Learn what Shockwave is and how you can use it

Learn what a browser is and why you need one

Prepare a Director movie for distribution over the Internet

APPROXIMATE TIME
It usually takes about 1 hour to complete this lesson.

LESSON FILES
Media Files
Lesson15\Media
Starting Files
Lesson15\Shocker.dir
Lesson15\Shocker.HTML
Completed Project
Lesson15\Complete\Shocker.dcr

OBTAINING SHOCKWAVE AND THE BROWSER SOFTWARE

Shockwave includes two distinct functional parts: Afterburner, a Director Xtra that compresses a standard Director movie into a shocked Director movie and converts it to DCR file format designed specifically for the Web; and the Shockwave Plug-In for Director, which allows movies to be incorporated into the browser page layout.

Versions of Afterburner and Shockwave for Director are available on the CD-ROM provided with this book. The most up-to-date versions can always be downloaded for free from Macromedia's Web site (http://www.macromedia.com). A Shockwave developer's kit, which includes information on server configuration, tips and techniques, troubleshooting, and more, can also be downloaded.

shockwave tip *Before using Shockwave or Afterburner, you should visit Macromedia's Web site to be sure you have the latest version of the software.*

1] If you don't already have Afterburner and Shockwave on your computer, install the files from the CD-ROM now.

For the most up-to-date versions of Afterburner and Shockwave, go to Macromedia's home page and download them now. The location is http://www.macromedia.com. Find the Shockwave Center and follow the instructions for downloading and installing the software. You will not be able to follow the steps for this task if you do not have this software installed on your computer.

2] If you don't already have a Web browser that supports the Shockwave plug-in, download that now.

A Web browser is software that is used to navigate around the World Wide Web and view files published there. Netscape Navigator versions 2.02 and later and Microsoft Internet Explorer version 3.0 are two popular browsers that support Shockwave. Both are available for downloading from the Web. To download Netscape Navigator, go to http://www.netscape.com. To download Internet Explorer, go to http://www.microsoft.com.

SHOCKING A MOVIE

In this task, you will shock a movie for playback on the Internet. A movie has already been created for you (with sound) to shock, and an HTML document is provided that will run the shocked file. All you need to do is shock the movie and test it using your browser.

1] Copy the Lesson15 folder from the CD to your MyWork folder.

You'll need access to all of these files, and you will be saving your work in this lesson to the Lesson15 folder.

2] Open Shocker.dir in the Lesson15 folder now on your hard drive and play the movie.

This is the movie you're going to shock. It's an electronic version of a sketch toy. To play with the sketcher, run the movie and use the arrow keys on the keyboard to draw lines. To change a dot color, click a new color. To create a new dot, click New Dot. You may need to click the stage first to make it active before you can play the movie and use the keyboard to draw lines.

3] Choose Xtras › Shockwave for Audio Settings .

You use this Shockwave Xtra only when your Director movie includes sound files (as this one does). A dialog box will open.

4] Check the Enabled box to enable compression for the audio embedded in the movie. Close the dialog box.

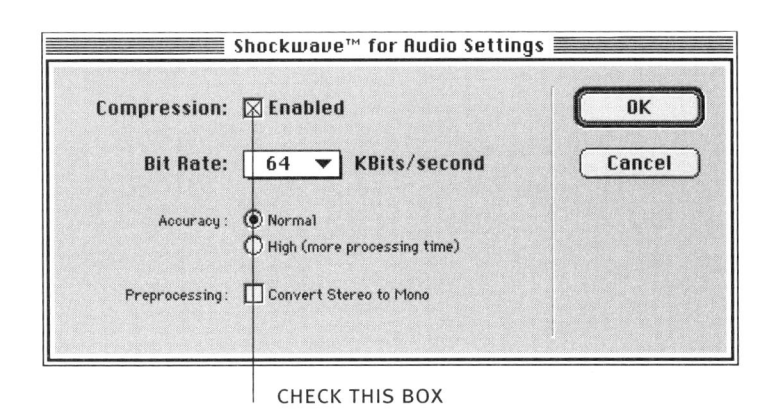

CHECK THIS BOX

You'll use the default settings for the other controls in the dialog box. These allow you to set a bit rate for the sound and convert stereo to mono sound. The bit rate determines both file size and output quality. A low bit rate produces a small file but can result in the loss of sound quality. A stereo sound will automatically be converted to mono if you choose a bit rate of 32 Kbps or less.

Now you'll run the movie through Afterburner.

5] Choose Xtras > Afterburner.

A dialog box appears prompting you to type a name and choose a location for saving the file.

6] Save the file as Shocker.dcr in the Lesson15 folder in your MyWork folder.

Director runs the file through Afterburner, and the result is a shocked file. You now have an icon that looks like this in the Lesson15 folder:

7] Close Director.

The shocked movie is now ready to be embedded into a Web page.

8] Open the text file Shocker.HTM (Windows) or Shocker.HTML (Macintosh) in the Lesson15 folder and review the contents.

This file is a pure text file and can be opened in any text editor or word processor.

The text you see is in HTML, the hypertext markup language that is use to create Web pages. This simple file includes a few lines that describe the document to the browser, one line of text to be displayed in the browser window, and the HTML <EMBED> tag, which tells the browser to include the shocked movie. This same line tells the browser to display the movie at 528 x 413 pixels (the size of this movie's stage).

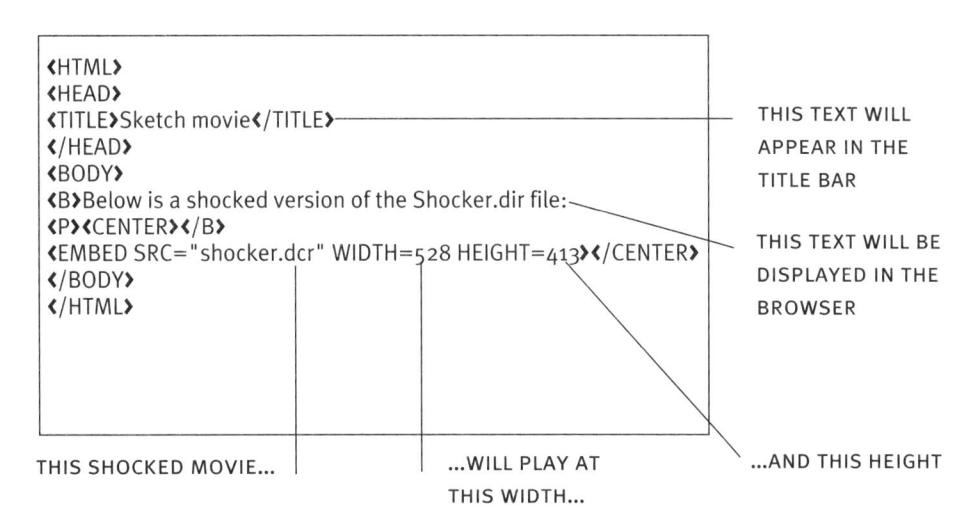

```
<HTML>
<HEAD>
<TITLE>Sketch movie</TITLE>
</HEAD>
<BODY>
<B>Below is a shocked version of the Shocker.dir file:
<P><CENTER></B>
<EMBED SRC="shocker.dcr" WIDTH=528 HEIGHT=413></CENTER>
</BODY>
</HTML>
```

THIS TEXT WILL APPEAR IN THE TITLE BAR

THIS TEXT WILL BE DISPLAYED IN THE BROWSER

THIS SHOCKED MOVIE... ...WILL PLAY AT THIS WIDTH... ...AND THIS HEIGHT

9] Close Shocker.htm (Windows) or Shocker.html (Macintosh) and drag it to a browser that supports Shockwave.

This should open the file in the browser. If it does not, open the file by using the browser's File › Open command. The text is displayed, and the movie opens in the browser.

10] Use the arrow keys on the keyboard to draw using the electronic sketch toy. To change a dot color, click a new color. You may need to click the sketch toy first to make it active, so it plays.

It works! You've just shocked a Director movie.

You can find out more about Shockwave from the *Shockwave Developer's Guide* at Macromedia's World Wide Web site: http://www.macromedia.com.

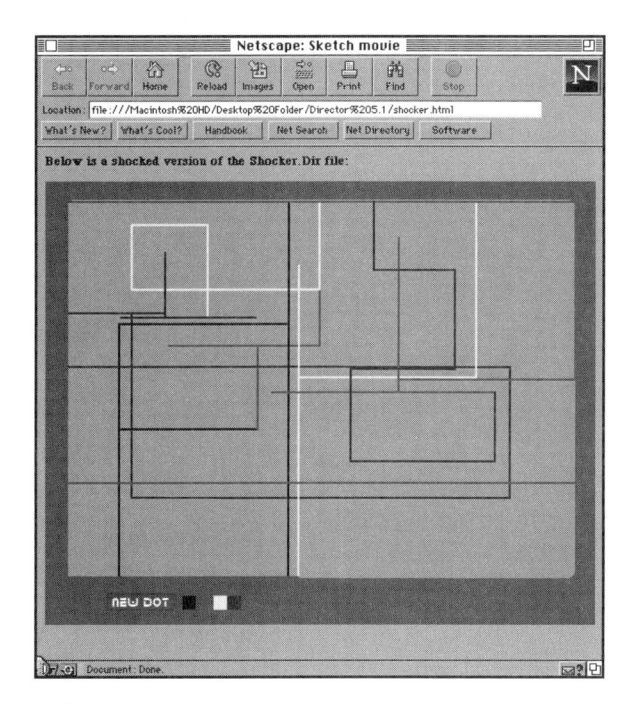

WHAT YOU HAVE LEARNED
In this lesson you have:

Learned why you need a browser to view Shockwave movies [*page* **218**]

Shocked a Director movie for playback on the Internet [*page* **219**]

Embedded a Shockwave movie in an HTML document [*page* **220**]

CONCLUSION

Congratulations! You have just completed all the lessons in the Director Multimedia Studio Authorized course. In this course, you've created animations with in-betweening, screen transitions, film loops, color cycling, and more. You've also developed scripts to branch to various sections of a movie, created buttons, and added sound for extra impact. You have learned numerous authoring tips and Shockwave tips and been introduced to the Director Multimedia Studio. We hope you've enjoyed learning Director basics, and most of all, we hope the techniques in these lessons will help you in your own Director Shockwave and multimedia development.

For more advanced Director techniques for building sophisticated interactivity into your programs, see *Lingo for Director 5 Authorized* from Macromedia Press.

shortcuts

windows

APPENDIX A

Director offers lots of shortcuts that, once you learn them, will make it easier to get your work done. Many are already described in the lessons in this book. This appendix is a quick reference to all the shortcuts in Director's interface.

NUMERIC KEYPAD SHORTCUTS

You can use the numeric keypad to control the score, play the movie, and move the playback head.

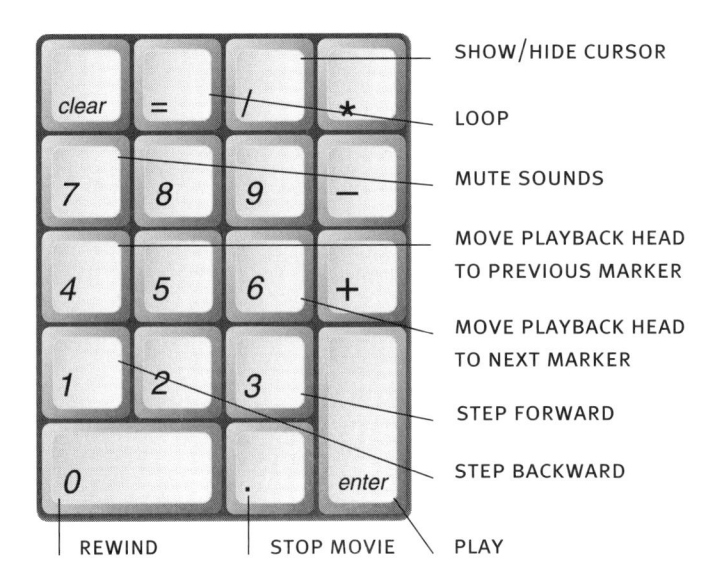

- SHOW/HIDE CURSOR — *
- LOOP — *
- MUTE SOUNDS — −
- MOVE PLAYBACK HEAD TO PREVIOUS MARKER — +
- MOVE PLAYBACK HEAD TO NEXT MARKER
- STEP FORWARD — 3
- STEP BACKWARD — enter
- REWIND — 0
- STOP MOVIE — .
- PLAY — enter

SHORTCUT MENUS

Right-clicking a sprite, a cast member, or any window displays a shortcut menu that offers quick access to commonly used commands for that item.

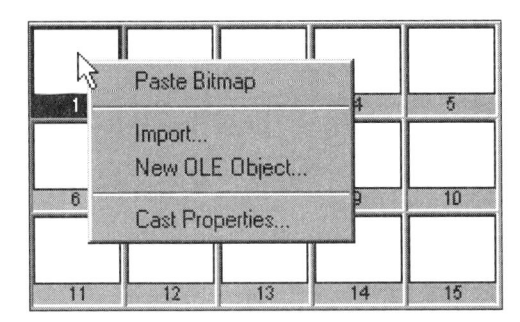

KEYBOARD SHORTCUTS

Many menu commands are also available as keyboard shortcuts. This section lists the keyboard shortcuts for commands in each menu.

FILE MENU

Command	Shortcut
New Movie	Control+N
New Cast	Control+Alt+N
Open	Control+O
Close	Control+F4
Save	Control+S
Import	Control+R
Export	Control+Shift+R
Page Setup	Control+Shift+P
Print	Control+P
General Preferences	Control+U
Exit	Alt+F4

EDIT MENU

Command	Shortcut
Undo	Control+Z
Repeat	Control+Y
Cut	Control+X
Copy	Control+C
Paste	Control+V
Clear	Delete
Duplicate	Control+D
Select All	Control+A
Find Text	Control+F
Find Handler	Control+Shift+; (semicolon)
Find Cast Member	Control+; (semicolon)
Find Selection	Control+H
Find Again	Control+Alt+F
Replace Again	Control+Alt+E
Exchange Cast Members	Control+E

KEYBOARD SHORTCUTS [cont'd]

VIEW MENU

Command	Shortcut
Next Marker	Control+right arrow
Previous Marker	Control+left arrow
Zoom In	Control+ + (plus)
Zoom Out	Control+ - (minus)
Show Grid	Control+Shift+Alt+G
Snap to Grid	Control+Alt+G

INSERT MENU

Command	Shortcut
Insert Frame	Control+] (right square bracket)
Remove Frame	Control+[(left square bracket)

MODIFY MENU

Command	Shortcut
Cast Member Properties	Control+I
Cast Member Script	Control+' (apostrophe)
Sprite Properties	Control+Shift+I
Sprite Script	Control+Shift+' (apostrophe)
Movie Properties	Control+Shift+D
Movie Casts	Control+Shift+C
Font	Control+Shift+T
Paragraph	Control+Shift+ Option +T
In Between	Control+B
In Between Special	Control+Shift+B
Bring to Front	Control+Shift+ up arrow
Move Forward	Control+up arrow
Move Backward	Control+down arrow
Send to Back	Control+Shift+ down arrow
Align	Control+K
Tweak	Control+Shift+K

KEYBOARD SHORTCUTS [cont'd]

CONTROL MENU

Command	Shortcut
Play	Control+Alt+P
Stop	Control+. (period)
Rewind	Control+Alt+R
Step Backward	Control+Alt+left arrow
Step Forward	Control+Alt+right arrow
Loop Playback	Control+Alt+L
Volume: Mute	Control+Alt+M
Toggle Breakpoint	F9
Watch Expression	Shift+F9
Ignore Breakpoints	Alt+F9
Step Script	F10
Step Into Script	F8
Run Script	F5
Recompile All Scripts	Control+Shift+Alt+C

WINDOW MENU

Command	Shortcut
Toolbar	Control+Shift+Alt+B
Tool Palette	Control+7
Text Inspector	Control+T
Stage	Control+1
Control Panel	Control+2
Markers	Control+Shift+M
Score	Control+4
Cast	Control+3
Paint	Control+5
Text	Control+6
Field	Control+8
Color Palettes	Control+Alt+7
Video	Control+9
Script	Control+0
Message	Control+M
Debugger	Control+` (back single quote)
Watcher	Control+Shift+` (back single quote)

WINDOWS SHORTCUTS

DIRECTOR WINDOW SHORTCUTS

Many shortcuts are also available from directly within the Stage, Score, Cast, and Paint window. This section lists the available shortcuts in these windows.

STAGE

To do this	Do this
Open cast member	Double-click sprite editor
Display ink pop-up	Control+click menu
Toggle record light on/off	Alt+click
Perform real-time recording	Alt+spacebar+drag sprite on the stage
Display shortcut menu for selection	Right-click
Change contents of stage to black	Keypad minus (-)

SCORE WINDOW

To do this	Do this
Duplicate selection of cells	Alt+drag
Open cast editor for selected sprite	Double-click cast thumbnail
Select entire range of a cast member	Double-click cell with a sprite in it
Select channel	Double-click channel number
Select multiple channels	Double-click channel number and drag up or down
Toggle step recording	Alt+click channel number
Move playback head to end of movie	Tab
Move playback head to first frame	Shift+Tab
Move playback head to beginning/end of movie	Control+Shift+left/right arrow
Open settings dialog box	Double-click tempo, palette, or transition channel
Go to next marker comment (or jump 10 frames)	Control+right arrow
Previous marker comment (or go back 10 frames)	Control+left arrow
Shuffle backward	Control+up arrow
Shuffle forward	Control+down arrow

DIRECTOR WINDOW SHORTCUTS [cont'd]

CAST WINDOW

To do this	Do this
Open cast member editor	Double-click a paint, text, palette, or script Select the cast member and press Enter
Open cast member script	Control+' (apostrophe)
Switch selected cast member with score selection	Alt+double-click thumbnail
Open script in new window	Alt+Script button
Place button	Control+Shift+L (places selected cast member in center of stage)
Cast to Time (Option-Place button)	Control+Shift+Alt+L
Add button (new cast member)*	Control+Shift+A
Left arrow (previous cast member)*	Control+left arrow
Right arrow (next cast member)*	Control+right arrow
Scroll up/down one window	Page up, Page down
Scroll to top left of cast window	Home
Scroll to show last occupied cast member	End
Select cast member by number	Type number
Find selected cast member in the score	Control+H

* To execute the same function in a new window, press the Alt key as you use the shortcut.

shortcuts

macintosh

APPENDIX B

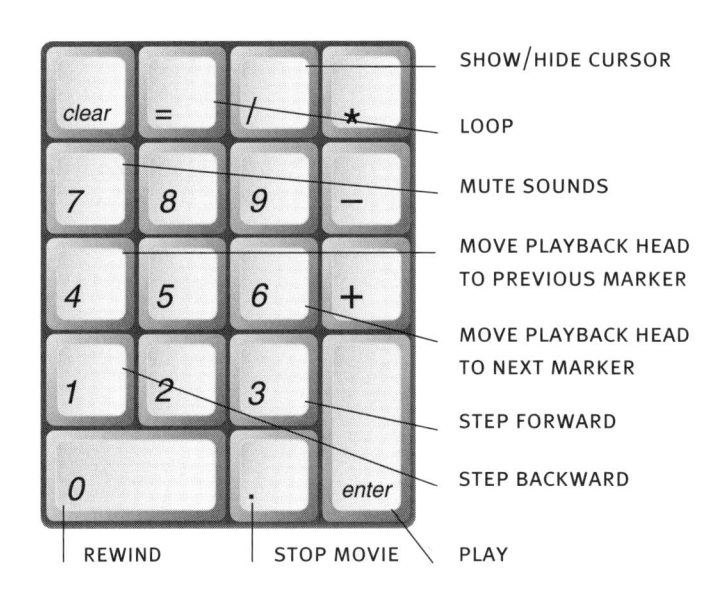

Director offers lots of shortcuts that, once you learn them, will make it easier to get your work done. Many are already described in the lessons in this book. This appendix is a quick reference to all the shortcuts in Director's interface.

NUMERIC KEYPAD SHORTCUTS

You can use the numeric keypad to control the score, play the movie, and move the playback head.

- SHOW/HIDE CURSOR
- LOOP
- MUTE SOUNDS
- MOVE PLAYBACK HEAD TO PREVIOUS MARKER
- MOVE PLAYBACK HEAD TO NEXT MARKER
- STEP FORWARD
- STEP BACKWARD
- PLAY
- STOP MOVIE
- REWIND

SHORTCUT MENUS

Control+clicking a sprite, a cast member, or any window displays a shortcut menu that offers quick access to commonly used commands for that item.

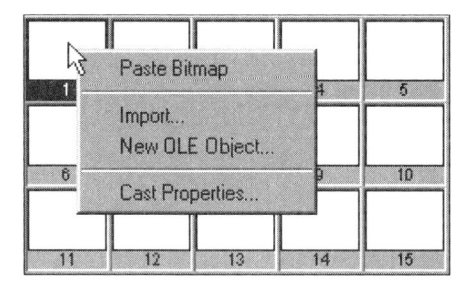

KEYBOARD SHORTCUTS

Many menu commands are also available as keyboard shortcuts. This section lists the keyboard shortcuts for commands in each menu.

FILE MENU

Command	Shortcut
New Movie	Command+N
New Cast	Command+Option+N
Open	Command+O
Close	Command+W
Save	Command+S
Import	Command+R
Export	Command+Shift+R
Page Setup	Command+Shift+P
Print	Command+P
General Preferences	Command+U
Quit	Command+Q

EDIT MENU

Command	Shortcut
Undo	Command+Z
Repeat	Command+Y
Cut	Command+X
Copy	Command+C
Paste	Command+V
Clear	Delete
Duplicate	Command+D
Select All	Command+A
Find Text	Command+F
Find Handler	Command+Shift+; (semicolon)
Find Cast Member	Command+; (semicolon)
Find Selection	Command+H
Find Again	Command+Option+F
Replace Again	Command+Option+E
Exchange Cast Members	Command+E

SHORTCUT MENUS [cont'd]

VIEW MENU

Command	Shortcut
Next marker	Command+right arrow
Previous Marker	Command+left arrow
Zoom In	Command++ (plus)
Zoom Out	Command+ - (minus)
Show Grid	Command+Shift+Option+G
Snap to Grid	Command+Option+G

INSERT MENU

Command	Shortcut
Insert Frame	Command+] (right square bracket)
Remove Frame	Command+[(left square bracket)

MODIFY MENU

Command	Shortcut
Cast Member Properties	Command+I
Cast Member Script	Command+' (apostrophe)
Sprite Properties	Command+Shift+I
Sprite Script	Command+Shift+' (apostrophe)
Movie Properties	Command+Shift+D
Movie Casts	Command+Shift+C
Font	Command+Shift+T
Paragraph	Command+Shift+Option+T
In Between	Command+B
In Between Special	Command+Shift+B
Bring to Front	Command+Shift+up arrow
Move Forward	Command+up arrow
Move Backward	Command+down arrow
Send to Back	Command+Shift+down arrow
Align	Command+K
Tweak	Command+Shift+K

KEYBOARD SHORTCUT MENUS [cont'd]

CONTROL MENU

Command	Shortcut
Play	Command+Option+P
Stop	Command+. (period)
Rewind	Command+Option+R
Step Backward	Command+Option+left arrow
Step Forward	Command+Option+right arrow
Loop Playback	Command+Option+L
Volume: Mute	Command+Option+M
Toggle Breakpoint	Command+Shift+Option+K
Watch Expression	Command+Shift+Option+W
Ignore Breakpoints	Command+Shift+Option+I
Step Script	Command+Shift+Option+down arrow
Step Into Script	Command+Shift+Option+right arrow
Run Script	Command+Shift+Option+up arrow
Recompile All Scripts	Command+Shift+Option+C

WINDOW MENU

Command	Shortcut
Toolbar	Command+Shift+Option+B
Tool Palette	Command+7
Text Inspector	Command+T
Stage	Command+1
Control Panel	Command+2
Markers	Command+Shift+M
Score	Command+4
Cast	Command+3
Paint	Command+5
Text	Command+6
Field	Command+8
Color Palettes	Command+Option+7
Video	Command+9
Script	Command+0
Message	Command+M
Debugger	Command+` (back single quote)
Watcher	Command+Shift+` (back single quote)

MACINTOSH SHORTCUTS

DIRECTOR WINDOW SHORTCUTS

Many shortcuts are also available from directly within the Stage, Score, Cast, and Paint window. This section lists the available shortcuts in these windows.

STAGE

To do this	Do this
Open cast member editor	Double+click sprite
Display ink pop+up menu	Command+click
Toggle record light on/off	Option+click
Real+time record	Control+Spacebar+drag sprite on the stage
Display shortcut menu for selection	Control+click
Change contents of stage to black	Keypad minus (-)
Invert everything on stage	Keypad /
Cursor shows/hides	Keypad =

SCORE WINDOW

To do this	Do this
Duplicate selection of cells	Option+drag
Open cast editor for selected sprite	Double+click cast thumbnail
Select entire range of a cast member	Double+click cell with a sprite in it
Select channel	Double+click channel number
Select multiple channels	Double+click channel number and drag up or down
Toggle step recording	Option+click channel number
Move playback head to end of movie	Tab or Command+Shift+right arrow
Move playback head to first frame	Shift+Tab or Command+Shift+left arrow
Open settings dialog box	Double+click tempo, palette, or transition channel
Go to next marker comment (or jump 10 frames)	Command+right arrow
Previous marker comment (or back 10 frames)	Command+left arrow
Shuffle backward	Command+up arrow
Shuffle forward	Command+down arrow

APPENDIX B

DIRECTOR WINDOW SHORTCUTS [cont'd]

CAST/CAST EDITOR WINDOWS

To do this	Do this
Open cast member editor	Double+click a paint, text, palette, or script cast member
	Select the cast member and press Return
Cast member script	Command+' (apostrophe)
Switch selected cast member with score selection	Option+double+click thumbnail
Open script in new window	Option+script button
Place button	Command+Shift+L (places selected cast member in center of stage)
Cast to Time (Option+Place button)	Command+Shift+Option+L
Add button (new cast member)	Command+Shift+A*
Left arrow (previous cast member)	Command+left arrow*
Right arrow (next cast member)	Command+right arrow*
Scroll up/down one window	Page up, Page down
Scroll to top left of cast window	Home
Scroll to show last occupied cast member	End
Select cast member by number	Type number
Find selected cast member in the score	Command+H

* To execute the same function in a new window, press the Option key as you use the shortcut.

DIRECTOR WINDOW SHORTCUTS [cont'd]

PAINT WINDOW

To do this	Do this
Undo	~ (tilde)
Next/Previous cast member	Keypad left/right arrow keys
Turn selected tool into foreground eyedropper	D key, while pressed
Turn selected tool into background eyedropper	Shift+D key, while pressed
Turn selected tool into destination eyedropper	Option+D key, while pressed
Turn selected tool into hand tool	Spacebar, while pressed
Nudge selection rectangle or lasso	Keypad arrows with selection rectangle or lasso
Change airbrush size (while painting)	Keypad up/down arrows with airbrush selected
Change airbrush flow (while painting)	Keypad left/right arrows with airbrush selected
Change foreground color (while not painting)	Keypad up/down arrows, all tools
Change background color (while not painting)	Shift+Keypad up/down arrows, all tools
Change destination color (while not painting)	Option+Keypad up/down arrows, all tools
Draw border with current pattern	Option+shape or line tools
Select background color	Shift+eyedropper
Select destination color	Option+eyedropper
Toggle between custom and grayscale patterns	Option+click pattern
Polygon lasso	Option+lasso
Duplicate selection	Option+drag
Stretch	Command+drag
Draw with background color	Option+pencil tool
Open Gradient Settings dialog box and set ink to gradient	Double+click paintbrush, rectangle, paint bucket, or polygon tool
Open Airbrush Settings dialog box	Double+click airbrush
Clear visible part of window	Double+click eraser
Open color palettes window	Double+click foreground, background, or destination color chip
Open Pattern Settings dialog box	Double+click pattern chip
Open Brush Settings dialog box	Double+click paintbrush
Open Paint Window Preferences	Double+click line width selector
Open Transform Bitmap dialog box	Double+click color resolution indicator
Toggle Zoom In/Out	Command+click in window or double+click pencil tool

index

1-bit color, 162, 165
3D text, 147–151
32-bit images, importing to 8-bit stage, 32–33

A
add-on tools. See Xtras
Afterburner
    installing, 218
    obtaining, 218
    overview, 218
    running movies through, 20, 220
    versions of, 218
    See also Shockwave
AIS cast member, 173, 214
aligning
    buttons, 69, 172
    snapping to grid, 170–171
    sprites, 69
    text, 71
    See also positioning
Align tool, 172
animation, 16–41, 84–95
    beginning frame, 38–39
    with color cycling, 192–203
    creating a movie, 18–19
    creating text cast members, 19–22
    cursor movement simulation, 90
    with film loops, 114–121
    four-step process, 17
    handwriting simulation, 94
    with In Between, 25–31
    with In Between Special, 84, 88–90
    incorporating from other movies, 124–125
    with key frames, 105–106
    placing sprites in score, 22–25
    with real-time recording, 84, 91–94
    reversing, 57, 125
    See also in-betweening; tempo
Animation Wizard, 38–41
    creating animated bullets, 39–41
    illustrated, 39, 40
    opening, 39
    starting frame, 38–39
arrow pointer, toggling, 50
assets. See cast members
audio compression, 219
Audiosyncrasy, 216
Authorware licensing policy, 82

B
background color
    in Extreme 3D, 148
    movie, 158
    selecting from Color Picker, 142–143
    stage, 45–46, 86, 90, 158
    transparent, changing, 183–186
background images
    importing, 32–33, 86
    in-betweening, 50
    ink effects on, 48–49
    moving to lowest layer, 34–36
    See also graphics

background sound, 62–64, 111–112, 174
  See also sounds
Bevel Extrude tool (Extreme 3D), 150
  Extrude Depth field, 151
Bitmap Cast Member Properties dialog box, 161
bitmap files, reducing size, 161–162
Bkgnd Transparent ink
  for background image, 48–49
  with black-and-white images, 183–186
  for cast members, 162
  changing color, 183–186
  for lines, 183
  for sprites, 69
  for text, 36–37, 182
blending
  blurring with xRes, 138–146
  defining color gradient, 197–200
  dimming text blocks, 187–188
blurring with xRes, 138–146
Boiling.aif, 111
Branch.dir, 123, 124
branching
  to animation loop, 130–134
  to menu, 134–135
Bullet.dir, 10, 18
bullet points
  animating, 25–31, 38–41
  creating cast members, 19–22
  during playback, 28
  placing in score, 22–24
buttons, 122–135
  aligning, 68, 172
  for branching to animation loop, 130–134
  for branching to menu, 134–135
  creating, 125–127
  dimming, 187–188
  dragging, 68, 127, 172
  highlighting, 186–187
  navigational elements, 172–173
  positioning, 68
  and relative markers, 212
  in shocked movies, 127
  uses for, 122
  See also Control Panel; scripts; toolbar; tool palette
Button tool, 126–127

C

case of marker labels, 78, 129
cast
  defined, 11
  maximum members, 11
  organizing, 159–160
  viewing, 11
Cast Editor window shortcuts, 235
Castle, Mark, 216
Castle Productions, 216
cast members
  creating text cast members, 19–22
  defined, 11
  dragging, 48, 68, 69, 73, 100, 101, 170–171
  editing, 168–169
  exchanging
    creating frames, 206–208
    film loop, 116–117
    lightning effect, 58–60
    paper flapping effect, 110–111
  field, 20
  importing, 46–48, 98–99, 156–157
  in-betweening, 49
  maximum number, 11
  naming, 166, 167
  organizing, 159–160
  reusing, 167, 193
  scripts, 188–190, 210–213
  sound, 62–64, 111–112
  text, 19–22, 181–182
  transition, 61
  viewing, 11
  viewing names, 159
cast member scripts, 188–190, 210–213
Cast window
  Cast Member Properties button, 62, 118, 161, 166
  Cast Member Script button, 210, 211, 212, 213
  exchanging cast members, 59–60
  illustrated, 11
  Macintosh shortcuts, 235
  opening, 46
  overview, 11
  resizing, 11
  viewing cast members in, 11
  Windows shortcuts, 228

CD-ROM
    Afterburner version on, 218
    Lessons folder, 2–3
    Made with Macromedia (MwM) folder, 82
    Read Me files, 4
    running files from, 2
    Shockwave version on, 218

cells
    defined, 22
    dots at top, 50, 51
    identifying in-betweened cells, 50, 51
    illustrated, 22
    selecting all, 93, 124

centering
    full-screen graphics, 162
    text in Extreme 3D, 150

Center Out, Square transition, 61

channels
    and animation layers, 108
    copying, 178
    defined, 22
    dragging, 178
    empty, 165
    illustrated, 12, 22
    layering sprites, 108–109
    as layers, 34
    on/off toggle, 65
    overview, 11–12
    palette, 12
    RGB mode (xRes), 143, 146
    script, 12
    selecting frames in, 104
    shuffling, 35–36, 108–109, 120
    sound, 12
    sprite, 12
    storing selection (xRes), 144
    tempo, 12, 45–46
    transition, 12

Channels window
    opening, 143
    RGB channel, 143, 146
    storing selection in new channel, 144

closing
    Control Panel, 19
    Director at end of movies, 79
    Extreme 3D, 151
    Macromedia xRes, 146
    score, 23
    Script window, 77
    SoundEdit 16, 153
    Sound Forge XP, 153
    toolbar, 54

color
    1-bit sprites, 162, 165
    background
        changing transparent color, 183–186
        in Extreme 3D, 148
        selecting from Color Picker, 142–143
        setting for movie, 158
        stage, 45–46, 86, 90, 158
    blending colors, 187–188
    depth of, 162
    edge color, 26–27, 56
    foreground, 92, 164, 180
    highlights around hot area, 186–187
    index color numbers
        defined, 163
        defining color gradient, 199
        finding, 163–165, 184–185, 186–187, 197–198
        numbering scheme, 163, 164
        uses for, 163
    movie palette, 157–158
    remapping images to Macintosh palette, 99
    remapping images to Windows palette, 157
    RGB mode (xRes), 143, 146
    selecting from Color Picker, 142–143
    stage background, 45–46, 86, 90, 158
    system requirements, 5
    See also background color

color cycling, 192–203
    animating with, 201–202, 208–211
    defined, 192
    defining color gradient, 197–200
    graphics requirements, 193
    of other sprites with same colors, 201
    overview, 192, 193
    rate, 201
    reusing your work, 208–210
    script with relative marker, 196–197, 209
    and system resources, 195, 208

Color Depth menu, 162

color gradient
    defining, 197–200
    direction of, 200
    selecting colors, 199

Color Picker, 142–143

Color window
    opening, 142
    Picker tab, 142–143

Command key shortcuts. See Macintosh shortcuts
commands, 8
  See also Macintosh shortcuts; Windows shortcuts; specific menus and commands
commands (Lingo)
  go marker, 196, 209, 211–212
  go to frame "marker"
    for Director Multimedia Studio button, 211
    for FreeHand Graphics Studio button, 189, 190
    for menu, 77, 134–135
    for navigation buttons on screen bottom, 211–213
    for Receive the Document button, 132
    for Send the Document button, 133
    using relative markers, 194–196, 209, 211–212
    variants, 189
  go to the frame, 76, 77, 179
  pause, 128–129
  quit, 79
  See also scripts
Complete folder, 3
compression, audio, 219
constraining dragging, 27, 55, 103
Control menu
  Macintosh shortcuts, 233
  Windows shortcuts, 227
Control Panel
  buttons, 10, 18
  closing, 19
  illustrated, 9, 18
  Loop Playback button, 107
  opening, 9, 18, 107
  Play button, 107
  Selected Frames Only button, 107
copying
  channels, 178
  frames, 117, 178, 195, 206
  reversing sequence, 57
  scripts, 208–209
  sprites, 26, 102–104
  transitions, 61
Copy ink, 49, 100, 169, 170, 173
  and animation speed, 100, 170
Create Film Loop dialog box, 118
Create Projector dialog box, 80, 81

creating
  bullet charts, 19–22
  buttons, 125–127
  color gradient, 197–200
  credits screen, 69–73
  custom stage, 98
  field cast members, 20
  film loops, 117–119
  folders, 18
  highlights, 186–187
  key frames, 87–88, 105–106, 119–120
  markers, 74–75, 129–130, 178–179
  menu screen, 68–69
  movies, 18–19, 38–41
  navigation scripts, 75–79
  projectors, 79–82
  text cast members, 19–22, 181–182
  See also animation
Credits button, 68, 78, 79
Credits marker
  creating, 75
  script using, 78
Credits.rtf, 47, 48
credits screen, 69–73
  alignment, 70–71
  in-betweening, 71
  ink effects, 69
  pause for, 72–73
Ctrl key shortcuts. See Windows shortcuts
cursor, simulating movement, 90
cutting and pasting. See copying; moving

D
DCR file format, 218
Debugger, 15
Default Palette menu (Macintosh), System-Win command, 157
delaying. See pausing; performance
deleting
  extraneous graphics parts, 169
  scripts, 195–196
  sprites from score, 93
deselecting, 144, 145
destination screen, 176–190
  adding sprites to stage, 180–183
  blending colors, 187–188
  changing background transparent color, 183–186
  highlights around hot area, 186–187
  markers, 178–179
  navigating to markers, 188–190
  pausing playback head for user input, 179–180

digital video, 73–74
dimming text blocks, 187–188
Director 5
  closing at end of movies, 79
  event messages, 128
  four-step process, 17
  frame-based playback by, 46
  licensing policy, 82
  making Xtras available, 62
  opening, 8
  platform for, 79–80
  play-only version, 81
  Shockwave Plug-In, 218
  system requirements, 5
Director marker
  creating, 206
  script using, 211
Director Multimedia Studio, 136–153
  demo version, 4, 18, 22
  Extreme 3D, 147–151
  overview of package, 1, 136
  run-time distribution agreement, 82
  Shockwave for Director, 215–223
  SoundEdit 16, 152–153
  Sound Forge XP, 152–153
  xRes, 138–146
Director Multimedia Studio button
  highlighting, 208
  script for, 210–211
displaying. See viewing
distribution
  licensing agreements, 80, 82
  and "Made with Macromedia" logo, 82
  Multimedia's licensing policy, 82
  platform for, 79–80
  using projectors, 79–82
  Xtra restrictions, 80
dots at top of cells, 50, 51
download speed
  and animation size, 60
  and ink effects, 49
  and looping sounds, 112
  reducing bitmap file size, 161–162
  See also speed

dragging
  buttons, 68, 127, 172
  cast members, 48, 68, 69, 73, 100, 101, 170–171
  channels, 178
  enabling drag and drop, 50
  markers, 74–75, 129–130, 178, 206, 208
  movies to browsers, 221
  objects off stage, 54
  playback head, 51
  real-time recording, 91–94
  with Shift key, 27, 55, 103
  sound cast members, 62, 64, 112
  sounds, 174
  sprites, 102–103, 167

E
Edit menu
  Cut Cells command, 26
  Macintosh shortcuts, 231
  Paste Cells command, 26
  Windows shortcuts, 225
Effects menu (SoundEdit 16), Fade Out command, 153
Effects menu (xRes), Blur, Gaussian, 145
empty channels, 165
enabling. See turning on and off
end statement, 76
enterFrame event, 128
entering text
  in Extreme 3D, 149
  in Text window, 19–20
Essex, Jeff, 216
events
  enterFrame, 128
  exitFrame, 76, 128–129
  handlers, 75, 128
  mouseDown, 128
  mouseUp, 128, 131, 134–135, 189
  playback head and event messages, 128
Exchange Cast Members tool, 59, 110, 116, 117, 206
exchanging cast members
  creating frames, 206–208
  film loop, 116–117
  lightning effect, 58–60
  paper flapping effect, 110–111
Exit button, 68, 78, 79
exitFrame event, 76, 128–129
exiting. See closing
Exit marker
  creating, 75
  script using, 78–79

Extreme 3D, 147–151
   centering text in, 150
   closing, 151
   Extrude Depth field, 151
   opening, 147
   overview, 136
   work area, 147, 149–150
   working plane, 147, 151
Extrude Depth field, 151
Eyedropper tool, 184–185

F

fading out sounds, 152–153
field cast members, 20
File menu
   Cast Preferences command, 11
   Create Projector command, 80
   Import command, 32, 47, 86, 90, 98, 156
   Macintosh shortcuts, 231
   New submenu, Movie command, 18, 86, 90, 98
   Open command, 10
   Preferences submenu
      General command, 9
      Score command, 50
   Save As command, 44
   Save command, 22
   Windows shortcuts, 225
File menu (Extreme 3D)
   Exit (Windows) command, 151
   Export submenu
      Bitmap (Windows) command, 151
      Paint PICT (Macintosh) command, 151
   Quit (Macintosh) command, 151
File menu (xRes)
   Exit command, 146
   Export submenu, PICT command, 146
   Open command, 139
files
   for lessons, 2–3
   opening, 44, 156
   PICT files, 98–99
   reducing bitmap file size, 161–162
   saving, 22, 41
   shocked, 220
   types of, 47
Files of Type menu (Windows), Macintosh PICTs command, 99
Filled Ellipse tool, 91–92
Film Loop Cast Member Properties dialog box, 118

film loops, 114–121
   creating, 117–119
   creating key frames with, 119–120
   defined, 114
   exchanging cast members, 116–117
finding index color numbers, 163–165, 184–185, 186–187, 197–198
flashing effect, 58–60
folders
   creating, 18
   Lessons, 203
   Made with Macromedia (MwM) folder, 82
   Media, 3, 99
   MyWork, 18
Font dialog box, 182
fonts
   in Extreme 3D, 148
   and projector, 20
   resizing, 148, 182
   selecting, 182
   and Text window, 20
foreground color, 92, 164, 180
fps (frames per second). See tempo
frames
   adding markers, 74–75, 129–130, 178–179, 206
   beginning frame, 38–39
   copying, 178, 195, 206
   copying sprites into, 26
   creating by exchanging cast members, 206–208
   defined, 22
   dropped during playback, 46
   duplicating, 195
   illustrated, 22
   last frame for sounds, 112
   looping frames with transitions, 77
   playback head moving through, 25, 28
   playing selected frames only, 107–108
   scripts, 190
   selecting, 25, 104
   See also key frames
frame scripts, 190
frames per second (fps). See tempo
frame, the phrase, 76
FreeHand Graphics Studio button
   highlighting, 186–187
   script for, 188–190
FreeHand marker
   creating, 178
   scripts using, 189, 190
Fruit.pct, 32

G

Gaussian Blur dialog box, 145
glow effect with xRes, 138–146
go marker command, 196, 209, 211–212
go to frame "marker" command
  for Director Multimedia Studio button, 211
  for FreeHand Graphics Studio button, 189, 190
  for menu, 77, 134–135
  for navigation buttons on screen bottom, 211–213
  for Receive the Document button, 132
  for Send the Document button, 133
  using relative markers, 194–196, 209, 211–212
  variants, 189
go to the frame command, 76, 77, 179
  pause command vs., 128, 179
Gradient ink, 198–199
gradients. See color gradient
Gradient Settings dialog box, 199–200
graphics
  centering, 162
  color depth, 162
  deleting extraneous parts, 169
  edge color, 26–27, 56
  reducing bitmap size, 161–162
  snapping to grid, 170–171
  See also background images; cast members; special effects; sprites
grid
  setting width and height, 170
  snapping to, 170–171
  turning on and off, 171

H

halting. See closing; pausing; stopping
Hammer.pct, 137, 139
handlers, 75, 128
hand pointer, toggling, 50
handwriting simulation, 94
hard disk space required, 5
hardware requirements, 5
height. See resizing
highlights around hot area, 186–187
horizontal constraint for dragging, 27, 55, 103
hot area highlights, 186–187
HTML (hypertext markup language), 221

I

Image Options dialog box, 86, 99, 157
images. See background images; graphics
Import dialog box
  importing background image, 32
  importing cast members, 47–48
  importing media elements, 156
importing
  background image, 32–33
  blended images, 187
  cast members, 46–48, 86, 90
  media elements, 98–99, 156–157
  PICT files, 99
  with same setting, 99, 157
  sounds, 111
  types of files, 47
In Between
  animating objects, 54–56
  animating text, 25–31
  on background image, 50
  for credits screen, 71
  In Between Special compared to, 84
in-betweening
  background image, 50
  bullet text, 25–31
  credits screen, 71
  defined, 49
  identifying in-betweened cells, 50, 51
  key frames, 96, 106, 120
  objects, 54–56
  sounds, 63, 112, 174
In Between Special
  animating with, 88–90
  In Between compared to, 84
  setting key frames, 87–88
  setting movie properties, 86
  uses for, 84
In Between Special dialog box, 88–89
index color numbers
  defined, 163
  defining color gradient, 199
  finding, 163–165, 184–185, 186–187, 197–198
  numbering scheme, 163, 164
  uses for, 163
ink effects
  Bkgnd Transparent, 36–37, 48–49, 69, 162, 182, 183–186
  Copy, 49, 101, 169, 170, 173
  and download speed, 49
  Gradient, 198–199
  Lightest, 181
  Matte, 49, 56, 58, 87
  memory intensity of, 49
  opening Ink menu, 58
  and performance, 100, 170

inserting frame copies, 195
Insert menu
    Frame command, 195, 208
    Macintosh shortcuts, 232
    Windows shortcuts, 226
installing
    demo software, 4
    Shockwave and Afterburner, 218
interactivity, 179–180
Internet Explorer, 218
Invert Selection tool, 140, 142

K

keyboard shortcuts. See Macintosh shortcuts; Windows shortcuts
key frames
    animation with, 105–106
    creating, 87–88, 105–106
    creating with film loops, 119–120
    in-betweening, 96, 106, 120
    See also frames

L

labels
    for markers, 75, 78, 129
    numbering relative markers, 194–195
Lasso tool (xRes), 141
layers
    animation problems, 108
    channels as, 34
    moving background to lowest, 34–36
    shuffling sprites, 35–36, 108–109, 120–121
    See also channels
Leader.aif, 137, 152, 153, 174
Left arrow button
    adding, 172
    script for, 211–212
length of movie, tempo and, 46
Lesson folder
    contents, 3
    running the files, 2
lessons
    features of, 2
    files for, 2–3
    list of, 1–2
licensing agreements
    and projector distribution, 82
    and Xtra distribution, 80
Lightest ink, 181
lightning flashes, 58–60

Lingo
    defined, 14
    handlers, 75, 128
    overview, 75
    See also commands (Lingo); scripts
Loop.dir, 115, 116
looping
    film loops, 114–121
    frames with transitions, 77
    for pausing movies, 132, 133, 190
    pausing vs., 128, 179
    playback, 10
    sounds, 63, 111–112

M

Macintosh
    minimum system requirements, 5
    projector creation for, 79–80
    system palette, 99, 157
Macintosh shortcuts
    about, 2
    Cast/Cast Editor windows, 235
    Command+2, 9, 18, 19, 107
    Command+3, 11, 19, 46
    Command+4, 11, 22, 23, 45, 100
    Command+5, 13
    Command+6, 13, 19
    Command+7, 126
    Command+', 15
    Command+], 208
    Command+., 78
    Command+A, 93, 124
    Command+B, 26, 50, 55
    Command+D, 144
    Command+E, 59, 116, 206
    Command+K, 68
    Command+N, 18, 86, 98, 156
    Command+O, 14
    Command+Q, 151
    Command+R, 32, 47, 86, 98, 156
    Command+S, 22, 86, 98, 125
    Command+Shift+1, 160, 180
    Command+Shift+B, 88
    Command+Shift+D, 44
    Command+Shift+Option+B, 9
    Command+Shift+T, 182
    Command+V, 26, 124
    Command+X, 26
    Control menu, 233
    Edit menu, 231

File menu, 231
Insert menu, 232
Modify menu, 232
numeric keypad, 230
Option+Command+Shift+P, 51
Paint window, 236
Score window, 234
shortcut menus, 231
Stage window, 234
View menu, 232
Window menu, 233

Macromedia
Authorized training courses, 1–4
licensing policy, 82
open architecture, 62
Showcase CD 5.0, 42, 154
user interface, 9
Web site, 218

Macromedia Authorized training courses
books in, 3
lesson plans, 2–3
overview of this course, 1–4

Macromedia Open Architecture (MOA), 62
Macromedia User Interface standard, 9
Macromedia xRes, 138–146
closing, 146
illustrated, 138
opening, 138
overview, 136, 138
using, 138–146

"Made with Macromedia" logo, 73, 82
Made with Macromedia (MwM) folder, 82
Magic Wand tool (xRes), 139
Magnifying Glass tool, 200, 209
Main button
adding, 172
script for, 213

Main marker, 178
main menu screen, 154–174
background music, 173
bitmap file size reduction, 161–162
cast organization, 159–160
editing cast members, 168–169
importing media elements, 156–157
index color numbers, 163–165
movie palette, 157–158
navigational elements, 172–173
snapping to grid, 170–171
sprite locations, 160
sprite properties, 165–168

markers
adding, 74–75, 129–130, 178–179, 206
defined, 74
dragging, 74–75, 129–130, 178, 206, 208
labels for, 75, 78, 129
navigating to, 188–190, 210–213
relative, 194–197, 209, 211–212
See also go to frame "marker" command; relative markers

Market1.dir, 44
Market2.dir, 53, 54
Market3.dir, 67, 68, 80
Market.dir, 43
Marquee tool, 168–169
Matte ink, 49, 56, 58, 87
media elements. See cast members
Media folder, 3, 99
memory
and ink effects, 49
system requirements, 5
menu bar, 8
Menu button
creating, 134
script for, 134–135
Menu marker
creating, 74, 129
script using, 77
menus
keyboard shortcuts, 8
Macromedia User Interface standard, 9
shortcut menus, 225, 231
See also menu screen
menu screen
branching to, 134–135
creating, 68–69
creating buttons with tool palette, 125–127
navigating to, 77
pausing at, 76–77
See also main menu screen
Microsoft Internet Explorer, 218
MOA (Macromedia Open Architecture), 62
modem speed and storage space, 162
modifying sounds, 152–153

Modify menu
- Align command, 69, 172
- Font command, 182
- Frame submenu
  - Sound command, 174
  - Tempo command, 64
- In Between command, 26, 28, 50, 55, 71
- In Between Special command, 88
- Macintosh shortcuts, 232
- Movie submenu, Properties command, 44, 86, 90, 98, 157
- Reverse Sequence command, 57, 125
- Sprite submenu, Properties command, 160, 162, 165, 167, 173, 188, 209
- Transform Bitmap command, 161
- Windows shortcuts, 226

mono sound, converting stereo to, 219
mouseDown event, 128
mouseUp event, 128, 131, 132, 134–135, 189
movie palette, 157–158
Movie Properties dialog box, 44–45
- Default Palette menu (Macintosh), 157
- illustrated, 44, 45
- Stage Color chip, 45, 86, 90, 158
- Stage Size menu, 98, 158

movies
- animations from, 124–125
- background color, 158
- closing Director at end, 79
- creating, 18–19, 38–41
- defined, 8
- embedding in Web pages, 220–221
- film loops, 114–121
- palette, 157–158
- pausing in loop, 132, 133
- playing, 10
- projectors for, 79–82
- reusing work, 204–215
- rewinding, 28
- running through Afterburner, 20, 219–220
- setting properties, 86
- "shocking," 127, 219–220
- stopping, 78
- See also tempo

moving
- background to lowest layer, 34–36
- shuffling sprites, 35–36, 108–109, 120
- simulating cursor movement, 90
- snapping to grid, 170–171
- See also aligning; navigation; positioning-
  - music. See sounds

MwM (Made with Macromedia) folder, 82
MyMrktng file, 81
MyWork folder, 18

N

names
- cast members, 159, 166, 167
- film loops, 118
- marker labels, 75, 78, 129
- saving files under different name, 44

navigation
- buttons for, 122–135, 172–173, 211–212
- creating scripts, 75–79, 210–212
- to markers, 188–190, 210–213
- markers for, 74–75, 129–130, 178–179, 206
- with relative markers, 194–197, 209, 211–212

Netscape Navigator, 218
numeric keypad
- Macintosh shortcuts, 230
- playback using, 51
- Windows shortcuts, 224

O

Object menu (Extreme 3D), Show Working Plane command, 151
on exitFrame statement, 76, 77, 128–129, 132, 133, 179, 190
on mouseUp statement, 131, 134, 189, 211, 212, 213
opacity. See Bkgnd Transparent ink
opening
- Animation Wizard, 39
- cast, 11
- Cast window, 46
- Channels window, 143
- Color window, 142
- Control Panel, 9, 18, 107
- Debugger, 15
- Director, 8
- Extreme 3D, 147
- files, 44
- Ink menu, 58
- Macromedia xRes, 138
- Paint window, 13, 168, 198
- score, 11, 22, 45, 100
- Script window, 14
- SoundEdit 16, 152
- Sound Forge XP, 152
- Text window, 13, 19, 70
- toolbar, 9
- tool palette, 91, 126
- See also creating

organizing the cast, 159–160

P

Paint Bucket tool
   defining color gradient, 198–199
   painting graphics, 200, 209

Paint window
   animating with color cycling, 201–202
   defining color gradient, 198–200
   finding index color, 184–185, 187
   illustrated, 13
   Macintosh shortcuts, 236
   opening, 13, 168, 198

palette channel, 12

Palette dialog box, 201–202

Palette menu, Remap to System-Win command, 157

palettes. See movie palette; system palette; tool palette

Paper.dir, 97, 98, 124

Paper Loop cast member, 119

pasting. See copying

pause command, 128–129
   go to the frame statement vs., 128, 179

pausing
   for credits screen, 72–73
   for digital video, 73–74
   looping vs., 128, 179
   for menu display, 128–129
   playback head for user input, 179–180
   script for, 76–77, 132, 179–180, 190
   for sound to finish, 64
   See also stopping

performance
   and blending, 187
   and color cycling, 195, 208
   and Copy ink, 100, 170
   and resizing, 167
   See also speed

PICT files, importing, 98–99

playback
   dropped frames during, 46
   frame-based playback, 46
   looping, 107
   projectors, 81
   rewinding, 28
   scrubbing (dragging playback head), 51
   selected frames only, 107–108
   using numeric keypad, 51
   using toolbar, 28
   while temporarily closing all open windows, 51
   See also Control Panel

playback head
   defined, 25
   dragging (scrubbing), 51
   and event messages, 128
   illustrated, 25
   Lingo function for frame location of, 76
   movement during playback, 25, 28
   pausing for menu display, 128–129
   pausing for user input, 179–180
   pausing while sound plays, 64
   relative markers and head position, 194–195
   See also tempo

pointer
   simulating movement, 90
   toggling, 50

positioning
   buttons, 69
   centering full-screen graphics, 162
   centering text in Extreme 3D, 150
   graphics on stage, 100–102, 169
   sprites, 160, 173
   See also aligning; moving

Process menu (Sound Forge XP), Fade, Out command, 153

Projector Options dialog box, 81

projectors
   creating, 80–82
   custom icon, 82
   defined, 8
   and fonts, 20
   licensing agreements, 82
   platform for, 80
   playing, 82

projects, steps for, 17

Q

QuickTime
   frames dropped by, 46
   version required, 5

quit command, 79

R

RAM
   and ink effects, 49
   system requirements, 5

rate. See speed

Read Me files, 4

real-time recording
   animating with, 91–94
   overview, 85
   setting up the movie, 90

Receive marker
    creating, 129
    script for, 131
Receive the Document button
    creating, 125–127
    script for, 130–134
reducing bitmap file size, 161–162
relative markers, 194–197
    defined, 194
    illustrated, 194–195
    and navigation buttons, 212
    numbering of, 194–195
    and playback head position, 194–195
    scripts using, 196–197, 209, 211–212
    See also markers
remapping images
    to Macintosh palette, 99
    to Windows palette, 157
Render menu (Extreme 3D), Set Background command, 147
resizing
    cast members, 167
    Cast window, 11
    deleting extraneous graphics parts, 169
    fonts, 182
    fonts in Extreme 3D, 148
    grid width and height, 170
    minimizing Shockwave movies, 20
    and performance, 167
    reducing bitmap file size, 161–162
    screen size vs. stage size, 160
    sprites, 167, 180
    stage, 98, 158
reusing work, 204–215
    cast members, 167, 193
    color cycling, 208–210
    creating frames by exchanging cast members, 206–208
Reverse Sequence feature, 57, 125
rewinding movies, 28
RGB mode (xRes), 143, 146
Rich Text Format files. See RTF files
Right arrow button
    adding, 172
    script for, 212
RTF files
    cast members from, 48
    and formatting, 70
    importing, 47–48

S

Same Setting for Remaining Images box, 99, 157
sampling rate, 63
saving
    files, 22, 41
    files under different name, 44
    running movies through Afterburner, 219–220
score
    adding sounds, 62–65, 110–111
    animating objects, 54–56
    channels, 11–12
    closing, 23
    defined, 11
    deleting sprites, 93
    empty channels in, 165
    enabling drag and drop, 50
    illustrated, 12, 22
    Macintosh shortcuts, 234
    opening, 11, 22, 45, 100
    placing text in, 22–24
    selecting all cells, 94, 124
    Shuffle Down button, 36, 108, 109, 120
    Shuffle Up button, 35, 36
    toggling hand and pointer, 50
    Windows shortcuts, 228
Score Window Preferences dialog box, 50
Score Window tool, 45
screen transitions, 60–62
    Center Out, Square, 61
    defined, 60
    looping frames with transitions, 77
    Wipe Left, 60
    Xtras, 62
script channels, 12
scripts
    branching to animation loop, 130–134
    branching to menu, 134–135
    cast member scripts, 188–190, 210–213
    copying, 208–209
    creating navigation scripts, 75–79, 130–135
    defined, 14, 75
    deleting, 195–196
    frame scripts, 190
    for pausing, 76–77, 132, 179–180
    relative markers in, 194–197, 209, 211–212
    sprite scripts, 130–134
    See also commands (Lingo); Lingo
Script window
    closing, 77
    illustrated, 14
    opening, 14
    Trails box, 94

scrubbing, 51
selecting
  all cells in score, 94, 124
  colors from Color Picker, 142–143
  deselecting, 144, 145
  fonts, 182
  frames, 25, 104
  images, 139–140
  inverting selection, 140, 142
  playing selected frames only, 107–108
  rectangular areas, 168–169
Select menu (xRes)
  Inverse command, 140, 142, 143
  None command, 144, 146
  Store submenu, New command, 144
Send marker
  creating, 130
  script for, 131
Send the Document button
  creating, 125–127
  script for, 130–134
Set Background dialog box (Extreme 3D), 147
Shape Cast Member Properties dialog box, 167
Shift key dragging constraint, 27, 55, 103
Shocker.dcr, 220
Shocker.dir, 219
Shocker.HTM, 221
Shocker.HTML, 221
"shocking" movies, 127, 219–220
Shockwave, 215–223
  Afterburner, 20, 218
  developer's kit, 218
  embedding movies in Web pages, 220–221
  installing, 218
  minimizing movie size, 20
  obtaining, 218
  overview, 216, 217
  Plug-In for Director, 218
  "shocking" movies, 127, 219–220
  sound files and, 219
  system requirements, 5
  versions of, 217, 218
  Web browser support, 218
Shockwave Developer's Guide, 222
Shockwave for Audio Settings dialog box, 219–220
shortcut menus
  Macintosh, 231
  Windows, 225
shortcuts. See Macintosh shortcuts; Windows shortcuts

Showcase CD 5.0, 42, 154
showing. See viewing
Show menu (Macintosh), Picture command, 98
shuffling
  down, 36, 108–109, 120
  up, 35–36, 109
simulating
  cursor movement, 90
  handwriting, 94
sizing. See resizing
Skater.dir, 85, 90
Skater.pct, 90
Smallsun.pct, 86
snapping to grid, 170–171
software
  Director Multimedia Studio package, 1, 136
  installing demo software, 4
  speaker support programs, 154
  system requirements, 4, 5
Sound Cast Member Properties dialog box, 63, 111–112
sound cast members
  dragging, 62, 64, 112
  looping, 63, 111–112
sound channels, 12
SoundEdit 16
  closing, 153
  editing sounds, 152–153
  opening, 152
  overview, 136, 152
Sound Forge XP
  closing, 153
  modifying sounds, 152–153
  opening, 152
  overview, 136, 152
sounds
  adding to score, 62–64, 110–111, 174
  audio compression, 219
  background, 62–64, 111–112, 174
  converting stereo to mono, 219
  cut off, 112
  dragging, 174
  fading out, 152–153
  in-betweening, 63, 112, 174
  last frame for, 112
  listing available sounds, 174
  looping, 63, 111–112
  modifying, 152–153
  sampling rate, 63
  Shockwave Xtra for, 219
  speech, 63
  turning on and off, 64–65
  waiting until finished, 64

spacing, grid, 170
Speaker2.dir, 177, 178
Speaker3.dir, 193, 195
Speaker4.dir, 205, 206
Speaker.dir, 155
speaker presentation, 154
speaker support programs, 154
special effects, 52
    exchanging cast members, 58–60, 110–111
    flapping paper, 110–111
    glow effect with xRes, 138–146
    with In Between Special, 84, 88–90
    lightning flashes, 58–60
    with real-time recording, 84, 91–94
    screen transitions, 60–62
    See also ink effects; sounds
speech, sampling rate, 63
speed
    color cycling rate, 201
    download speed
        and animation size, 60
        and ink effects, 49
        and looping sounds, 112
        reducing bitmap file size, 161–162
    performance
        and blending, 187
        and color cycling, 195, 208
        and Copy ink, 100, 170
        and resizing, 167
    sampling rate, 63
    sound bit rate, 219
    tempo
        changing, 18
        and Copy ink, 100
        and length of movie, 46
        requested vs. absolute frame rate, 100
        setting in Animation Wizard, 40
        setting in Tempo dialog box, 45–46
sprite channels
    defined, 12
    illustrated, 12
    placing in score, 22–24
    shuffling, 35–36, 108–109, 120
Sprite Properties dialog box
    Blend, 188, 209
    positioning sprites, 160, 165, 180
    resizing sprites, 165, 180

sprites
    1-bit color, 162, 165
    adding to stage, 180–183
    aligning, 68–69
    color cycling, 192–203
    copying into frames, 26
    copying to new location, 102–104
    deleting from score, 93
    dragging, 102–103, 167
    exchanging cast members, 58–59
    ink effects on, 49
    layering, 108–109
    modifying properties, 165–167
    real-time recording, 90
    resizing, 167, 180
    reversing sequence, 57
    scripts, 130–134
    setting location of, 160, 173
    shuffling, 35–36, 108–109, 120
    for text cast members, 22–24
stage
    adding sprites, 180–183
    background color, 45–46, 86, 90, 158
    creating custom, 98
    dragging objects off, 54
    illustrated, 8
    importing 32-bit image to 8-bit stage, 32–33
    Macintosh shortcuts, 234
    positioning graphics, 100–102
    resizing, 98, 158
    screen size vs. stage size, 160
    Windows shortcuts, 228
Start.dir, 43, 44, 54, 68, 178, 195
starting. See creating; opening; turning on and off
stereo sound, converting to mono, 220
stopping
    movies, 78
    See also closing; pausing
storing
    modem speed and storage space, 162
    selection (xRes), 144
Sun.dir, 85, 86
system palette
    index color numbers, 163–165, 184–185, 186–187, 197–198
    remapping to Macintosh, 99
    remapping to Windows, 157
system requirements, 5
system resources. See performance

T

tempo
  changing, 18
  and Copy ink, 100
  and length of movie, 46
  requested vs. absolute frame rate, 100
  setting in Animation Wizard, 40
  setting in Tempo dialog box, 45–46
  See also pausing; speed

tempo channel
  defined, 12
  illustrated, 12
  setting tempo, 45–46

Tempo dialog box, 45–46
  requested vs. absolute frame rate, 100
  Wait for End of Digital Video radio button, 73
  Wait for End of Sound radio button, 64
  Wait radio button, 72–73

text
  3D, 147–151
  aligning, 71
  animating with In Between, 25–31
  centering in Extreme 3D, 150
  creating cast members, 19–22, 181–182
  credits screen, 69–73
  dimming text blocks, 187–188
  entering in Extreme 3D, 149
  entering in Text window, 19–20
  placing in score, 22–24
  transparent background, 26–27
  white boxes around, 26–27

Text.pct, 137
Text tool (Director), 181–182
Text tool (Extreme 3D), 148
Text Tool Preferences dialog box (Extreme 3D), 148

Text window
  Align Center button, 71
  entering text, 19–20
  and fonts, 20
  illustrated, 13
  opening, 13, 19, 70
  Plus button, 21

Ticket.pct, 47, 48
time for download. See download speed
toggling. See turning on and off

toolbar
  closing, 54
  Exchange Cast Members, 59, 110, 116, 117, 206
  illustrated, 8, 9
  Invert Selection, 140, 142
  opening, 9
  Play, 28
  Rewind, 28
  Score Window, 45
  screen partly hidden by, 54
  Stop, 78
  tooltips, 9

tool palette (Director)
  Align tool, 172
  Button tool, 126–127
  Eyedropper tool, 184–185
  Filled Ellipse tool, 91–92
  foreground color, 92
  Magnifying Glass tool, 200, 209
  Marquee tool, 168–169
  modifying objects created with tools, 167
  opening, 91, 126
  Paint Bucket tool, 198–200, 209
  Text tool, 181–182
  Unfilled Rectangle tool, 186

tool palette (Extreme 3D)
  Bevel Extrude tool, 150
  Text tool, 148

tool palette (xRes)
  Lasso tool, 141
  Magic Wand tool, 139
  Zoom tool, 140

tooltips, 9
Trails box, 94
Transform Bitmap dialog box, 161–162
transition channel
  defined, 12
  illustrated, 12
  using screen transitions, 60–62

Transition dialog box, 61
transitions. See screen transitions
transparency. See Bkgnd Transparent ink
triangular markers. See markers
troubleshooting
  layer problems, 108
  sound cut off, 112

251

INDEX

turning on and off
   audio compression, 219
   enabling drag and drop, 50
   grid, 171
   movie toggles, 65
   pointer/hand toggle, 50sounds, 64–65
   tooltips, 9

U
Unfilled Rectangle tool, 186
user input, pausing for, 179–180
user interface standard, 9

V
vertical constraint for dragging, 27, 55, 103
video, digital, 73–74
viewing
   cast, 11
   cast member names, 159
   cast members, 11
   grid, 171
   in-betweened cells, 50, 51
   sounds available, 174
   tooltips, 9
   zooming, 140, 200
   See also opening; screen transitions
View menu
   Grid submenu
      Settings command, 170
      Show command, 171
   Macintosh shortcuts, 232
   Snap To command, 171
   Windows shortcuts, 226

W
waiting. See pausing
Web browsers, 218
Web pages
   embedding movies, 220–221
   for Internet Explorer, 218
   for Macromedia, 218, 222
   for Netscape Navigator, 218
Web, the, 216, 217
white
   boxes around text, 26–27
   edges around objects, 56
width. See resizing

Window menu
   Cast command, 11, 19, 46
   Color Palettes command, 164, 187, 197
   Control Panel command, 18, 19
   Debugger command, 15
   Macintosh shortcuts, 233
   Paint command, 13
   Score command, 11, 22
   Script command, 14
   Text command, 13, 19
   Toolbar command, 54
   Tool Palette submenu
      Field command, 20
      opening tool palette, 91
   Windows shortcuts, 227
Window menu (xRes)
   Channels command, 143
   Palettes submenu, Picker command, 142
Windows (Microsoft)
   minimum system requirements, 5
   projector creation for, 79–80
   system palette, 99, 157
Windows shortcuts
   about, 2
   Alt+Ctrl+Shift+P, 51
   Alt+F4, 151
   Cast window, 228
   Control menu, 227
   Ctrl+2, 9, 18, 19, 107
   Ctrl+3, 11, 19, 46
   Ctrl+4, 11, 22, 23, 45, 100
   Ctrl+5, 13
   Ctrl+6, 13, 19
   Ctrl+7, 126
   Ctrl+', 15
   Ctrl+], 208
   Ctrl+., 78
   Ctrl+A, 93, 124
   Ctrl+B, 26, 50, 55
   Ctrl+D, 144
   Ctrl+E, 59, 116, 206
   Ctrl+K, 68
   Ctrl+N, 18, 86, 98, 156
   Ctrl+O, 14
   Ctrl+R, 32, 47, 86, 98, 156
   Ctrl+S, 22, 86, 98, 125
   Ctrl+Shift+1, 160, 180
   Ctrl+Shift+Alt+B, 9
   Ctrl+Shift+B, 88
   Ctrl+Shift+D, 44

Ctrl+Shift+T, 182
Ctrl+V, 26, 124
Ctrl+X, 26
Edit menu, 225
File menu, 225
Insert menu, 226
Modify menu, 226
numeric keypad, 224
Score window, 228
shortcut menus, 225
Stage window, 228
View menu, 226
Window menu, 227
Wipe Left transition, 60
work area (Extreme 3D), 147, 149–150
working plane (Extreme 3D), 147, 151
World Wide Web, 216, 217

X
xRes. See Macromedia xRes
Xronos, Inc., 42, 154
Xtras
Afterburner, 20, 218, 219–220
Animation Wizard, 38–41
defined, 38
and distribution, 80
list of Xtras available, 38
making available to Director, 62
screen transitions, 62
Xtras menu
Afterburner command, 219
Animation Wizard command, 39
Animwiz command, 39
Shockwave for Audio Settings command, 219

Z
zooming
with Magnifying Glass tool, 200
with Zoom tool, 140
Zoom tool (xRes), 140

MACROMEDIA TECH SUPPORT NUMBER: 415-252-9080

LICENSING AGREEMENT

The information in this book is for informational use only and is subject to change without notice. Macromedia, Inc., and Macromedia Press assume no responsibility for errors or inaccuracies that may appear in this book. The software described in the book is furnished under license and may be used or copied only in accordance with terms of the license.

The software files on the CD-ROM included here are copyrighted by Macromedia, Inc. You have the non-exclusive right to use these programs and files. You may use them on one computer at a time. You may not transfer the files from one computer to another over a network. You may transfer the files onto a single hard disk so long as you can prove ownership of the original CD-ROM.

You may not reverse engineer, de-compile, or dis-assembl e the software. You may not modify or translate the software or distribute copies of the software without the written consent of Macromedia, Inc.